The Trent & Mersey Canal

Trade and Transport 1770-1970

A pair of Mersey Weaver boats above King's Lock at Middlewich. The King's Lock public house astern of them survives but the small lockside toll office is long vanished. Below the lock, the canal heads straight towards the town wharf and a flight of three further locks amongst the salt works that continue the route to Anderton, Preston Brook and the Bridgewater Canal. The rise in the road to the left marks the entrance to the Wardle Canal, a very short arm of the T&M that gives access to the first lock of the Shropshire Union Canal's Middlewich Branch – 'The New Cut' to boatmen. NEIL PARKHOUSE COLLECTION

The Trent & Mersey Canal
Trade and Transport 1770-1970

Tom Foxon

Black Dwarf Publications

London Wharf, Shardlow, showing a wide boat. Wide boats were used for some of the local traffic on this part of the canal. SHARDLOW HERITAGE CENTRE

Contents

Introduction	page 7
CHAPTER ONE: THE POTTERIES TRADE	PAGE 13
CHAPTER TWO: CANALSIDE WORKS AND WHARVES IN THE POTTERIES	PAGE 23
Tunstall	page 25
Longport	page 27
Port Vale and Middleport	page 30
Newport	page 31
The Burslem Arm	page 32
Etruria	page 36
Shelton Bridge	page 40
Stoke	page 41
The Newcastle Canal	page 43
Hanley	page 44
The Canal Company's Railways	page 46
Outside the Potteries	page 47
CHAPTER THREE: THE POTTERIES TRADE BEFORE 1840	PAGE 49
CHAPTER FOUR: THE POTTERIES TRADE AFTER 1840	PAGE 69
CHAPTER FIVE: THE IRON AND COAL TRADES	PAGE 91
Iron	page 91
Coal	page 106
CHAPTER SIX: GENERAL MERCHANDISE, FOODSTUFFS AND BUILDING MATERIALS	PAGE 113
General Merchandise	page 113
Grain and Foodstuffs	page 121
Cheese and Milk Products	page 125
Sugar	page 126
Other Foodstuffs	page 127
Ale	page 128
Wool	page 129
Timber and Building Materials	page 129
Paper	page 130
Non-Ferrous Metals	page 131
Shoes	page 132
Lime and Limestone	page 132
Plaster	page 135
CHAPTER SEVEN: SALT, CHEMICALS AND LIQUID FUELS	PAGE 137
Salt	page 137
Chemicals	page 142
Liquid Fuels	page 149
CHAPTER EIGHT: A WORKING WATERWAY	PAGE 151
CHAPTER NINE: THE DECLINING YEARS 1913-1970	PAGE 167
Appendix	page 187
Index	page 188

© Black Dwarf Publications & Tom Foxon 2015
Designed by Alan Kittridge
British Library Cataloguing-in-Publication Data. A catalogue record for this book is available from the British Library
ISBN: 9781903599 22 8

All rights reserved. No part of this publication may be reproduced, stored in a retrieval system or transmitted in any form or by any means, electronic, mechanical, photocopying, recording or otherwise, without the written permission of the publisher.

BLACK DWARF LIGHTMOOR PUBLICATIONS LTD
Unit 144B, Lydney Trading Estate, Harbour Road, Lydney, Gloucestershire GL15 5EJ
www.lightmoor.co.uk
BLACK DWARF PUBLICATIONS is an imprint of BLACK DWARF LIGHTMOOR PUBLICATIONS LTD

The Trent & Mersey Canal – Trade and Transport 1770-1970

An LM&SR map showing the canals under the railway's ownership in the Midlands and North West England, along with the other canals that they connected with. The Trent & Mersey can be seen running from the River Trent at Derwentmouth in the east to connect with the Bridgwater Canal at Preston Brook in the north west. The Caldon and Leek branches are simply indicated as part of the T&M. The map clearly indicates the competing route offered by the Shropshire Union Canal, the two waterways running parallel to each other from the Midlands to the Mersey. When the North Staffordshire Railway, owners of the Trent & Mersey Canal, and the London & North Western Railway, lessees of the Shropshire Union Canal became part of the newly formed LM&SR, the traffic between the Mersey Ports and south Staffordshire formerly passing by means of the T&M /Staffordshire & Worcestershire Canal route now left the T&M for the SU at Wardle Junction. However, agreements between the principal carrier on this route and the Manchester Ship Canal (Bridgewater Department) meant that, until 1948, most of this traffic continued to travel via Preston Brook and Wardle Junction rather than via Ellesmere Port. Successors to the 2nd Duke of Sutherland, who was one of the initial subscribers to the Liverpool & Manchester Railway and who also had substantial canal interests, were among the LM&SR Directors until the company was nationalised in 1948.
BASIL JEUDA COLLECTION

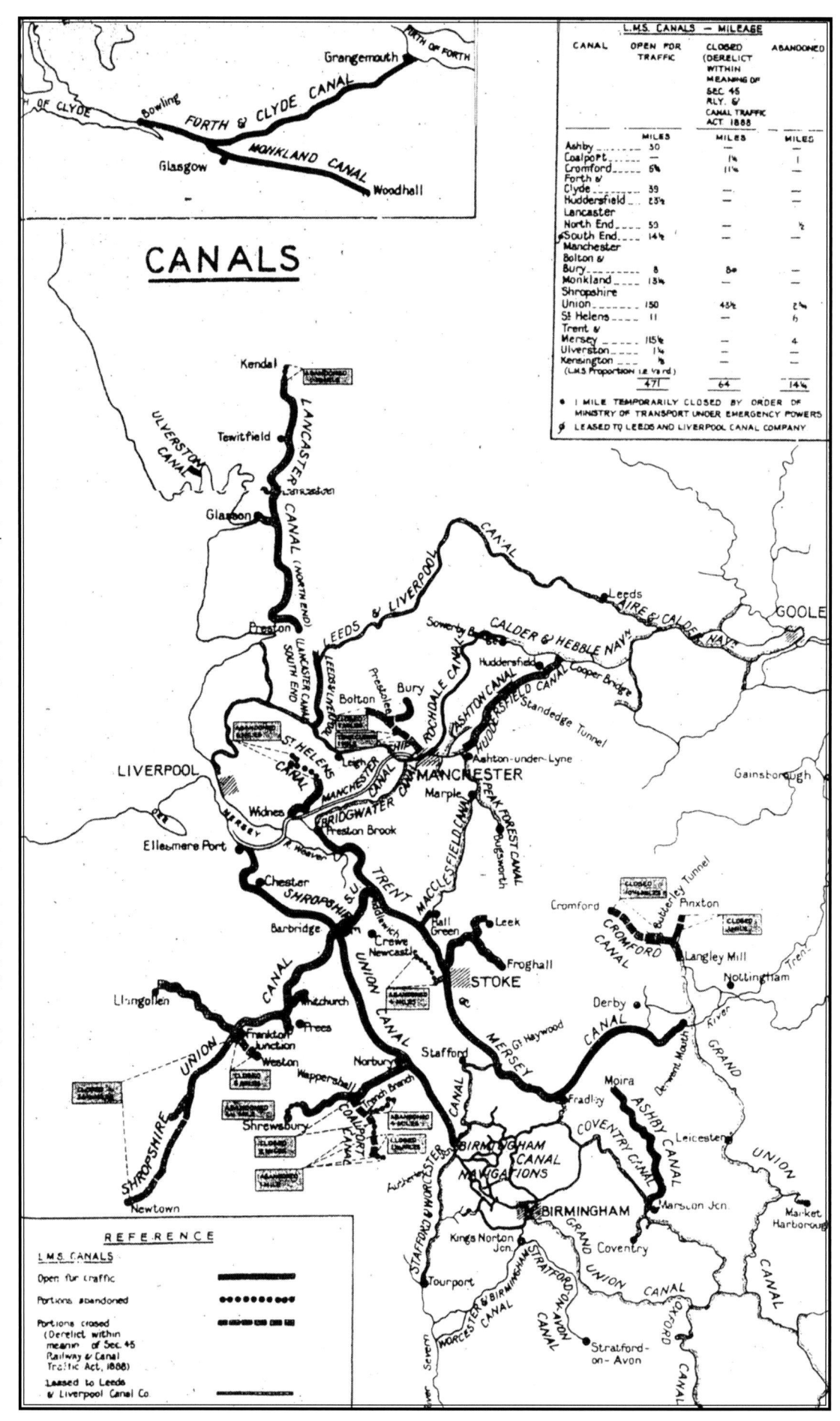

INTRODUCTION

As a young boatman in the 1950s, my travels often took me on to the Trent & Mersey Canal (T&M). Sometimes we entered the canal at Preston Brook or Anderton and left it at Wardle Junction (Middlewich) bound for Birmingham or Wolverhampton. On other occasions, we would climb the great flight of Cheshire Locks to the 408 foot summit level and be towed through Harecastle Tunnel by the electric tug, emerging into waters busy with boats and lined with factories and wharves almost the whole way from Tunstall to Stoke. By contrast, the eastern part of the canal, which we followed from Stoke as far as Fradley, bore hardly any traffic and, apart from the small towns of Stone and Rugeley, was quiet and rural. Later, as an owner boatman, I sometimes loaded coal at Sideway or gravel at Port Vale for the Mersey, Weaver & Ship Canal Carrying Company and had the sad task of carrying redundant equipment to Braunston when the Middleport boat dock closed. That trip, loaded on 15th May 1958, was my last cargo carrying voyage on the T&M. In the days when it still performed the function it was built for, the T&M was a fascinating waterway and this book has been very much a labour of love. In later years, as a student of and a researcher into canal history, I became conscious that very little information had been published about the commercial activities of and on the Trent & Mersey. The standard history, *The Trent & Mersey Canal* by Jean Lindsay,[1] appeared in 1979. It covers the events leading up to and the process of construction of the

Seal of the Trent & Mersey Canal Company.

The basin below the Anderton Lift, probably in the 1890s. Three salt chutes can be seen.
NEIL PARKHOUSE COLLECTION

*Anderton Company boats **Kate** (which had been converted to a motor boat in 1924) and **Protection** at Runcorn Docks in the 1930s. From left to right: John Wakefield, G. Grimes, R. Bailey. BASIL JEUDA COLLECTION*

*Mersey, Weaver motor boat **Spain**, taken over from the Anderton Company in 1953. The Steerer is Albert, son of 'Chocolate Charlie' Atkins. GORDON BRIGGS*

A portion of Bradshaw's Map of Canals situated in the Counties of Lancaster, York, Derby & Chester, published circa 1830, showing the Trent & Mersey Canal, here referred to as the Grand Trunk Canal, from Harecastle to Runcorn. HUGH POTTER COLLECTION

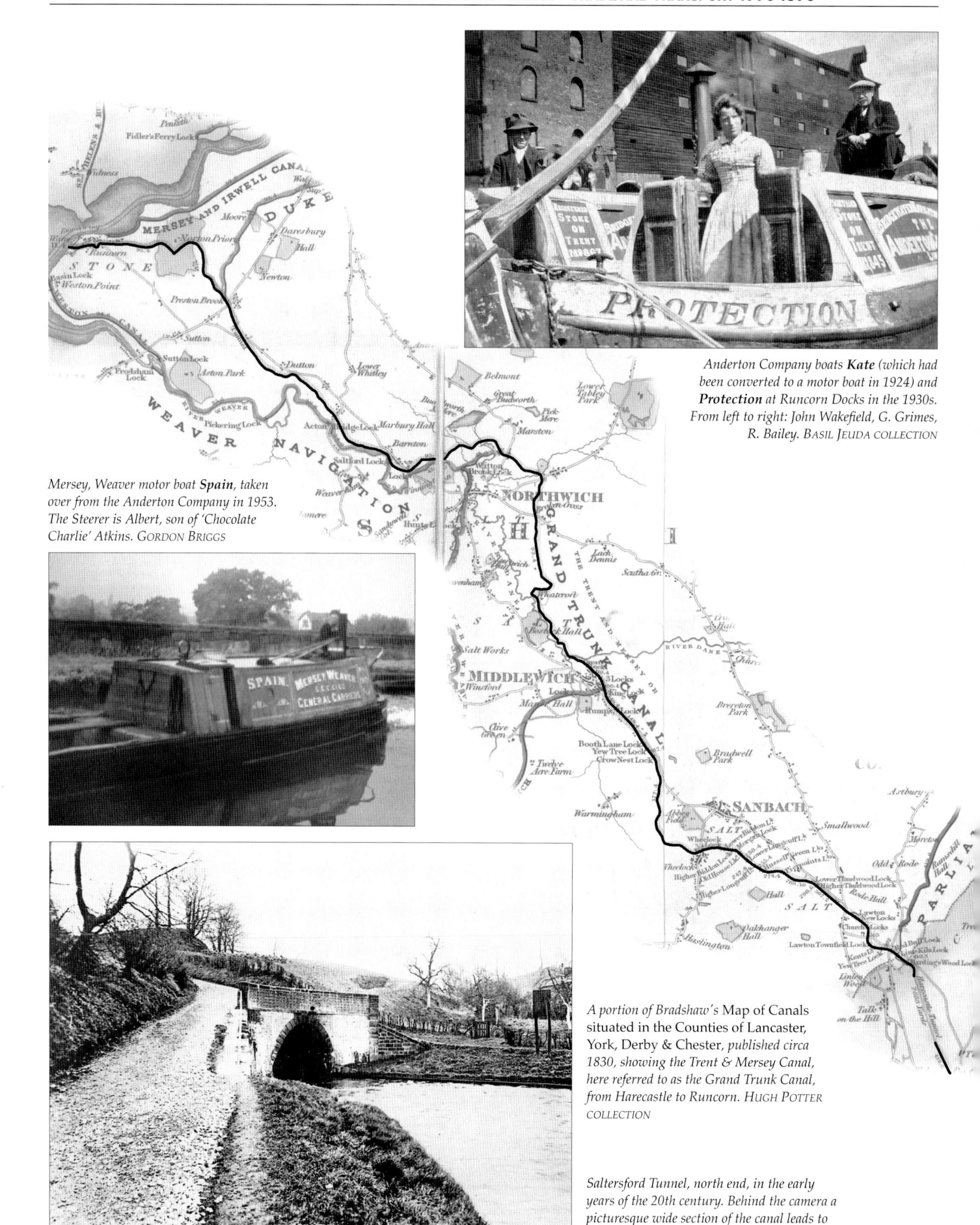

Saltersford Tunnel, north end, in the early years of the 20th century. Behind the camera a picturesque wide section of the canal leads to Barnton Tunnel. NEIL PARKHOUSE COLLECTION

The southern portal of Preston Brook Tunnel at Dutton, circa 1908. A scene that is little changed today. BASIL JEUDA COLLECTION

canal, its branches and major engineering works but its length of only 182 pages meant that commercial aspects could be given little space. Peter Lead, in *The Caldon Canal and Tramroads*,[2] covered canalside works and traffic more fully but concentrated on the section between Milton and Froghall, leaving the four miles of heavily industrialised canal between Etruria and Milton virtually untouched. He has also published an excellent photostudy, *The Trent & Mersey Canal*,[3] which, unlike most of its genre, has very useful and accurate captions. *After the Canal Duke* by F.C. Mather[4] unravels many of the complications in the relationship between the T&M and adjoining waterways. I am indebted to articles by Mike Clarke and Alf Hayman published in Volume 5 of *Waterways Journal* (Spring 2003)[5] for additional information on the effects of two World Wars and on the Bridgewater terminals in Liverpool.

In more recent years, the trend in canal history has been to investigate aspects of commercial operation more deeply, particularly on the Birmingham Canal Navigations where the *Industrial Canal and Working Boats*[6] series deal with traffic and early carriers respectively. Historians have long felt the need for a commercial history of the Trent & Mersey but have been hampered by the destruction of the canal's records in a fire at Stone in 1950. However, every transaction has two (or more) parties so that research into the records of the canal's customers and those of connecting waterways has thrown a great deal of light on what happened on the T&M.

This book is not, therefore, an attempt to update the works of my predecessors. Rather it sets out to describe the way industry used the canal and the way carriers and the canal company responded to their demands. It describes the cut and thrust of competition between the T&M, its carriers and other canal routes, and later with railways and road transport, competition that led inevitably to a sometimes complicated series of agreements and traffic conferences which managed to retain traffic on the canal until 1970. Because no

Canal Bridge, Wheelock Wharf, looking north along Crewe Road circa 1910. The properties on the right all still exist, including the Cheshire Cheese public house in the right foreground. On the left, the chimney is long gone but the whitewashed warehouse still remains. JOHN RYAN COLLECTION

ANAL – TRADE AND TRANSPORT 1770-1970

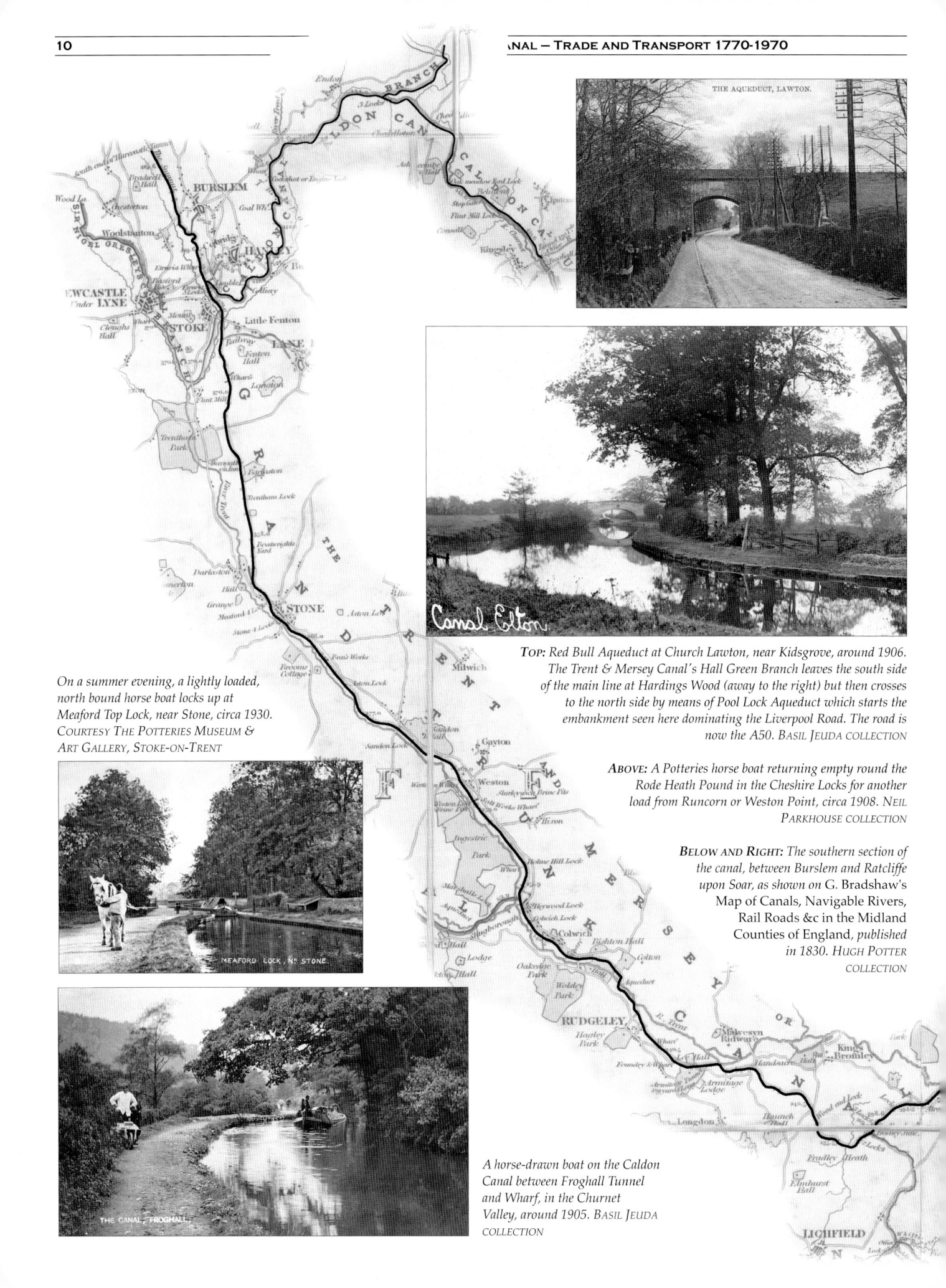

On a summer evening, a lightly loaded, north bound horse boat locks up at Meaford Top Lock, near Stone, circa 1930. COURTESY THE POTTERIES MUSEUM & ART GALLERY, STOKE-ON-TRENT

TOP: Red Bull Aqueduct at Church Lawton, near Kidsgrove, around 1906. The Trent & Mersey Canal's Hall Green Branch leaves the south side of the main line at Hardings Wood (away to the right) but then crosses to the north side by means of Pool Lock Aqueduct which starts the embankment seen here dominating the Liverpool Road. The road is now the A50. BASIL JEUDA COLLECTION

ABOVE: A Potteries horse boat returning empty round the Rode Heath Pound in the Cheshire Locks for another load from Runcorn or Weston Point, circa 1908. NEIL PARKHOUSE COLLECTION

BELOW AND RIGHT: The southern section of the canal, between Burslem and Ratcliffe upon Soar, as shown on G. Bradshaw's Map of Canals, Navigable Rivers, Rail Roads &c in the Midland Counties of England, published in 1830. HUGH POTTER COLLECTION

A horse-drawn boat on the Caldon Canal between Froghall Tunnel and Wharf, in the Churnet Valley, around 1905. BASIL JEUDA COLLECTION

canal - and particularly the Trent & Mersey - existed in isolation, I have gone into a certain amount of detail on adjoining waterways, particularly as many of the important places where traffic was transferred between ship or river barge to boats operating on the T&M were outside its own waters. Preston Brook and Runcorn were on the Bridgewater Canal and Weston Point on the River Weaver. Transshipment at Anderton involved both the T&M and the Weaver. Shardlow was the only inland port actually on the T&M.

No writer could hope to research a volume like this without assistance. That help has unstintingly been given to me by many people, not least my fellow members of the Railway & Canal Historical Society. I would like to thank in particular Ray Shill, Christopher Jones, Tony Lewery, Sheila Cooke and Alan Faulkner. My thanks also go to the late Roy Jamieson, former archivist at the British Waterways Gloucester Archives and the current archivist Caroline Jones, and to the staff at Stafford Record Office, the William Salt Library, the Public Record Office, Birmingham Central Library, Manchester and Derby City libraries. Illustrations are individually credited but particular thanks for help in assembling such a varied collection to choose from should go to Basil Jeuda for generously allowing me to choose liberally from his extensive archive of T&M images collected over many years, to Harry Arnold of Waterways Images, and to John Ryan and Neil Parkhouse.

Any errors are my own. I must also thank my editor Euan Corrie for providing advice and encouragement. No research is ever fully completed and I hope this book will encourage others to delve further into the history of the Trent & Mersey Canal.

NOTES TO INTRODUCTION
1. David & Charles, 1979; in the *Canals of The British Isles* series
2. 2nd edn, Oakwood Press 1990
3. Moorland Press 1980
4. Manchester 1970
5. Boat Museum Society, Ellesmere Port
6. Heartland Press, Birmingham

ABBREVIATIONS USED
PRO - Public Records Office
SRO - Staffordshire County Records Office
WSL - William Salt Library
DRO - Derbyshire County Records Office
BW GLOS - British Waterways Archives, Gloucester

Froghall top basin in 1903, showing a boat being loaded by hand with limestone brought down by rail from Caldon Low Quarries.
BASIL JEUDA COLLECTION

Marl hole at Longton circa 1900. The marl was conveyed directly into Blake's Pottery, which is behind the hole. Marl was one of the local clays used by the early potters and its use continued in the manufacture of certain products such as glazed bricks or tiles. Marl was carried on the canal to Armitage and also en route to Ireland. BASIL JEUDA COLLECTION

CHAPTER ONE
THE POTTERIES TRADE

The manufacture of Pottery in north Staffordshire dates back to the 17th century. In Burslem, the trade started in 1644 and the industry came to dominate the area to such an extent that the locality became known as 'the Potteries'. The area broadly comprises the six towns of Hanley, Burslem, Stoke, Longton, Fenton and Tunstall, situated along and around the headwaters of the River Trent in north Staffordshire. Another name for the district is 'The Five Towns', coined by the author Arnold Bennett and used in many of his novels set against a thinly disguised background of the Potteries. 'The Five Towns' was subsequently adopted as an alternative name for the area, although there are actually six towns in the Potteries - Bennett excluded Fenton.

'The Potteries' was not an official name but one descriptive of the area, just like the use of the term 'Black Country' in south Staffordshire. The City of Stoke-on-Trent, which comprised the six Pottery towns, received its charter on 31st March 1910, causing some argument as both Hanley and Burslem claimed to be larger and more important than Stoke.

At first the pottery industry relied on the local supplies of clay and coal but the use of materials from outside the district had become established well before the canal age. Cornish and Dorset clay and stone, and flints from south east England, were shipped coastwise either to Liverpool, whence they were barged up the River Weaver to Winsford; to Bristol, proceeding then by the River Severn to Bewdley; or to Gainsborough, for onwards transport by the River Trent to Wilden Ferry or Willington depending on the state of the river. Final delivery was by packhorse. The finished ware was distributed in the same way.

The history of the events leading up to the promotion of the Trent & Mersey Canal (T&M) has been well documented elsewhere.[1] The Trent & Mersey, or Grand Trunk, Canal was a response to growing demand for transport by producers and manufacturers along its route. It ran from a junction with the Duke of Bridgewater's Canal at Preston Brook, giving it access to Manchester and Liverpool, to Derwentmouth on the River Trent. The Trent provided access, via the ports of Gainsborough and Hull, to the east coast and London. The main line

An early print showing Burslem, right, and Longport, to the left, in the 1840s. The foreground is rural but many pottery chimneys can be seen in the background. NEIL PARKHOUSE COLLECTION

The 'Preston Sheds' at Preston Brook. A group of three warehouses enclosed a wharf and two cranes with a full boat's length basin running under the northernmost one. They were equipped with steam hoisting equipment driven by a beam engine which was still working in the 1930s. Hoists were fitted over the covered basin and steam drove the two wharf cranes but most boat loading was done with jiggers, which were attached to cat heads projecting over the boats. Thus the goods were lifted by steam hoists, trucked by hand to their storage position on an upper floor and, when required, trucked to the jiggers and lowered by gravity. In the foreground, an Anderton Company boat is receiving bags from a flat. Behind is another narrowboat, to the right of which is a chute used for loading goods from an upper floor. Two flats are in the covered arm and the stables can be seen in the left background. WATERWAY IMAGES COLLECTION

Preston Brook Tunnel, north end circa 1910. The cottage was demolished many years ago. WATERWAY IMAGES COLLECTION

of the canal was 93 miles long and branches were subsequently made to Froghall, Newcastle-under-Lyme, Leek, Burslem, Wardle Lock and Hall Green. These are discussed more fully later in the book.

The Trent & Mersey opened throughout in 1777 and was soon connected to other canals. It held a strategic position and, in its early days, all inland waterway traffic between Lancashire and London, Bristol, south Staffordshire, Birmingham and the east Midlands had to pass over it. It was taken over by the North Staffordshire Railway (NSR) in 1846. The NSR became part of the London Midland & Scottish Railway (LM&SR) in 1923. The LM&SR and its canals, including the T&M, were nationalised in 1948.

The present book is intended to explain the interaction between the canal and industry in areas served by it and how the canal trade was conducted. To do this it is first necessary to list the main ingredients used in the pottery trade and which formed the principal cargoes on the canal, after which I have summarized the pattern of trade. White ware was first produced by John Astbury in 1720. A typical modern recipe for porcelain was:

China clay 55%

The Potteries Trade

Potash Feldspar 25%
Quartz 15%
White bentonite 5%

This was glazed with a mixture of:
Feldspar 25%
China clay 25
Flint.................................. 25%
Whiting 25%

The main ingredients of the body of bone china typically consist of:
China clay 25%
Feldspar 25%
Bone Ash 50%

A major cargo on the canal was Cornish (or china) stone used as a flux in bodies and a constituent of glazes. One common composition was:
Cornish stone 35%
China clay 10%
Siliceous fireclay 5%
Gypsum 50%

Gypsum was also used to make Plaster of Paris, used for pottery moulds.

The number of materials which are used in the pottery industry is enormous. Some of the others carried by canal were borax, soda, salt, syenite, lead, ball clay and hydrochloric acid.[2] China clay and unground china stone, feldspar, bones and flints were carried in uncovered boats and stored in the open or in open sided sheds. Borax, soda, syenite, ball clay and bentonite clay, were among cargoes which had to be protected from the weather and warehouse accommodation was provided for these.

Coastal and short sea shiploads of pottery materials were ordered by merchants from whom the pottery manufacturers and millers of pottery materials bought as required. These vessels could use the smaller Mersey ports at Runcorn, Weston Point and Ellesmere Port.

China clay and many other materials could be used directly in the potworks but flints, feldspar, quartz, bones and china stone had first to be ground. Only the largest manufacturers did their own grinding. There were a number of firms which specialised in providing ground materials to smaller potworks, sometimes in a slurry state. In the early days of the canal trade, clay was often packed in casks and carried in small quantities but the growth of consumption and the concentration of purchasing soon led to boatload quantities being carried in bulk. Irish granite was imported to line the potter's grinding mills and there was a return trade to Ireland of ground flints, ground stone and saggars

A posed picture at Waterloo Bridge, Runcorn, on the Bridgewater Canal circa 1907. At the far left a flat occupies the top lock of the 'new' flight. All the other craft are Manchester Ship Canal Company Bridgwater Department tugs, often referred to as 'Little Packets', so this may be some sort of official company view. **Stretford** *in the foreground is in a dry dock which was positioned between the top locks of the original and new flights. The camera was positioned close to the top gates of the top pair of staircase locks of the original flight, where another 'Little Packet' (far right) is lying in the approach channel.* NEIL PARKHOUSE COLLECTION

Anderton Company boatmen and boatwoman on the narrow boat **Thames**, *awaiting a return load to the Potteries in the dock below Runcorn Locks, also circa 1907. The flat in the background carries the two white bands around her cabin chimney that the Bridgewater Navigation inherited from the Mersey & Irwell Navigation and passed on to the Manchester Ship Canal Company.* NEIL PARKHOUSE COLLECTION

Sailing coasters in Weston Point Docks in the 1890s.
BASIL JEUDA COLLECTION

for the Arklow Pottery Company. Materials carried in deep sea ships were ordered by the merchants in 'parcels', sometimes of several hundred tons; borax, most of which came from California, was in this category. Deep sea goods would be discharged at Liverpool and lightered to the transshipment points between estuarial barges and narrow canal boats at Preston Brook, Anderton, or Ellesmere Port.

At one time, bones were an important cargo from Liverpool, because many imported animals were slaughtered there for the processed meat trade. After the opening of the Manchester Ship Canal Company's terminal docks in Manchester in 1894, some cargoes of pottery materials, e.g. syenite, a substitute for feldspar, and ground flints, arrived there, where they could be transshipped directly from ships to narrow boats. The manufacturers were concerned to find and protect reliable sources of clay and even investigated supplies from America. Wedgewood and some other large potters had clay leases in Cornwall by 1775, in which year the price was 3 shillings per ton at the mine and 16 shillings per ton at Liverpool. Some idea of the quantities passing sixteen years later is evidenced by the 1791 agreement between the Wedgwood family and twelve other potters, to deliver a minimum of 1,200tons per year. This syndicate was enlarged by a further twelve signatories in 1797.

Of interest, because it had at least one wharf in the Potteries, is the Hendra Company, a consortium of eight important manufacturers who acquired mineral rights on Hendra Common in Cornwall in 1799. The company owned a sloop, **Hendra**. Peter Lead gives the wharf as being at Longport while the Wedgwood archives refer to *'a clay wharf in the Potteries on land near the towing path on the south west side of the Trent & Mersey Canal for a term of 18 years*

Flint crushing circa 1850. NEIL PARKHOUSE COLLECTION

The Potteries Trade

Flint grinding circa 1850.
NEIL PARKHOUSE COLLECTION

1138.—Flint-grinding.

1198.—Mill-room, where the Ingredients for Pottery are mixed.

Mixing Pottery ingredients circa 1850. NEIL PARKHOUSE COLLECTION.

An advertisement from the Slop, Flint & Stone Trade Calculator, *September 1886, showing some of the machinery used in the making of pottery and tiles.* BASIL JEUDA COLLECTION

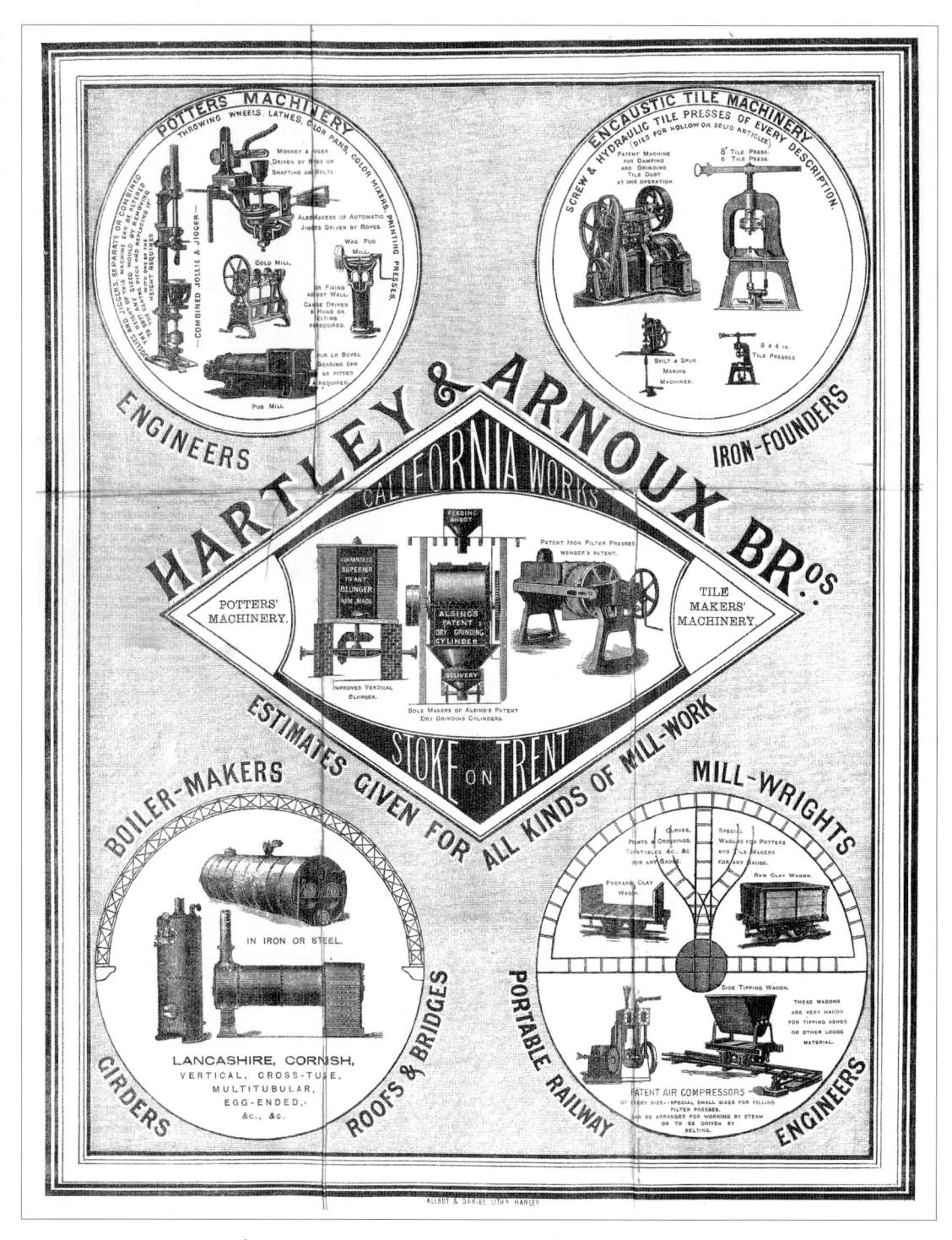

at a rental of £21.' In 1818, the Hendra Company was said to have *'too much stock of clay and Cornish stone at Charleston and at the wharf at Stoke'*.[3] The company was dissolved in 1821. The Hendra Company was the last of its kind amongst the North Staffordshire potters.

Between 1730 and 1850, the potters, individually and often collectively, did all in their power to secure a regular supply of ball clay, china clay and Cornish stone from south west England and Europe. Great quantities of flint were used for body and glaze, coming from south east England and the French coast, supplemented by chalkpit flints. Wedgwood feared that a monopoly in the supply of flints had formed when the price doubled in June 1777.[4] He arranged to buy flints from Gainsborough and supply other potters. Two months later, these steps had removed the threat of rising prices.[5] Gypsum was readily obtained, there being several quarries in Staffordshire and Derbyshire, with mills on the Trent & Mersey and further supplies were available close to the River Soar in Leicestershire and on the Grantham Canal.

Manufactured pottery, or ware, was packed in straw in casks, boxes or large open sided crates, originally with a wooden framework but later

Mr and Mrs Gorton with their Anderton Company boat **Nora** *at Hanley in the 1920s.* BASIL JEUDA COLLECTION

made of wire mesh. In canal records all these types of packed ware are referred to as crates. The sale of ware was commonly handled by merchants but some firms performed this function themselves by making a merchant their partner. Josiah Wedgewood was in partnership with Thomas Bentley, a Liverpool merchant. An interesting feature of the trade was the practice of some small potworks buying materials, and even sometimes crates and packing casks, from a larger manufacturer. Wm Adams' pottery at Tunstall sold 'composition' to S. & T. Cartledge, J. & R. Hall and other small potters, and acted as a merchant for the sale of ware for them via his own warehouse in Liverpool.[6] Albutt's 1802 map of the Potteries lists 144 separate works between the north of Tunstall and Lane End at the eastern end of the Potteries. Locations were at Green Lane, Golden Hill, Red Street, Tunstall, Newfield, Smithfield, Brownhills,

The Anderton Company's boat dock at Middleport in 1952. Boats were lifted in and out of the water by slings attached to electric hoists. BASIL JEUDA COLLECTION

*Boats below the Anderton lift in the 1930s. The narrow boats on the left are waiting to transship their salt cargoes into Henry Seddon's steam packet **Weaver Belle** and her flat **Gowanburn**. WATERWAY IMAGES COLLECTION*

Longport, Newport, Burslem, Cobridge, Booden Brook, Shelton, Hanley, Vale Pleasant, Etruria, Stoke Lane, Cliffgate Bank, Lower Lane, Lane Delph, Folley and Lane End.

Early potworks were sited on the coal measures, because the quantity of coal used to make a given amount of ware exceeded the total quantity of other raw materials. In 1823-35, clay was twice as expensive as coal. There was no great rush to follow the example of Josiah Wedgwood and move to canalside premises. There seem to have been few canalside works before the 1820s but later, in the 19th century, a number of works were built at Longport and Middleport. The Caldon Canal between Etruria and Ivy House Wharf, where the canal crosses the coalfield, was also favoured. Elsewhere, canalside works were built over the years, some as late as the early 1900s. There were only a few canalside potworks in Shelton and Stoke.

Unlike on the Birmingham Canal Navigation, it was not usually the practice for works on the towpath side to have a basin and side-bridge, and the movement of boat horses was hindered by boats unloading across the towpath using wheelbarrows and also by many towpath cranes, used for loading crates into boats and at warehouses. Nearly all the

John's Pottery at Armitage in the first decade of the 20th century. BASIL JEUDA COLLECTION

A circa 1908 view of Brook's (or Ashbrook's) Bridge at Little Leigh, between Saltersford and Bartington, nowadays more often called Taylor's Bridge. The bridge had been rebuilt with an iron span so that it could be easily raised in the event of subsidence. BASIL JEUDA COLLECTION

early, and much of the later, canal traffic in pottery materials and ware had therefore to be dealt with at canal wharves, and carted to and from the works. This put the canal at a disadvantage when railway and, later, road competition developed, particularly because the canal was considerably lower than most works, which were on the coalfield, with the result that the heavy clay had to be carted uphill, sometimes for a mile or more. The main line of the North Staffordshire Railway also followed the valley floor but the Potteries Loop Line, opened to Burslem in 1873 and completed in 1875, and the Tunstall Branch (1875) penetrated the coalfield and was close to a number of potworks. To assist in overcoming these cartage difficulties, the canal built three tramroads; from Burslem Basin to near St. John's Square; Etruria Basin to Hanley Market Place; and Stoke Basin to Lane End in Longton. Premises marked on maps as flint mills often ground china stone and other raw materials as well as flint. Many were earlier water powered flour mills that remained on their original sites even when converted to steam power. Not all were close to the Potteries but few were far from the canal although still requiring cartage to and from the waterway. In later years, some steam mills were specially built on the canal. A few of the larger potworks were integrated and contained their own milling facilities. Occasionally, a flint mill would

The canal at Barlaston Wharf in the 1930s, with the North Staffordshire Railway station in the right background. The warehouse on the left has gone, with the site now a car park but the cottages beyond remain. JOHN RYAN COLLECTION

RIGHT: *British Waterways (ex-Fellows, Morton & Clayton) motor boat* **Perch** *southbound above Middlewich Top Lock circa 1960.* AUTHOR'S COLLECTION

BELOW: **Action**, *owned by the Holland family, carried milled pottery materials in slop form in three large tubs. This was pumped out at the receiving works, in this case the Newport Pottery. The pump house is on the tow-path side and the slop was carried into the works through the pipes over the canal. Such craft were colloquially referred to as 'buttermilk boats'.* BASIL JEUDA COLLECTION

BOTTOM: *An Anderton Company motor boat bound for the Potteries approaches Wheelock Lock.* GRAHAM HOVEY

have railway sidings put in, mainly for the supply of coal but also competing for the flint traffic. Rail competition does not appear to have made a great difference to the Cornish and imported traffic, much of which was left to the canal until road haulage became a serious threat. Initially, rail took about 10% of the raw material traffic from Runcorn and about one third of the ware but canal traffic continued to increase due to rising production. We have seen something of the history, operation and location of works in the north Staffordshire pottery industry. Now it is time to look at the facilities provide for this trade by the Trent & Mersey Canal.

NOTES TO CHAPTER ONE
1. Lindsay. J., *The Trent & Mersey Canal*. David & Charles 1979
2. Hamer, F. & J., *The Potters Dictionary of Materials*. London 1986
3. Thomas J., *The Rise and Fall of the Staffordshire Potteries*. Adams & Dart 1971
4. Wedgwood to Bentley, 16th June 1777
5. Wedgwood to Bentley, 23rd June 1777
6. Thomas J., *op cit*

CHAPTER TWO
CANALSIDE WORKS AND WHARVES IN THE POTTERIES

Wharves are an integral part of a waterway and without them it could not operate. There were two main factors in choosing the site for a wharf; it needed to be as close as possible to the works or district it was to serve and it had to have good road access. In the days of horse-drawn cartage on unmetalled roads, it was important to minimise the cartage distance for heavy goods. On the other hand, the flyboat services carrying lighter and more valuable traffic could not make frequent stops and still maintain their schedules. The Manchester to London flyboats, for instance, were allowed only five days for the journey. Cartage distances for flyboat traffic could therefore be longer. Once built, there are very few instances known where wharves have been closed or re-sited until the period of massive urban reconstruction in the mid 20th century but, during the time when the canal was still in use for freight, they were often extended and new wharves built. Wharves were often built by the canal company, who either charged wharf rent for space on them or leased them outright to carriers.

Canal wharves in the Potteries were fairly simple affairs. They needed a metalled surface, usually of brick or cobblestones, warehouses to accommodate vulnerable goods, one or more cranes, a weighbridge and an office. The office was often accommodated in a dwelling house provided for the wharfinger. On early plans, warehouses may be indicated as such, or as clay & flint sheds, or crate sheds. Crate sheds were specifically for the storage of ware waiting to be despatched by boat.

Some outdoor storage areas were described as clay or flint 'beds' and had a surface of brick with a stone surround. In general, goods could be, and

*A pair of British Waterways narrow boats waiting to unload feldspar from Runcorn at Dolbey's Mill, Stoke-on-Trent on 25th June 1962. The motor is probably **Effingham**, built at Pimblotts of Northwich in 1959 and her butty, on the outside, is Yarwoods-built **Keppel**, which entered service in April 1960.* WATERWAYS IMAGES COLLECTION

A sketch map of waterside premises in the Potteries in 1889. BASIL JEUDA COLLECTION

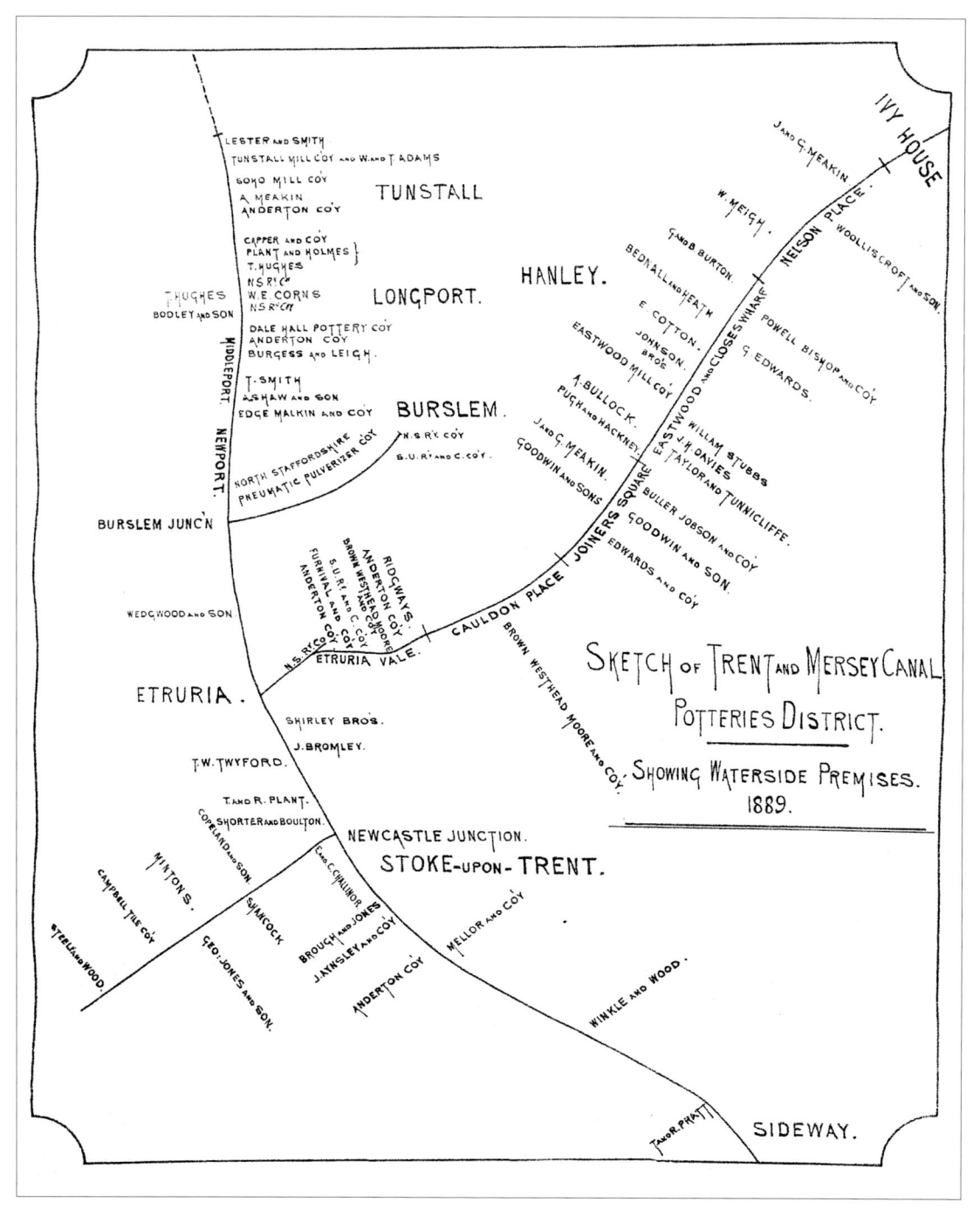

were, handled manually, so that cranes were not always necessary. In the Potteries, however, because of the need to lift heavy crates of ware, simple hand operated cranes proliferated, far more than could be found on most other sections of canal. Few of the Potteries warehouses had more than two floors and it appears that cranes, rather than hoists, were often used to raise goods from boats to the landing place for the upper floor. The canal company's wharf at Church Street, Stoke was exceptional in having a covered gantry over the towpath and canal. It may be appropriate to mention early methods of materials handling at wharves and warehouses. Bulk commodities like coal and china clay were shovelled out of the boat and moved by wheelbarrow to the appointed heap on the wharf. Bagged and cased goods were either craned or lifted manually out of the boat and moved about by 2-wheeled trucks with long handles, known as sack trucks. In the Potteries, as elsewhere, these methods survived until the end of canal traffic. The handling of bulk commodities was rarely mechanised, for instance by the provision of mechanical grabs, although at least one potworks graduated to loading ware into boats by forklift truck.

When ware was packed in casks, these could be moved by rolling. Fred Bloor has recounted his early working life in a carrier's office in 1936, when he was sent to Wood's potworks to roll a cask of ware to the Anderton Company's Burslem Wharf.[1]

The method of packing varied and packing cases or large open sided hampers were also used. The hampers originally had a wooden framework but, later, 3 inch square wire mesh was used.

The mills grinding pottery materials like flint, bones and china stone were often a long way from the potworks in which these materials were used. There was therefore a substantial canal trade in ground materials. Grinding reduced these materials to a fine powder which was hazardous to health, so they were often carried in the slop state, i.e. mixed with water. In this state they could be carried in barrels or tubs. Wm Podmore & Sons carried ground china stone and calcined flint between their Crowgutter and Consall mills on the Caldon Canal and their Caledonian Works at Shelton until 1950. This was conveyed in both the dry and slop condition. The slop flint from Crowgutter Mill was pumped directly into the hold of the boat and pumped out again at the other end. Following the general reduction in tolls from 1½d to 1d per ton-mile that had been made in 1832, the tolls on slop flint and slop china stone were further reduced to ½d per ton-mile from 22nd May 1843. Sometimes the water was evaporated and the flint, or other ground material, formed into blocks for carriage and use by the potters.

A problem with describing wharves and works in detail is that these premises often changed hands. It has not been possible to record all these changes in this book.

Tunstall

Starting from the north end of the Potteries district, there had been several potteries at Tunstall since the 14th century and, by 1818, there were eighteen. One more had been opened by 1863.[2] Many of these works were tileries for which, in many cases, the clay could be dug on site. As the 19th century progressed, Tunstall began to develop a large trade with the United States for its products, led by Alfred Meakin from 1875 and followed by Johnson Bros

*Another aspect of **Keppel** and **Effingham** whilst unloading feldspar at Dolbey's Mill on 25th June 1962.* WATERWAYS IMAGES COLLECTION

*Two motor boats belonging to the carrier John Knill of London tied up at the Trent & Mersey Canal Company's wharf, Church Street, Stoke on Trent in 1950. **Columba** (left) and **Kenelm** are loaded with salt on its way from Middlewich to Reading and Newbury. The owner is on the counter of the right hand boat.* COURTESY THE POTTERIES MUSEUM & ART GALLERY, STOKE-ON-TRENT

Mersey, Weaver boats in their original black and white livery at Port Vale Wharf. Leighton's Pottery is in the background.
BASIL JEUDA COLLECTION

The original site was later used by a boatyard and an iron works. The new wharf occupied 180 yards of main line canal frontage and had three arms giving a total water frontage of 1,700 feet. Up to twenty-three boats could be accommodated at any one time and it extended back between 300 and 400 yards from the canal.

Tunstall Wharf is sometimes referred to as Brownhills, or Brownhills Bridge, Wharf. It had access to the town via roads either from Peake's accommodation bridge or from Brownhills Bridge (No. 128). In 1847, Peake's brick wharf occupied land between the northern arm of Tunstall Wharf and a basin halfway between Peake's Bridge and Tunstall Bridge. Part of this land was later occupied by the Atlas Iron Foundry.

An early user of Tunstall Wharf was the carrying firm of Alexander Reid, who became the Anderton Company in 1836. They used the wharfage on each side of the southernmost arm. One of Reid's customers was Hugh Henshall Williamson who, in 1834 and 1835, received hundreds of tons of Gravesend and Newhaven flints, merchanted by the Weston Salt Company of Staffordshire and sent via the inland waterway route from London. They cost him, per ton, 22s (from Newhaven) and 26s (from Gravesend) *'delivered at A. Reid's wharf, Brownhills Bridge'*. In later years, the three arms were used (from the north) by the Shropshire Union Railways & Canal Co. and Peake's brickworks,[4] Adams & Meakins (pottery manufacturers) and the Anderton Company. In 1872, the Trader's North Staffordshire Carrying Company used Tunstall Wharf. The Shropshire

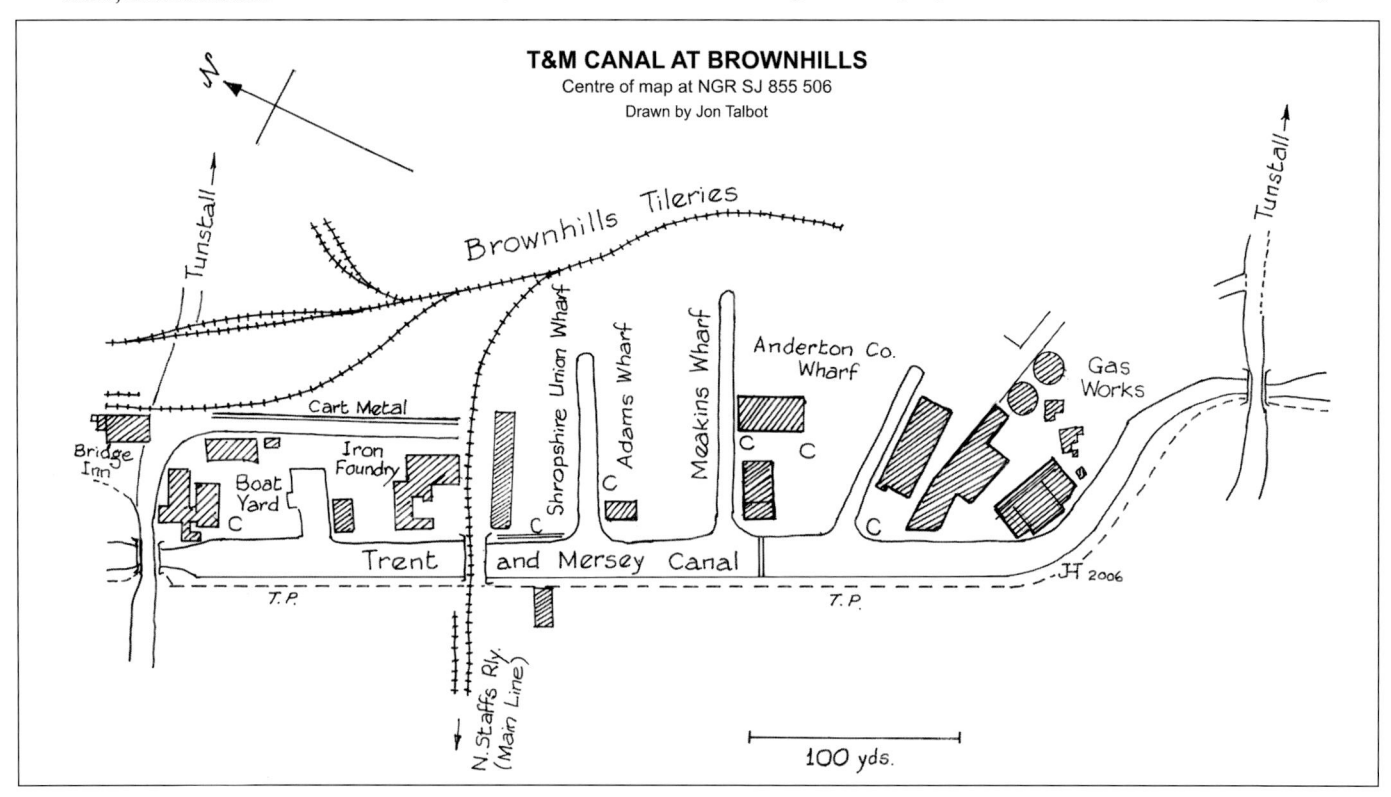

and W.H. Grindley & Co. in the 1880s.[3]

There was a wharf at Tunstall Bridge (No. 129) by 1781 and a *'new wharf'* at Tunstall was referred to in 1834, which was 130 yards to the south of the bridge.

Union had a hand operated travelling crane and a 30-cwt portable hand crane at their wharf, which was given up in 1921. In that year, the warehouse was described as being *'an old two-storey building'*. The stables had nine stalls and there were five clay and two flint beds. The Shropshire Union operated 100 foot of wharfage on the main line and the arm was 230 feet long. The Mersey, Weaver & Ship Canal Carrying Company later established a wharf on the site of the former Atlas Foundry styled, rather grandiloquently, Colonial Wharf.

Over the years, vast quantities of pottery materials, ware, bricks and tiles were handled over Tunstall Wharf, as well as general merchandise, groceries and flour. Even in the 1930s, Tunstall Wharf was still served by a regular Mersey, Weaver flyboat service conveying Liverpool goods to and from their depot at Anderton, on the River Weaver, where traffic was transshipped between canal boat and Mersey flat. Flour was still being unloaded at Tunstall in 1943 and pottery material in 1950 but the whole wharf had become disused by 1954. One of the reasons for its comparatively early demise was the introduction of motor cartage by the carriers, which enabled them to reduce the number of depots and increase the cartage area of each.

Between Tunstall Wharf and Brownhills Bridge lay Brownhills Gas Works. On the south side of the bridge, Williamson once had a wharf which was vacant land by 1899. The Tunstall Chemical Company, later Staffordshire Chemicals Ltd, had a sulphuric acid plant by the canal below Watergate Street.[5]

Longport

The name 'Longport' was first adopted in 1777, on completion of the canal, being originally known as Longbridge. Until the opening of the Burslem Branch in 1805, Longport, and its adjoining district of Middleport, had the nearest canal wharves to the important pottery town of Burslem. Public wharves here were first mentioned in 1790,[6] although some almost certainly date back to the opening of the canal. An early carrier at Longport was Richard Podmore of Chester who, by 1st May 1780, was trading between Wheelock (for Chester and Nantwich), Longport (Crosby's Wharf), Wolverhampton and Birmingham. The site of Crosby's Wharf has not been identified but William Crosby was a wharfinger and carrier based at Cavendish Bridge near Shardlow, who traded between Birmingham, Cavendish Bridge and the Potteries between about 1775 and 1781, when he was declared bankrupt.[7]

The first identifiable wharf going south is Appleby's, sited where the Scotia Brook enters the canal.[8] By 1847, the wharf appeared to have been absorbed in the premises of the Bradwell Pottery,[9] although the *Staffordshire Advertiser* of 23rd August 1851 carried a notice offering *'To be let, Longport Wharf, formerly in occupation of Appleby & Co and now in occupation of the Anderton Carrying Co'*. This wharf was described as being midway between Tunstall and Longport.[10] In 1802, Thomas Appleby was agent to William Kenwright, carrier and timber merchant, who used a wharf at Longport.[11] Geo Appleby, probably his son, was one of many carriers who flourished before the effects of railway competition were felt on the Potteries trade. In 1818,[12] he was

The remains of Mersey, Weaver's Colonial Wharf at Tunstall, photographed on 17th October 1971. WATERWAY IMAGES COLLECTION

Boats unloading at Middleport in the 1930s. BASIL JEUDA COLLECTION

A horse boat passing a British Waterways pair of boats (a new 'Admiral' Class motor paired with an ex-LM&SR 'Station' boat butty) immediately north of Longport Bridge on 25th June 1962. WATERWAY IMAGES COLLECTION

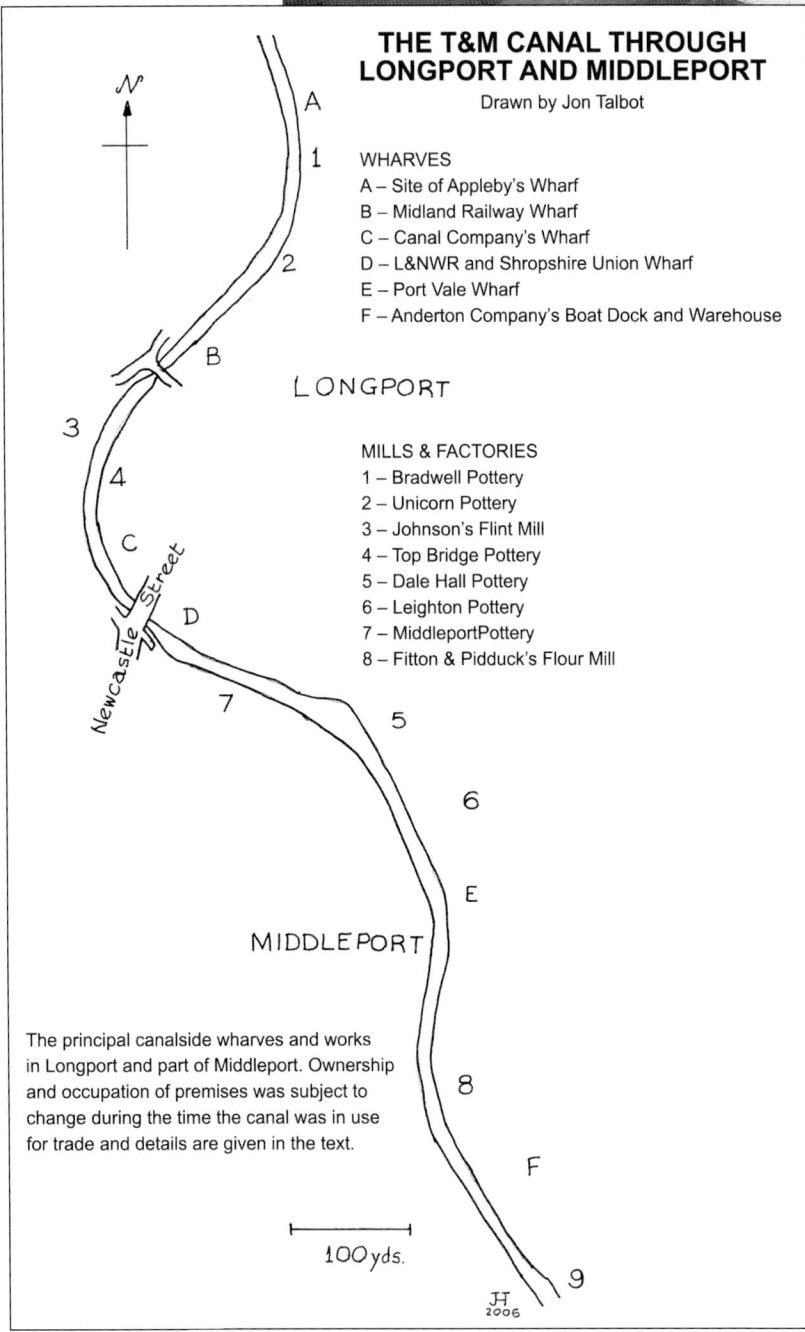

THE T&M CANAL THROUGH LONGPORT AND MIDDLEPORT

Drawn by Jon Talbot

WHARVES
A – Site of Appleby's Wharf
B – Midland Railway Wharf
C – Canal Company's Wharf
D – L&NWR and Shropshire Union Wharf
E – Port Vale Wharf
F – Anderton Company's Boat Dock and Warehouse

MILLS & FACTORIES
1 – Bradwell Pottery
2 – Unicorn Pottery
3 – Johnson's Flint Mill
4 – Top Bridge Pottery
5 – Dale Hall Pottery
6 – Leighton Pottery
7 – Middleport Pottery
8 – Fitton & Pidduck's Flour Mill

The principal canalside wharves and works in Longport and part of Middleport. Ownership and occupation of premises was subject to change during the time the canal was in use for trade and details are given in the text.

advertising as a carrier to Manchester and Liverpool from his Longport Wharf. In 1822, he was an agent for Crockett & Salkeld, carriers between Lancashire and the West Midlands. Appleby was also a maltster and a dealer in porter (ale). By 1834,[13] he had changed his address to the canal company's Longport Wharf. In 1840, he advertised as a carrier of passengers and parcels for the Grand Junction Railway between Newcastle-under-Lyme and Witmore station, and was still in the Manchester and Liverpool canal trade in 1846. In 1851, Hamlet Appleby was a wharfinger at Tunstall for the Anderton Company and the Bridgewater Trustees, a post he was still occupying ten years later.

In 1802, the canal company had only one wharf at Longport, located on the north side of Longport Bridge (No. 126). Kenwright's timber yard and wharf was south of Bridge No. 127.[14] By 1847, there was another company's wharf on the north side of Bridge No. 127 that, by 1872, had been leased by the North Staffordshire Railway (NSR) to the Midland Railway (MR), who were still there in 1896. All three of these wharves had become the property of the NSR by 1873. This layout was still extant in 1881 but, by 1894, the wharf south of the bridge was vacant land and the buildings had been demolished. This left the canal company with only one wharf at Longport.

These wharves had a combined canal frontage of about 500 feet. In practical terms each could accommodate three boats at a time. In 1802, there were two potteries adjacent to the canal company's original wharf, belonging to John Davenport and Henshall, Williamson & Co. By 1847, these had become one pottery, the Top Bridge Works, which had its own wharf and crane. In the same year, the canal company's wharf had two warehouses but, in 1857, enlargements were made to the crate

*ABOVE: Ex Fellows, Morton & Clayton single motor boat **Tench** ready to unload coal at the former LM&SR wharf at Longport on 25th June 1962.*

*BELOW: Awaiting unloading close to the bridge at Longport on the same day was Tench's butty **Raven**, which had been built as **Hydrus** for the Grand Union Canal Carrying Company by Harland & Wolff at North Woolwich in 1935. Sold in October 1943, she was bought back for the nationalised fleet in 1950. Mechanical handling equipment was rare at Potteries wharves. The pair of boats seen on page 28 are visible lying empty, facing south, alongside the towpath beyond the bridge. BOTH WATERWAY IMAGES COLLECTION*

A stretch of the T&M at Port Vale circa 1927. Right foreground is the Anderton Company's Middleport Wharf, behind which is Mersey, Weaver's Port Vale Wharf. Piles of clay stone lie in the open air on both wharves. Out of sight on the right is Albion Pottery, whilst in the centre background is Price Brothers Top Bridge Pottery, with Keeling pottery behind and on the skyline centre right the works of John Maddocks & Son Ltd, manufacturers of hotel tableware. BASIL JEUDA COLLECTION

sheds at the company's Longport wharves. Because the canal company eventually had three wharves in Longport, it is difficult to link carriers with a specific wharf. However, the wharves were so close together that they were probably treated as one unit. Geo Appleby and the canal company's carrying arm, Hugh Henshall & Co., were early users of the Longport wharves, as was William Henshall, who commenced a flyboat service between London, Manchester, Liverpool and Chester in 1827.[15]

After 1847, when the Trent & Mersey Canal became part of the NSR, the railway company had their own fleet of boats that called at Longport. Mellor, Colsell & Co., carriers to Manchester, Liverpool and London, were serving Longport in 1872, whilst according to Peter Lead, the Hendra Company had a wharf there in the early 1800s.[16] The public wharves at Longport were also used by numerous smaller carriers. Another canalside building there in 1847 was the Longport (later the Unicorn) Works, on the north side of the company's wharf at Bridge No. 127. Flanking this was the Bradwell Works, which had a covered arm from the canal. By 1880, they had been joined by A.E. Hughes (later, Johnsons) flint mill, which had a gantry over Canal Street and a towpath crane.

It would appear that the pattern of usage of canalside land at Longport had already been established by 1847 and was to have only minor additions and alterations until the end of canal carrying in the 1960s. There was a potworks (in 1802, Williamson & Henshall) on the south side of Longport Bridge (No. 126), immediately south of which was Pickfords Wharf, with a frontage of 500 feet and a covered basin. When Pickfords gave up their long distance carrying activities around 1847, this wharf was taken over by the carrying department of the Grand Junction Canal Company. It is not known when the Grand Junction gave up this wharf. They were advertising services to Manchester, Liverpool, Birmingham, Shrewsbury and London from here in 1872. Their carrying subsidiary was finally dissolved in July 1876 and this is the probable date.

By 1880, the wharf (and also the adjacent potworks) had been cleared of buildings and by 1896 the combined land was being used jointly by the London & North Western Railway (L&NWR), the Shropshire Union Railways & Canal Co. and the MR, who had built a 130 foot long shed in 1896, fronting the canal. It was known officially as Longport Railway Depot. There were rails for a travelling crane on the wharf but no record of such a crane. In 1921, the wharf had four 30 cwt and one 25 cwt hand cranes. There was a clay bed let out to J. Cooper of Burslem and opposite Pickfords' wharf was the New Bridge Pottery, worked in 1802 by Shirley, Lindop & Co. The Shropshire Union was a carrier on the canal from 1837 to 1921.

Port Vale and Middleport

Pickfords Wharf was separated by the Dale Hall Pottery from Port Vale Wharf. This was a large wharf with a canal frontage of about 420 feet, able to accommodate six boats. In addition, there was a covered arm capable of taking two boats. By 1838, it was occupied by the Anderton Company who were still there in 1896 but, by 1912, occupation had passed to the Mersey, Weaver & Ship Canal Carrying Company, whose headquarters it became.

Mersey, Weaver had a salt packing shed here, as well as warehouses, crate sheds and a large outdoor storage area. It remained in Mersey, Weaver hands until that company sold out to British Waterways in 1958. It then ceased to be used, the remaining carrying operations in that part of the Potteries being transferred to Navigation Road.

In 1848-51 a toll gate and house were erected in Newport Street at Dale Hall, to cover traffic using Port Vale Wharf.[17] Leighton's Pottery was located immediately behind and adjacent to the wharf. Between Port Vale Wharf and Bridge No. 125, there were, in 1847, only a bone mill immediately south of the wharf, and a corn mill (built in 1844 and owned by Samuel Fitton between 1848 and 1854), again with its own arm. These small mills often sent flour to each other. There is a letter dated 27th April 1846 in respect of thirty-one loads (about 14 tons) of flour taken by Sutton's from Port Vale mill to Minshull mill, near Middlewich, at 5 shillings per ton. In 1850, Fitton was prosecuted and fined for selling adulterated flour.[18] The bone mill disappeared in subsequent development but the corn mill remained, becoming Fitton & Pidduck's Hungarian Roller Flour Mills. By 1940 it was used by Price & Son as a bakery. The Fitton family may have had some connection with the Mersey, Weaver company because they renamed one of their boats *Fitton* in 1938.

By the end of the century, the Middleport Pottery (Burgess & Leigh) was established. Burgess & Leigh were important customers of the Anderton Company for both raw materials and the despatch of finished ware, and the works is featured in the 1945 film *Painted Boats*, showing the Anderton Company's first motor boat, **Westminster**, loading crates there, with boats unloading clay in the background. Adjacent is the Anderton Company's boatyard (with warehouse added in 1908) and these, together with Fitton's Mill, occupied the entire canalside between Port Vale Wharf and Bridge No. 125. On the south side of Bridge No. 125 was built Middleport Mills, where potters' materials were ground. John Walley, carrier and flint merchant, was still bringing china stone here in the 1950s. Burslem Corporation wharf lay between Middleport Mills and West Street. The Coventry carrier, William Bache had a wharf in Middleport, which he relinquished on 21st February 1846 but it has not been possible to establish its exact situation.

Newport

Between Middleport Mills and the junction of the Burslem Arm lies the district of Newport, whose canalside, in 1802, contained only the Newport Pottery of Walter Daniel. By the end of the century, it had been joined by the Royal Staffordshire Pottery and two flint mills (Malkins), one on each side of the Newport Lane Bridge (No. 123).

*Port Vale Wharf, Middleport, headquarters of the Mersey, Weaver & Ship Canal Carrying Company circa 1945. The motor **Empire** was converted from a horse boat at the Anderton Company's boatyard in 1941. At this date nearly all their fleet was horse drawn. The boat to the left is unloading sacks of borax by hand crane. The salt packing shed is to the right of and behind the crane, whilst raw materials for the pottery industry are stacked on the extensive wharf, behind which is the six-kiln Leighton Pottery.* COURTESY THE POTTERIES MUSEUM & ART GALLERY, STOKE-ON-TRENT

The Trent & Mersey Canal – Trade and Transport 1770-1970

A 1930s aerial view of A.&J. Wilkinson's Royal Staffordshire Pottery, Burslem, left front. To the right is the same company's Newport Pottery. The famous pottery artist Clarice Cliff began work here in 1916. The canal can be seen in the left foreground. Note how the boat unloading at Wilkinson's is being worked over a long plank, presumably because the canal is too shallow for it to get alongside the wharf without lightening a little. AUTHOR'S COLLECTION

The Burslem Arm in the 1930s. Malkin's flour mill is on the left. Centre right is the Mersey, Weaver (formerly Shropshire Union) wharf and warehouse, behind which is the Anderton Company's wharf.
BASIL JEUDA COLLECTION

The Burslem Arm

The Burslem Arm, 3 furlongs in length, was dug in 1805 and its terminal basin was connected at the same time with the centre of Burslem by a tramroad, on which there were two potworks. There was little development on its banks. At the junction with the main line was the Mersey, Weaver & Ship Canal Company's Newport boatyard. On the outside bank (opposite the towpath), the Burslem Cooperative Society established a bakery, which was still receiving 60 tons of flour weekly from Sun Mills in Manchester Docks in the late 1950s. Adjacent to this was Malkins flour mill. The terminal facilities consisted of the Shropshire Union Basin (formerly a coal and ironstone loading basin), wharf and warehouse below Dimsdale Street footbridge, and the canal company basin and wharf above it. The latter wharf had a warehouse and crate shed, the shed being extended in 1852. The arm terminated in another basin, surrounded with open storage and flanked by the Trent New Wharf Pottery of Wood & Sons. Materials could be wheelbarrowed into their works and ware in casks rolled to the crate shed. This was one of the last potworks to receive its raw materials by water. Adjacent to the potworks was the Furlong Flint Mill.

The *North Staffordshire Mercury* of 23rd August 1845 advertised the '*Sale of earthenware manufactory facing Newcastle Street called Furlong Middle and Lower Middle including two biscuit ovens and four glost*

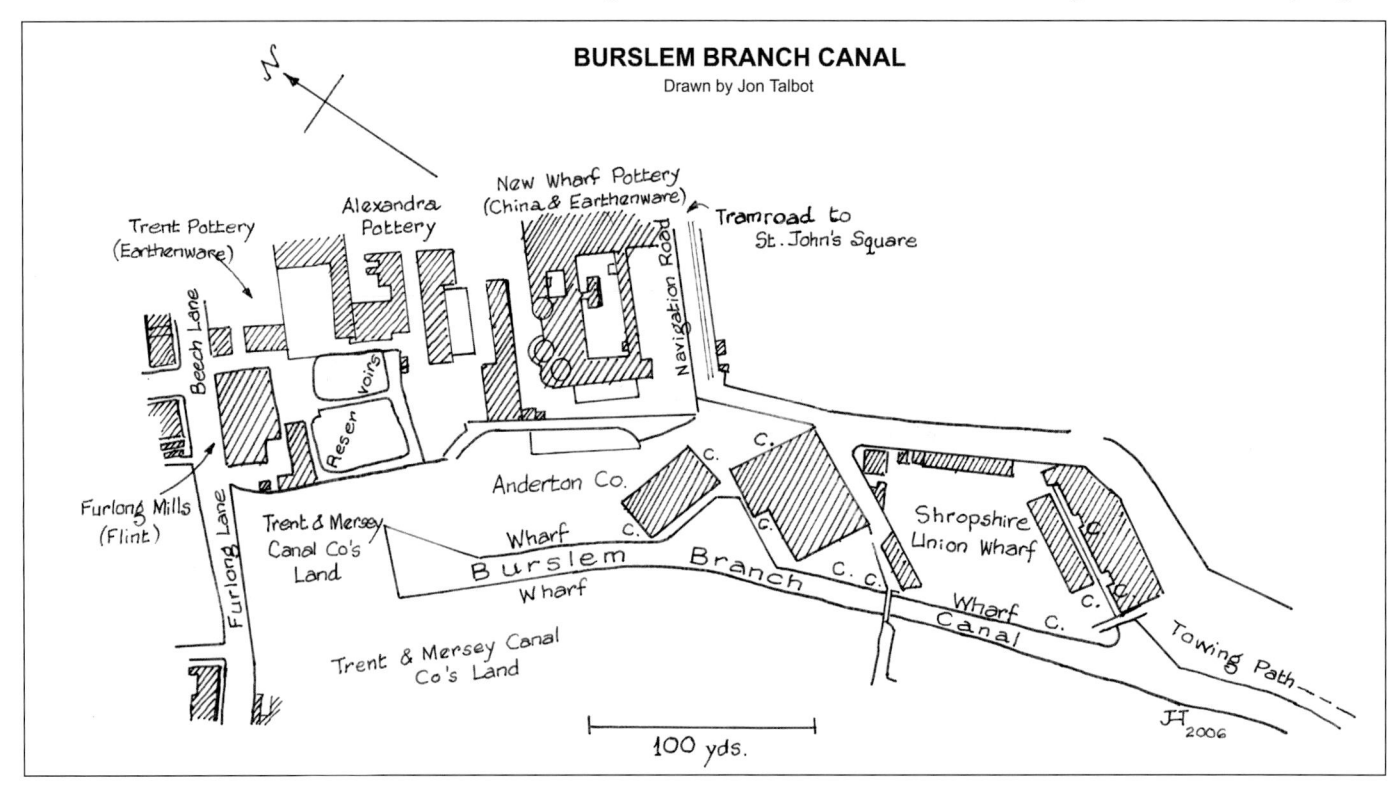

LEFT: *The end of the Burslem Arm in 1935, with china stone on the wharf. In the background is Wood's Trent New Works.* BASIL JEUDA COLLECTION

BELOW: *The yard of the Anderton Company's wharf at the terminus of the Burslem Arm circa 1960. The houses across and above the arm would have had an enviable view of the activities below.* E.J.D. WARRILOW, KEELE UNIVERSITY COLLECTION

BOTTOM: *Back on the main line of the canal, this is the rear of the Anderton Company premises at Etruria Basin, circa 1960.* BASIL JEUDA COLLECTION

ovens and also a flint mill capable of 1500 flints a week. Late Enoch Wood.' The canal company's depot was leased to the Anderton Company in 1894, as part of an agreement whereby the Anderton Company took over the NSR carrying business, being required to continue to provide public wharfage at this wharf. The Shropshire Union wharf passed to the Mersey, Weaver Company when the Shropshire Union ceased carrying operations in 1921. It had a two-storey warehouse, an open crate shed, an open clay shed and three clay beds, the largest being 1320 feet by 35 feet. The stables had twelve stalls. Wharf frontage to the branch was 240 feet and the basin was 150 feet long and 16 feet wide. There was one 5-ton crane, two of 25 cwt and and two of 20 cwt. Fred Bloor started work at the Anderton Co. wharf in 1936, at the age of fourteen. In a recorded interview with Arthur Wood he described his work there as a clerk. The company employed men to unload and load boats but he was sometimes sent to Wood's works to roll a cask of ware down to the wharf. The crate boats would often call at several wharves and works to make up a load, which was then despatched to Runcorn to await merchant's orders. China clay and flints were stored in the open but ball clay went into the shed. Remarkably, for 1936, the Burslem office had no typewriter, nor did it use carbon paper, copies of handwritten documents being copied in a copying press. The Burslem Arm wharves were still in use by British Waterways in 1958, when they took over Mersey, Weaver. They were the only wharves in use in the Longport and Burslem area by that date.

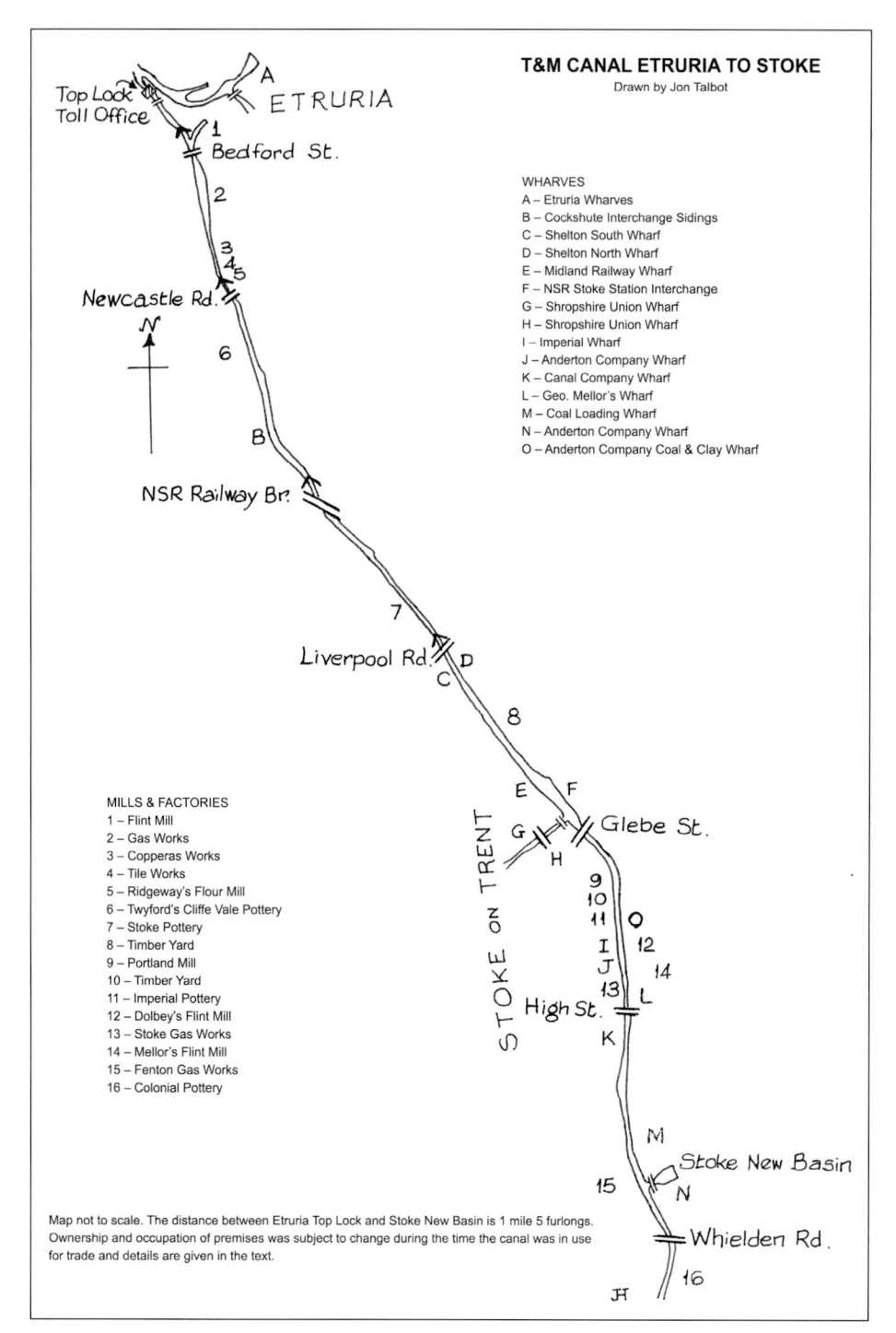

The Trent & Mersey Canal – Trade and Transport 1770-1970

T&M CANAL ETRURIA TO STOKE
Drawn by Jon Talbot

WHARVES
- A – Etruria Wharves
- B – Cockshute Interchange Sidings
- C – Shelton South Wharf
- D – Shelton North Wharf
- E – Midland Railway Wharf
- F – NSR Stoke Station Interchange
- G – Shropshire Union Wharf
- H – Shropshire Union Wharf
- I – Imperial Wharf
- J – Anderton Company Wharf
- K – Canal Company Wharf
- L – Geo. Mellor's Wharf
- M – Coal Loading Wharf
- N – Anderton Company Wharf
- O – Anderton Company Coal & Clay Wharf

MILLS & FACTORIES
1 – Flint Mill
2 – Gas Works
3 – Copperas Works
4 – Tile Works
5 – Ridgeway's Flour Mill
6 – Twyford's Cliffe Vale Pottery
7 – Stoke Pottery
8 – Timber Yard
9 – Portland Mill
10 – Timber Yard
11 – Imperial Pottery
12 – Dolbey's Flint Mill
13 – Stoke Gas Works
14 – Mellor's Flint Mill
15 – Fenton Gas Works
16 – Colonial Pottery

Map not to scale. The distance between Etruria Top Lock and Stoke New Basin is 1 mile 5 furlongs. Ownership and occupation of premises was subject to change during the time the canal was in use for trade and details are given in the text.

Etruria

Until recently, the canal at Etruria was dominated by the Shelton Iron & Steel Works. In 1841, Earl Granville had blown in three blast furnaces at Hanley, connected by tramway to the canal at Etruria. This was known as the Shelton Iron & Coal Works. Much of the pig iron produced here was converted into wrought iron by a nominally separate company, the Shelton Bar Iron Company. In 1852, a forge and rolling mill were added. The works was extended to a canalside location in 1858 and, in 1860, was producing 50,000 tons of pig iron. As the Shelton Iron, Steel & Coal Co., it produced its first steel in 1889 and it amalgamated with the Shelton Bar Iron Company in the same year. In 1919, the concern was acquired by John Summers & Co. and at that time included five coal mines, along with three furnaces, producing 2,000,000 tons of coal, 215,000 tons of pig iron and 200,000 tons of steel a year. Somewhat confusingly, the entire complex was known locally as 'Shelton Bar'.

Tom Rolt described the scene as he experienced it in 1939:

> 'Cressy's white windows … now looked directly into a clangorous rolling mill, lofty as the nave of a cathedral, where white hot billets of steel were being flattened as easily as pastry under a rolling pin, or grappled by the electric cranes which rumbled high overhead … A damp white mist shot through by the sunlight with miniature rainbows momentarily enveloped us as we passed the cooling towers, and beyond these the coke ovens were belching steam and flame alternately. Opposite them, towering above us, reared the fiery heart

An early engraving of Wedgewood's Etruria Pottery. WATERWAY IMAGES COLLECTION

Wedgwood's Etruria Pottery looking north. The sailing vessel is artistic licence. The roundhouse at the left hand end of the frontage, which may once have been a glost oven but was later used as a counting house, is the only part of Wedgwood's original works to survive. As a result of mining subsidence it now stands several feet below towing path level. WATERWAY IMAGES COLLECTION

of this monstrous organisation - the blast furnaces. Lifts were creeping up and down their pitiless steel sides, feeding them with fuel, and, as we passed, one of the cones that close their throats was lowered to admit a charge, the air above shimmering in the sudden blast of intense heat which shot skywards.[19]

In 1847, Earl Granville's Wharf was opposite Wedgwood's Etruria Pottery, connected by tramway with his mines and ironworks at Hanley. By the turn of the century, the wharf had disappeared under extensions to the Shelton Iron & Steel Works.

Wedgwood's Pottery, the first to be built alongside the canal and completed in 1768, closed in 1939 and operations were transferred to Barlaston. In 1847, on the south side of Bridge No. 118, was an '*engine manufactory*' but this had disappeared by the end of the century. Nearby, the Mersey, Weaver & Ship Canal Carrying Co. established a wharf and warehouses at Belmont Road, between the wars. The warehouses

Wedgewood's Etruria Works circa 1910, from a similar perspective to the engraving above. The Shelton Iron & Steel Works features in the right background. BASIL JEUDA COLLECTION

A circa 1930 aerial view of Wedgwood's Etruria Pottery. The canal runs diagonally from left to right across the top of the picture, beneath the bridge, top centre, from which the picture on the previous page was taken. WATERWAY IMAGES COLLECTION

were constructed with iron frames to withstand the effects of subsidence and had gantries which projected over the canal. Among the cargoes unloaded and stored here was flour for the Silvertown Co-op, a traffic that was lost in the early 1950s.

The canal company had premises at Etruria Basin,

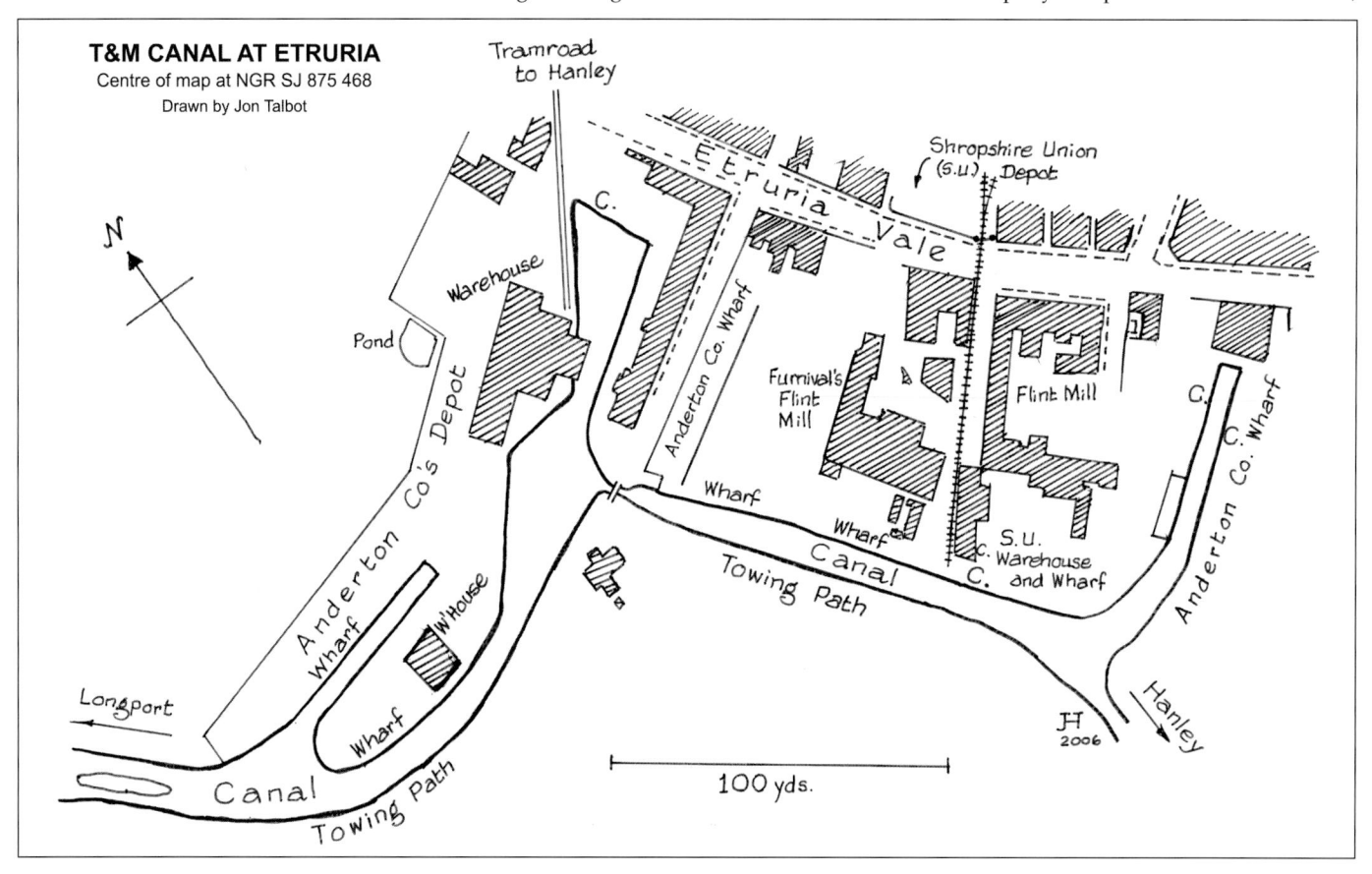

at the junction of the main line and Caldon Canal. The basin was in existence by 1783 and was, in 1802, connected by a tramroad to the centre of Hanley. Like Burslem and Stoke basins, this was leased to the Anderton Company in 1894, with the same proviso as to arrangements for public wharfage. The Anderton Company had other wharves at Etruria. One was a narrow strip of land between the canal company's basin and Furnivals (later Mellors) flint mill, with a canal frontage of only one boat's length. The other was on the south side of an arm about 350 feet long, originally built to serve Samuel Hollins Pottery and in use by 1802. On 24th November 1832, M. & K. Hollins advertised in the *Staffordshire Mercury*: '*19 casks of china clay now lying at Vale Pleasant Wharf upwards of 12 months. Notice is given if owner does not pay wharfage within 21 days they will be sold to defray same.*' It appears that Hollins had established a wharf on the arm adjacent to their works by this date. The north side was used by the Shropshire Union, who also used wharfage between the flint mill and the arm, connected by a short tramroad to their warehouse on Etruria Vale Road. The *1912 Kelly's Directory* gives the following street numbers in Etruria Vale: Unnumbered - Anderton Co; No. 75 - SUC and Anderton Co.; No. 79 - Anderton Co. wharf. These numbers rise from Bedford Street towards Etruria Basin, which is No. 79. The L&NWR, MR and Shropshire Union Co. had premises on the opposite side of the road at No. 64. On the road side of Etruria Vale, the depot had a two-storey warehouse, stalls for eight horses and a 30 cwt hand crane. On the canal side of the Vale, there was another two-storey warehouse and another 30 cwt hand crane, whilst the wharf frontage measured 117 feet.

The Anderton Company's wharves at Etruria passed to the Bridgewater Trustees when they took them over in 1848, and were handed back in 1948 when the Manchester Ship Canal Company (successors to the Trustees) terminated the agency agreement with the Anderton Co. Etruria Basin suffered from mining subsidence and the inner part, beyond the junction of the basin and the Caldon Canal, was infilled in 1940. The Anderton Company/Shropshire Union arm was still in water in 1958. *Painted Boats* has a shot of the wharfage on the Caldon Branch adjacent to the arm, with boats unloading. Below the top lock at Etruria, a short arm served the Etruscan Bone & Flint Mills, built in 1856 by Alderman Jesse and Councillor H.B. Shirley. Calcined bone from South America was milled here and the works also calcined bone from other sources. China stone and flint was also

Johnson's Lock (No. 39), also known as Etruria 2nd Lock, with the canal company maintenance yard in the right background. Shirley's Etruscan bone and flint mill survives as a museum below the lock off the right hand side of the picture. The narrow boat **Margaret** *locks through on 25th June 1962.* WATERWAY IMAGES COLLECTION

One of the Anderton Company's wharves at Etruria with two of their boats alongside. Situated on the arm below Bedford Street Locks, it was still being used despite severe subsidence. BASIL JEUDA COLLECTION

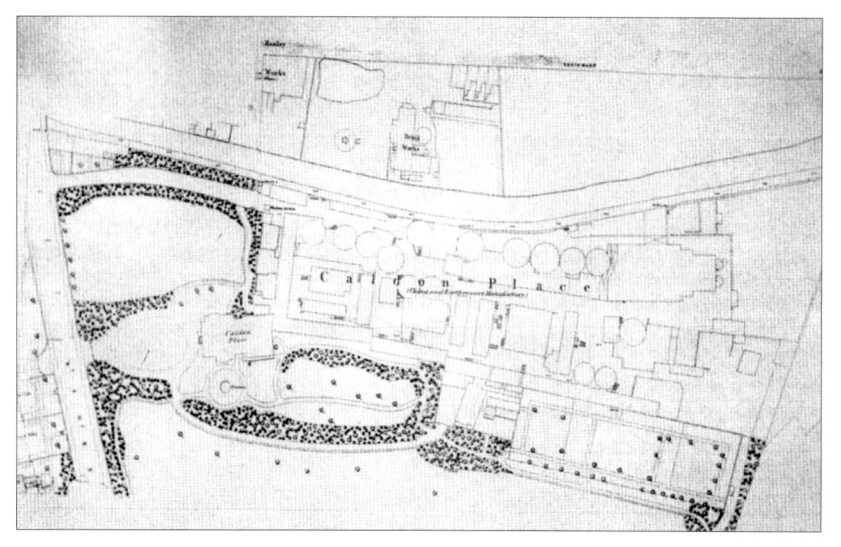

Caldon Place Works, Etruria, an extract from an OS map of 1866.

The original Stoke Bottom Lock on 22nd March 1974. It was re-sited, and a new house built, during construction of the city's D road, the A500, which has since been altered again, causing further adjustment of the canal. WATERWAY IMAGES COLLECTION

milled, and colours and glazes manufactured. Between there and the Newcastle Road Bridge (No. 115) were situated Etruria Gas Works, which were equipped with a coal hoist, a copperas works, the Etruscan Tile Works (later Castlefield Pottery) and Ridgeway's flour mill, which had an elevator.

In 1847, on the towpath side below Bridge No. 115 was a works belonging to Thos Brassey, the site of which was to become part of the 1887 Cliffe Vale Works of Twyford & Co. China clay was still being brought here in 1958 by the boats of Potter & Son (Runcorn) Ltd. Adjacent to Cliffe Vale was Cockshute railway sidings, where raw materials, particularly flints, brought by rail were transshipped across the towpath, using shovels and wheelbarrows, to canal boats serving local works.

Shelton Bridge

Above Shelton, or Liverpool Road, Bridge (No. 114) the small Stoke Pottery was on the towpath side. In the early days of the canal, an important wharfage area had grown up around the crossing of the canal by the turnpike from Trent Vale, built in 1791-2. Shelton South Side Wharf was in existence by 1791 and the North Side by 1802. In actual fact, both of these wharves were on the outside (north side) of the canal and lay respectively east and west of the bridge. In 1802, Wm Kenwright's timber yard and wharf lay west of the bridge. By 1837, this was the timber yard and sawmills of J. & T. Dimmock & Co., who were also boat builders.

J. Smith & Sons of Burton on Trent occupied a wharf on the eastern side of the bridge in 1802 and advertised it for sale in 1841:

> 'Sale of freehold and tithe free wharf and warehouse in Wharf St, Shelton on banks of Trent & Mersey Canal. The warehouse is two storeys high 44ft 8in long x 18ft 8in broad. There is a crate shed 65ft 6in long x 21ft broad with tiled roof and supported by metal pillars. Premises in occupation of John and Ralph Smith.'[20]

By 1847, the position had changed. The NSR one chain survey of that year shows no wharf on the west side of the bridge but wharves on both the towpath side and outside banks of the canal east of the bridge. A later reference to one of the east side wharves states, 'a freehold wharf at Shelton lately owned by Spode, formerly held by the Bridgwater Trustees in succession to Pickford offered for sale 1850'.[21]

The Bridgewater Trustees entered the Potteries trade in 1841 and may have given up Shelton Wharf when they acquired the Anderton Company and its wharves in 1847. In 1834, carriers calling at Shelton included: Robins, Mills & Co.; Jos. Smith (Shardlow and London via Gainsborough); John Whitehouse & Sons; Crowley, Hicklin, Batty & Co. (all parts); John Kenworthy. William Ebbern also had a wharf, shed and crane here which he advertised to be let in 1850. He advertised some boats for sale at the same time but was still selling whiting and cement at his Liverpool Road Wharf in the following year. By 1900, the wharfage east of the bridge on the outside of the canal had disappeared under extensions to the NSR goods yard but there was a small wharf and crane on the towpath side, apparently used by Parker's Brewery. West of the bridge, the timber yard now belonged to Bass & Smith and had tramways and cranes. Between Parker's Brewery and the junction with the Newcastle Canal were: the Atlas Works; Midland Nut & Bolt Co; a steam joinery works; G. Pim, Brewers; an ironfounder; Showell's Brewery; stables; Midland Railway Wharf; hay and corn stores and the Shropshire Union clay wharf.

Anderton Company boats at the firm's Lytton Street Wharf, Stoke, in the 1930s. Two boats are unloading china clay from Runcorn or Weston Point and behind, a cart is loading from a large stack of coal. COURTESY THE POTTERIES MUSEUM & ART GALLERY, STOKE-ON-TRENT

Stoke

The area around the junction with the Newcastle Canal featured a number of important wharves, none of which was in existence in 1802. On the offside of the canal was the North Staffordshire Railway's railway and canal transshipment depot. On the towpath side, there had been a wharf since at least 1832.[22] In the *North Staffordshire Mercury* of 2nd October 1847, two boats were offered for sale '*at Mr Brassingtons Wharf, Stoke, beside* [the] *Newcastle-under-Lyme Canal*'. By the end of the century, there were two wharves, the northernmost one occupied in 1892 by W.U. Lester, a carrier to London, but by 1912 being used by the Midland and London & North Western railways. The other was used by Colsell, Walley & Co. in 1872. By 1892, the Shropshire Union had moved here from Wharf Street and used this wharf and another just round the corner on the Newcastle Canal until 1921. Their name, painted on one of the warehouses, could be read right up to the time these disappeared under the 'D' Road (A500). On the east side of Copeland Street, the main stables were built in 1899 and had stalls for twenty-six horses. There was a workshop, a clay shed, foreman's cottage and a 50 cwt hand crane on the towpath. The west side had two warehouses, No. 1 being a two-storey building built around 1880; No. 2 described as an '*old building*' also had two floors. There was a 5-ton crane, two of 30 cwt and two of 25 cwt, all hand operated. Copeland Street, serving the rear of these wharves was built in the last quarter of the 1800s.

The derelict remains of the Canal Company's Stoke-on-Trent wharf and warehouse on 22nd March 1974. The gantry was originally covered and extended over the towpath to project over the canal. WATERWAY IMAGES COLLECTION

Close to the adjacent Glebe Street Bridge (No. 113) were the offices of several canal and railway companies. Between Glebe Street Bridge and Church Street Bridge (No. 112), the canal is lined with wharves and works dating back at least to 1802. In that year, Wm Kenwright occupied a wharf on the site of the later gas works. The Burton Boat Company's wharf was next door, later to be the Anderton Company wharf. Opposite Kenwright's Wharf, on land later used for wharfage by Geo Mellor, was Cotton & Company's Wharf, agent John Brassington. In 1818, the flyboat carriers Crockett & Salkeld and Pickfords were using wharves in Stoke, John Brassington, Thos Stubbs and Thos Hindle being wharfingers. By 1830, Church Street and Glebe Street were connected, on the west side of the canal, by Wharf Street, which gave access to all the canalside premises between those bridges, their canal frontage being onto the towpath.

From Church Street going northwards, the first premises on Wharf Street was Kenwright's Wharf, later the Stoke, Fenton & Longton Gas Works, built in the early 1840s to replace the supply obtained from the British Gas Company at Shelton. Cargoes of coke were sent as far afield as the Linley cement works on the Rushall Branch of the Wyrley & Essington Canal, the boats travelling via Churchbridge Locks and returning with cement for Stoke or Macclesfield. The works closed in 1924 and the system was connected to Etruria Gas Works. Separated from the gas works by Gas Street, on the corner of which was the Duke of York public house, were houses and warehouses which, by 1846, belonged to the Anderton Company. The Anderton Company originally traded as Alexander Reid who, in 1834, was sharing a wharf (Wm Waite, wharfinger) at Stoke with several other carriers. The Anderton Company's Wharf Street premises became the property of the Bridgewater Trustees when they took over the Anderton Company in 1847. They were leased back to the Anderton Company when that concern regained its independence in 1876 and the freehold was transferred to them when the Bridgewater, by then part of the Manchester Ship Canal, finally severed its links with the Anderton Company in 1948. Shortly afterwards the Anderton Company, who had advertised Wharf Street as their head office for many years, sold the premises and moved their head office to Navigation Road Wharf at the end of the Burslem Arm. By 1951 part of the wharf was occupied by a printing works and the two cranes on the towpath had been removed.

Beyond the Anderton Wharf lay the Wharf Tavern, occupying a prime location for a pub because it was flanked on each side by a busy wharf. The northernmost wharf, which was much smaller, was occupied in 1867 by the Shropshire Union Railways & Canal Co. (Richard Bastard, agent). By 1892, the Shropshire Union had moved to larger premises at Copeland Street on the other side of Glebe Street Bridge and, by 1896, this wharf was used by W. Vernon, corn dealer. *Kelly's Directory of 1912* shows the Mersey, Weaver & Ship Canal Carrying Co. as occupants; they gave it the grandiose title of Imperial Wharf and remained here until bought out by British Waterways in 1958. Imperial Wharf had one crane on the towpath. Both wharves had extensive warehousing and were used more for general merchandise than for bulk raw materials.

Separated from Imperial Wharf by a 'Barge' Mission was Portland Mills, owned in 1876 by John Aynsley & Co. It had an overhead gantry spanning the towpath. Next door was a timber yard, which later became the site of the Princes Cinema, and a Parian manufactory (Parian ware was china figurines). The Parian works was superseded by a telephone exchange and warehouse. In 1802, the area on the other side of the canal was undeveloped except for Cotton's Wharf, lying between Church Street Bridge and the Trent aqueduct. By 1872, Geo Mellor had a flint mill, set back from the canal on the banks of the River Trent, which here passes under the canal, and with access to Cottons (later Mellors) Wharf. By 1892, the construction of Lytton Street had opened up the outside bank of the canal and a Directory of that year shows Mellor as occupying a wharf, with a crane, on that site. As Mellor, Colsell & Co., Mellor had been trading since 1856 as a general carrier to London, returning with flints from Gravesend and Newhaven and, later, Harefield. North of the aqueduct were some gasworks buildings and the Anderton Company's coal and clay wharf. The works of Dolbey & Co., potters' millers was later built on part of this land. Dolbeys, which never had a crane, the materials having to be shovelled direct into the works, became famous as the last firm to receive pottery materials by water. Its

The Anderton Company's Wharf Road depot in Stoke in the 1930s, with one of their horse boats unloading china clay. Behind it, bagged goods are being unloaded by hand crane while casks of ware wait to be despatched. On the opposite side of the canal another boat is discharging china clay. The building in the background with a gantry over the towpath is the Portland Flint Mill. BASIL JEUDA COLLECTION

last load of feldspar was delivered in 1969, the traffic only ceasing because the firm went into liquidation. The works stretch northwards to a point opposite Imperial Wharf. From there a row of houses extend to what was once Brunt's hay and straw yard, now a garage, adjacent to Glebe Street Bridge.

On the south side of Church Street Bridge (No. 112), the Canal Company's Stoke Wharf stood on the towpath side of the canal. Occupying a triangular piece of ground, its large warehouse had a covered gantry over the towpath and canal as well as two cranes. Dating back almost certainly to the opening of the canal, it was used by Hugh Henshall & Co., a firm of carriers who were, in effect, the canal company's nominees. It must have been a busy place in 1834 when Williams' Directory records it as being used by Henshall, Pickfords, Thos. Bache and John Furnival; although Wm Wayte's (later the Anderton Company) Wharf on the other side of Church Street Bridge was equally busy. In *Piggott's 1822 Directory* there are six wharfingers listed in '*Stoke*', including David Thomas's '*Severn Wharf*'. If we assume that the canal company's Stoke New Wharf and Basin came under the administration of the wharfinger at Church Street Wharf, they have a wharf each, there being three at Newcastle Junction and two at Wharf Street.

A little further south and just to the north of Whieldon Street Bridge (No. 110) lay the canal company's Stoke New Wharf and Stoke Basin, built at the expense of Thomas Whieldon in 1775 to handle the Fenton and Longton trade. There was a length of wharfage along the main line, with a coal tip and three cranes. The coal tip was served by tramroads from collieries in the Berry Hill area and later by the Biddulph Branch of the NSR. A low side bridge gave access to the basin, flanked by a warehouse, crate shed and two cranes. The canal company's tramroad from Fenton and Longton, authorised in 1802, terminated here. Both the MR and the Shropshire Union had depots adjacent to the tramroad in Longton. There were seven potworks and one tileworks on the tramroad. The wharf and basin appear to have dealt mainly with coal, ware and raw materials. When the NSR ceased carrying in 1894, they leased Stoke Basin to the Anderton Company and their boats were still loading ware at the basin in 1950. South of Whieldon Street Bridge, Winkle's Colonial Pottery on the outside and the basin of Winkle's Whieldon Sanitary Pottery on the towpath side, bring us to the end of the Potteries area as served by the main line of the canal.

Newcastle Canal

This canal was opened in 1794 and ran for 4 miles from the Trent & Mersey at Newcastle Junction to a wharf at Brook Lane, Newcastle-under-Lyme. It was leased to the NSR in 1863. Only the lower section in Stoke was used by the pottery industry, there being at one time eight potworks alongside the canal, of which the most important were Copeland and Minton, plus two flint mills and a

The entrance to the Newcastle-under-Lyme Canal, on 22nd March 1974. The buildings on the right are part of the former Shropshire Union Stoke Wharf. After the end of commercial traffic, the first few yards of the canal became moorings for Stoke-on-Trent Boat Club, as indicated on the towpath bridge, but the bridges and most of the buildings seen here disappeared under the D road in the mid-1970s. WATERWAY IMAGES COLLECTION

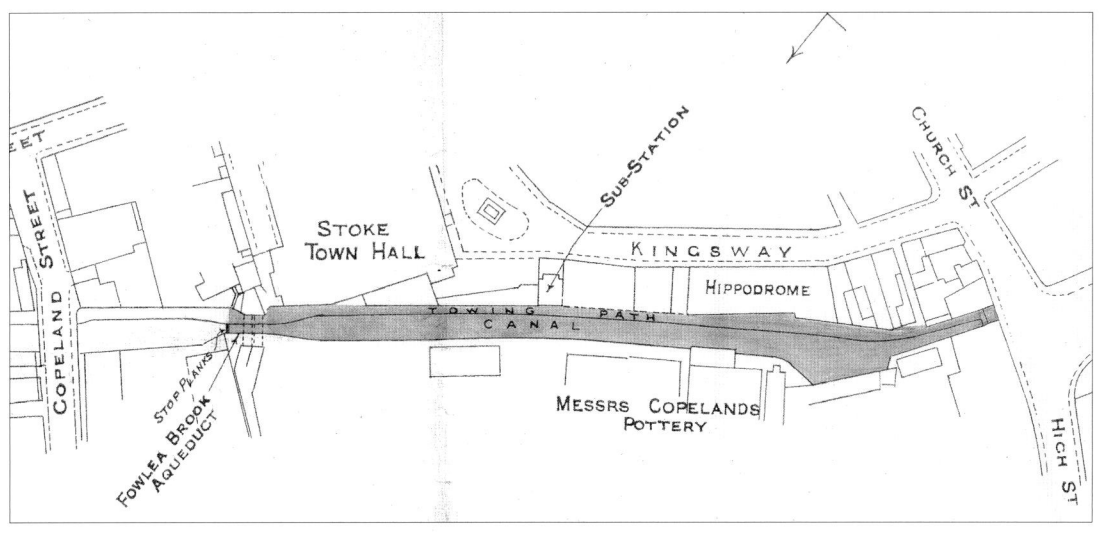

Plan of part of the Newcastle Canal in Stoke. BASIL JEUDA COLLECTION

The Newcastle Canal and London Road, Stoke-on-Trent circa 1930. The tunnel on the right carried a short branch into the Wolfe Street Pottery of Thomas Wolfe, established by 1781. On the left, the main line of the canal carries on beneath Stoke town centre towards its junction with the Trent and Mersey Canal. in the centre over the tunnels is a flint mill, whilst to the left are the imposing office buildings of the Minton Pottery. BASIL JEUDA COLLECTION

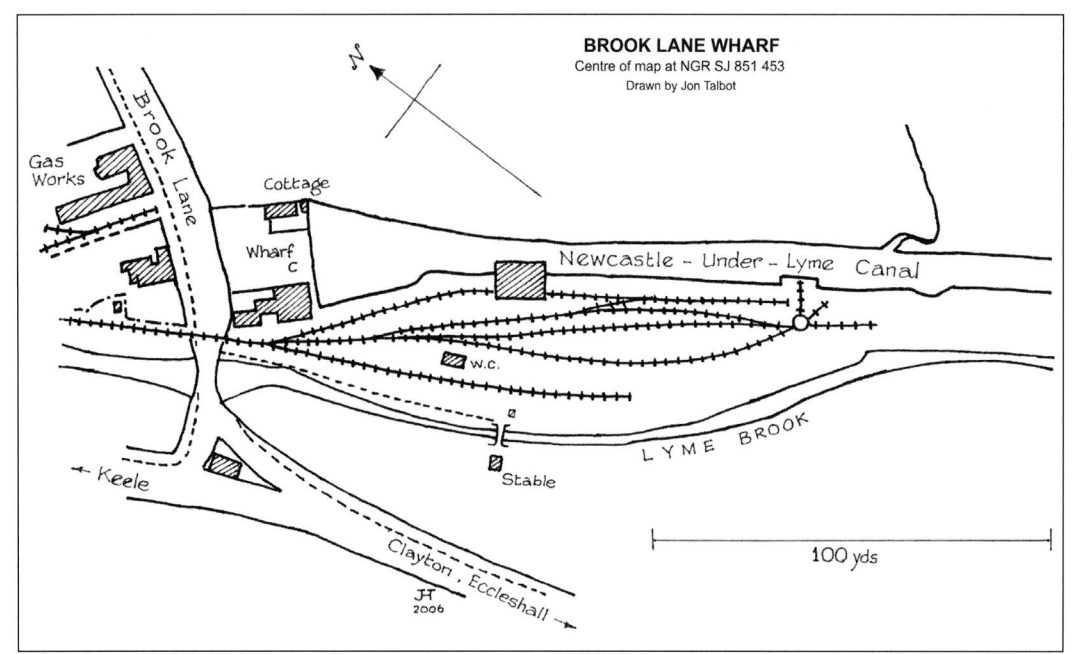

tile works. The only carrier's wharves were those of the Shropshire Union Company located between Copeland Street Bridge and the Fowlea Brook aqueduct, and between the junction with the main line and Copeland Street. The canal company had a wharf and 2-ton crane at the Newcastle terminus, where there were sidings and coal and ore chutes. A gas works was adjacent.

Hanley

Under the heading of 'Etruria', we dealt with the Caldon Canal (opened in May 1777) from its junction with the main line to the bottom of the first two locks. There were flyboat services to Leek and Uttoxeter on the Caldon Canal, most general traffic for Hanley being dealt with at the Etruria wharves but, in 1851, a service to Leek and Uttoxeter was advertised from the canal company's Cauldon Wharf (later leased to Brown, Westhead & Co.).[23] It has been suggested that this wharf may have been one of two wharves established at Joiner's Square by 1832, one of which, on the east side of Lichfield Road Bridge (No. 8), was still in use in the 1870s; or it may have been attached to the Cauldon Place Pottery, where there was a wharf in the 1870s.[24] These two miles of canal saw the greatest concentration of canalside industry to be found in the Potteries, the reason being that here the waterway passed over the coal measures. Early maps show little manufacturing industry on this section but, by the turn of the century, the canal bank through Cauldon and Eastwood was crowded. Numerous small collieries sprang up to serve these works, including one at Joiners Square with its own short tramway to the canal.

On the outside bank above Etruria locks, Geo Ridgeway built the Bedford Pottery. Between Bridge No's 3 and 4 lay Hanley Corporation roadstone wharf, opposite which was a brewery. Beyond Stoke Road Bridge (No. 4) the Falcon flint glass

Johnson Brothers' Eastwood Pottery alongside the T&M's Caldon Branch Canal at Hanley. This group of kilns were locally known as 'The Seven Sisters'. BASIL JEUDA COLLECTION

works and the Norfolk Pottery lay on the outside, with the Cauldon Place potworks, boasting no less than fifteen kilns, on the towpath side. A green interlude through Victoria Park intervened before the smoking chimneys of Eastwood appeared, with the electric light works on the outside opposite the Trent Earthenware Works and an adjacent flint mill. Trent Works had been owned by J.H. Davies in 1872, Johnsons in 1896 and Harrisons by 1951. The flint mill had been owned by Keeling & Adams in 1872, C.H. Adams in 1896 and later came into the hands of Johnsons. Opposite the flint mill was the Mousecroft Brick Works. Through Lichfield Street Bridge (No. 8), china clay was barrowed across the towpath into Harrisons Joiners Square works. This works and Trent Works between them consumed

An early 'bird's eye view' engraving of J. & G. Meakin's Eagle Pottery, less than a quarter mile further along the Caldon Branch. The canal is in the background and Ivy House Lift Bridge just visible at the left hand margin. BASIL JEUDA COLLECTION

A view across the canal at Hanley, circa 1904. BASIL JEUDA COLLECTION

A 1960s industrial scene on the Caldon Canal at Hanley, with Stoke Road Bridge and Planet Lock in the distance. The lock was built in 1909 to compensate for mining subsidence, which accounts for the height of the towing path, on the right, above canal water level. COURTESY THE POTTERIES MUSEUM & ART GALLERY, STOKE-ON-TRENT

150 tons of china clay each week and, together with Johnsons works, were among the last users of the canal. Harrisons had their own materials mill further up the Caldon Canal at Stanley.

On the opposite bank lay Eastwood Works, owned by C.H. Adams in 1876, J. & G. Meakin in 1896 and later worked by Johnsons. Imperial Pottery (towpath side) and Hanley Pottery (opposite) were also part of the Johnson empire. Hanley Pottery lay on both sides of Eastwood Road and faced Johnsons Trent Sanitary Works (twenty-three kilns). These two works occupied the entire area between Nelson Road and Ivy House Road bridges (No's 10 and 11). Beyond the latter, the outside bank boasted the Nelson Pottery (Elijah Cotton Ltd), Ivy House paper mills and J. & G. Meakin's Eagle Pottery. On the towpath side, C.H. Adam's Waterloo Pottery and flint mill was flanked by an encaustic tile works. The remaining space up to Bucknall Road (Bridge No. 12) was filled by the Ivy House iron foundry, whilst through the bridge lay Ivy House Wharf and crane. There were two nearby flint watermills which no doubt also used Ivy House Wharf.

On the towpath side, C.H. Adam's Waterloo Pottery and Flint Mill was flanked by an encaustic tile works. The remaining space up to Bucknall Road was filled by the Ivy House Iron Foundry. Through the bridge lay Ivy House Wharf and crane. Goods from Wincham in Cheshire were regularly sent here in the 1860s for the firm of Cartledge. There were two nearby flint watermills which no doubt also used Ivy House Wharf.

The Canal Company's Railways

The course of the Trent & Mersey Canal through the Potteries lay in the valley of the River Trent, well below the level of the established towns of Burslem, Hanley and Longton. The amount that each horse-drawn cart could carry from the canal to these centres was limited, particularly in the era of unmetalled roads. To alleviate this problem, railways, (so called, although they were actually tramroads) were authorised in 1801-02.

That from Burslem Wharf (at the end of the Burslem Arm) to Burslem was 2 3/4 furlongs long with a rise of 85 feet 9 inches; Etruria wharf to Hanley, 6 3/4 furlongs, rise 115 feet 5 inches, with a branch to Shelton of 3/4 furlong, 3 feet 0 inches rise: and Stoke Basin to Lane End, 2 miles 5 furlongs, rise 151 feet 8 inches, with a branch to Green Dock of 2 1/2 furlongs rise 25 feet 4 inches. The Lane End line was a conversion of an earlier coal tramroad.

These tramroads were not equipped with sidings but were to be used by their own and carriers' carts, which could be driven on or off the rails as required. They did, however, have passing loops. The NSR

Bylaws 1867 record the required dimensions of these vehicles:
  Gauge 3 feet 8 inches
  Maximum tare weight 10 cwt
  Maximum gross weight 2$^1/_2$ tons
  Maximum dimensions of carriage 6 feet long and 5 feet 6 inches wide
  No person was allowed to ride on the carriages

On 29th September 1892, Longton Corporation leased the tramroad *'leading to Foley and Longton'* and also that part between Heathcote Road and Bath Road in Longton, for a total of £40 per annum. The tramroads had gone out of use by the end of the century.

Outside the Potteries

We have now accounted for all the wharves and potworks (and much other canalside industry) within the main Potteries area. There were a few potworks and more potters' mills outside the area but on the canal. On the Caldon Canal, there was a flint wharf about a mile above Ivy House Wharf and a porcelain works and two corn mills at Milton. Adjacent to the junction with the Foxley Branch was Hardman's chemical works and Epstein's electric accumulator works. In later years, an aluminium works was built by the canal here. A wharf, crane and siding at Stanley served Victoria flint mill (Harrisons); Hercules flint mill was nearby. By 1815, two former corn mills at Cheddleton were converted to grind flint, one of which is now the Cheddleton Flint Mill Museum. They were operated by John Leigh between 1815 and 1840.

Consall Forge was leased to Thos Griffin, Francis Leigh and William Bill in March 1778, for conversion into a flint mill. Griffin and Bill had earlier converted a mill at Trentham to flint grinding, knowing that the Trent & Mersey Canal would soon be completed and that *'the Pottery trade at that time was extremely good.'*[25] Thomas Bill was a member of the management committee of the canal. In 1797, Griffin owned a single boat carrying flint to the mill. This mill also came into the possession of John Leigh and when he became bankrupt in 1841, all his mills were offered for sale with the enticement of annual profits between £3,000 and £4,000. Nearby was Crowgutter Mill, thought to have been a purpose built flint mill and known to be in production by 1811. In 1841, Consall Forge and Crowgutter were producing 350 tubs of slop per week. Cupola Mill at Froghall was grinding flint by 1812. At Froghall, the Caldon Canal joined the Uttoxeter Canal, opened in 1811. Uttoxeter was of interest to the early North Staffordshire potteries as an important market for butterpots.

Below Stoke, there were flint mills at Boothen

A circa 1930 aerial view of Harrison's Victoria Flint and Stone Mill, Stanley, near Endon, on the Caldon Canal. The mill was served by a short branch railway running from Endon station, on the Stoke to Leek line, which crossed the Caldon Canal by means of a swing bridge. There was also a short siding to a wharf on the canal. The base of the swing bridge remains in the centre of the canal today.
MARK MILLS COLLECTION

Bridge (No. 109), Sideway and Trentham, a ceramic insulator works at Stone and a pottery at Armitage. There were other flint mills along or near enough to be served by the canal, including eight on the Scotch Brook at Stone, Colton on the Trent at Rugeley, and Kings Mills on the Upper Trent Navigation near Weston Cliff. In 1818, S. Lloyd advertised as a carrier of flint from Kings Mills, near Weston in Derbyshire, to Shelton Lane Wharf.[26] The original corn mill at Kings Mills was mentioned in 1641. As well as flint, the mills ground gypsum from Humphrey Moore's quarries at Aston, connected to the canal by a tramway built in 1811. Moore was a partner in the Gainsborough Boat Co. and built a malt warehouse at Shardlow in 1799. The gypsum was taken along the canal to Weston Cliff, where it was transferred to a river boat and taken to Kings Mills. Some of the resulting plaster was sold to Pegg & Ellam a Derby paint firm. The gypsum and plaster was transshipped between canal and river at Weston Cliff.[27] Colton Mill, which was originally a corn mill mentioned in the Domesday Book, was grinding potters materials in the 1830s and had become a plaster and cement mill in 1876. Flints and china stone were delivered to a wharf at Brindley's Bank, on the Rugeley side of the aqueduct, shown on the 1816 T&M plan and squeezed between the canal and the River Trent. There was no road access and it appears that these materials reached the mill by transshipment to small craft on the river for the 1,100 yard journey to the mill.[28] A contract for flint for Colton Mill in 1834 was described as '*delivered at Brindley's Bank*'. In that year and until 1851, the mill was leased by Edward Johns, owner of the Armitage Pottery.[29]

To the north of the Potteries, Croxton Mill was built where the Trent & Mersey Canal crosses the River Dane on the northern outskirts of Middlewich. Like many other flint mills, it was originally a corn mill and it dated back at least to the 12th century. It was therefore a happy coincidence that the line of the canal should have been adjacent to it, so that a wharf could be made. The mill appears to have been grinding flint by 1819 but the date of its conversion to steam power is not known. In the period June-September 1832, the mill dispatched at least 225 tons 10 cwt of flint and, in June-September 1833, another 110 tons 6 cwt. Apart from 30 tons shipped to Preston Brook, all this traffic was destined for Red Bull or Longport. For at least the period 1828-54, the Phoenix Pottery in Tunstall was under the same ownership as Croxton Mill. It is thought the mill ceased to trade around 1910-14.[30]

Croxton Flint Mill was located in the angle formed by the canal and River Dane. It predates the canal but was grinding flint by 1816 and ceased to trade some time between 1910 and 1914. There are few visible remains. Flints were brought in by canal and ground flint was sent out in the same way.
ALBERT CLARKE/ MIDDLEWICH HERITAGE SOCIETY

NOTES TO CHAPTER TWO

1. Interview recorded by Arthur Wood, 7th April 1998
2. Malabar's Map of Tunstall, 1863
3. Thomas, J., op cit
4. Thos Peake, brick & tile manufacturer, established by the late 1820s; by 1861, this was the largest such works in the country
5. *Victoria County History - Staffordshire*, p104
6. *Universal British Directory*, 1791, iv 105
7. Shill, Ray, *Working Boat,* Heartland, 2001, p41 and *London Gazette*, 30th January 1781
8. SRO MS 3191/2, Map of Canal in the Potteries
9. BW GLOS, BW 4341.95, NSR, One Chain Survey, 1847
10. A possible explanation is that Appleby took the wharf formerly used by Kenwright
11. *Staffordshire Directory*, 1802
12. *Staffordshire Directory*, 1818
13. *Williams Directory*, 1834
14. Allbut's Map of the Potteries, 1802
15. *Staffordshire Advertiser*, 1st July 1827
16. Lead, Peter, *The Trent & Mersey Canal*, Moorland Press, 1980, p35
17. *Victoria County History - Staffordshire*, p108
18. *Staffordshire Advertiser*, 4th May 1850
19. Rolt L.T.C., *Narrow Boat*, London, 1944
20. *North Staffordshire Mercury*, 14th December 1841
21. WSL D1788 P2 B8
22. Hargreaves Map, 1832
23. *White's Directory*, 1851
24. *Victoria County History - Staffordshire*, p147.
25. Lead, Peter, *The Caldon Canal and Tramroads*, 2nd edn, Oakwood Press, 1990
26. *Staffordshire General and Commercial Directory*, 1818
27. Heath, John, *A Look at Shardlow's Past*, Paddock, 1985
28. BW 86.1, Plan of Trent & Mersey Canal, Derwentmouth to Stone, 1816
29. *Pigot's Directory*, 1834.
30. Walton, Mike. 'Croxton Flint Mill and its relationship with the Trent & Mersey Canal'. *Cheshire History No. 48*, 2008-2009

CHAPTER THREE
THE POTTERIES TRADE BEFORE 1840

In the early days of the canal, when the pottery industry was still quite small, a large number of carriers were involved in the carriage of pottery materials. Some of these were substantial general carriers like Henshall, Pickford or Gilbert & Worthington, for whom pottery materials, much of which was then carried in casks rather than in bulk, often formed only part of a boatload. Carriers in the Lancashire to London trade, in which there was considerably less northbound loading available than in the other direction, were keen to carry Gravesend and Newhaven flints brought by sea, transshipped to lighters in the Thames and then to boats on the Regents and Grand Junction canals. Their nationwide services, offered in conjunction with other carriers by inland waterway, road and coastal ship, made them natural carriers of finished ware.

From the start, there were manufacturers and merchants who operated their own boats. The Hendra Company, a consortium of manufacturers set up in 1799 to ensure a regular supply of clay, had their own ships, canal boats and a clay wharf in the Potteries '... *on land near the towing path on the southwest side of the Trent & Mersey Canal for a term of 18 years at a rental of £21.*'[1]

The Weston Salt Company, who also dealt in pottery raw materials, was an example of a merchant and manufacturer who had a fleet of boats. Manufacturers owning boats included the flint millers William Podmore & Sons, the large potters J. & G. Meakin and W. & F. Adams, the Davenport family, who had a number of interests, and Geo Ridgeway, who was a potter and corn miller. John Davenport was, until 1803, in a partnership with the carriers James Adams and Thos Sothern, that also included Thomas Kinnersley. Adams & Sothern traded between Birmingham, the Potteries, Stourport and the East Midlands.[2] Davenport built a warehouse at City Road Basin on the Regent's Canal in London in 1826. Potter & Son, merchants and shipbrokers, date back, as Simpson & Potter, to 1821. In the iron trade, Earl Granville, Robert Heath and the Wheelock Iron & Salt Co. were boatowners. To these must be added a large number of coal, salt and chemical companies. Many of these, in later years, handed over their traffic to professional carriers.

As time went by, professional carriers emerged who specialised in the potteries trade, though rarely to the complete exclusion of other cargoes. Competition from railways considerably reduced the number of carriers and led to increasing specialisation.

The eastern end of the canal was opened first, which meant that the Potteries were initially reached via the River Trent. Cargoes were unloaded from ships to Trent boats at Gainsborough and again transshipped into narrowboats, originally over the towpath at Weston Cliff and, when the canal was completed to Derwentmouth, at Cavendish Bridge on the Trent or Shardlow on the canal.

Although it was possible for Trent boats to go up the canal as far as Horninglow, most carriers transshipped between narrow boats and Trent boats at Shardlow, although the carriers Spilsbury & Smith had a wharf and basin at Willington in 1816 that was also possibly used for this purpose.

Paralleling the 16$^{1}/_{2}$ miles of canal between Derwentmouth and Burton was the Upper Trent Navigation, leased since 1762 by Lord Paget to the Burton Boat Company, a partnership of businessmen that included an ironmaster, two cheese factors and a timber merchant. There was no love lost between Paget and the Burton Company and the Trent & Mersey Canal. The Burton Company would have liked the canal to have joined the Trent at Burton and thus been able to take tolls on all traffic between that town and Derwentmouth. However, their navigation was prone to flood, drought and shoals,

Narrow boats and a wide boat by the Clock Warehouse at Shardlow circa 1910.
WATERWAY IMAGES COLLECTION

The canal at Weston Cliff, showing Bridge No. 10 circa 1905. The wharf, crane and warehouse can be seen through the bridge. Cargoes were transshipped here between canal boats and craft on the Upper Trent Navigation.
BASIL JEUDA COLLECTION

Boats of the Flixborough Shipping Company awaiting disposal at their base at Horninglow Wharf, Burton-on-Trent in 1950. This fleet was set up in 1946 to carry steel between Flixborough on the River Trent and Sankey's works at Bilston. The boats were sold in 1950, two of the motor boats, **Dunstable** *and* **Epsom**, *being bought by the carrier John Knill. They were re-named* **Dunstan** *and* **Kenelm**. **Kenelm** *worked in the salt trade between Middlewich and Reading, and* **Dunstan** *was employed in the Mersey to south Staffordshire trade, before being sold to the Potteries carrier John Walley. All of these buildings have disappeared to make room for roads but most of the basin survives as pleasure craft moorings, albeit comprehensively overshaddowed by the uncompromising concrete embankment of the adjacent A38.* WATERWAY IMAGES COLLECTION

hence its avoidance by the canal company. The 1860 turnpike Cavendish Bridge, replacing Wilden Ferry, was also an obstruction to navigation and boatmen attempted to hinder its construction by ramming the piles: '*Great damage lately done by watermen wilfully driving their boats against piles belonging to the bridge now building at Wilden Ferry. Trustees draw attention to clauses in the Act likely to deter offenders and warn of prosecutions against offenders in any more nonsense.*'[3]

Having failed in its attempt to get the Trent & Mersey to terminate at Burton, the boat company tried to get the canal company to agree not to navigate its boats below there. Instead, they wanted them to transship traffic there to the Burton Company's craft. A draft agreement was drawn up but was rejected by the T&M. Pamphlets were circulated condemning the crossing of the Trent by the T&M on the level at Alrewas rather than by an aqueduct, claiming that the lockage water thus taken by the canal was injurious to the Upper Trent Navigation and to other parties. Nevertheless, the Burton Company made a vigorous effort to attract trade to and from the canal, constructing the $1^{1}/_{2}$ mile Bond End Canal from the river to within about 40 yards of the T&M at Shobnall, and by buying a fleet of narrow boats and acquiring wharves at Birmingham (Aston), Stone and Stoke. In 1793, they advertised services from the Potteries to Liverpool, Manchester, Birmingham and Bristol, as well as to London via Coventry and Oxford.

The Potteries Trade Before 1840

An early engraving of a horse drawn boat heading downstream from Alrewas Lock towards Wychnor. The wooden barrier is to prevent craft from being swept over the weir ahead in times of high water. Boats were sometimes carried onto the barrier by the strength of the current and had to be assisted to extricate themselves. WATERWAY IMAGES COLLECTION

In 1773, Wedgwood, on behalf of the T&M, was authorised to bid up to £1,000 more than the Burton Boat Co. for a plot of land opposite his Etruria Pottery, which they wanted for a wharf.[4] Paget also complained that one of the side walls of the canal company's warehouse at Horninglow *'prevented Lord Paget from making and using a warehouse or from having any communication with the canal on either side at that place'*. Paget ordered his agent to take down a small part of the building, in retaliation for which the Reverend Falconer, one of the canal's proprietors, ordered the same to be done to the Burton Boat Company's warehouse at Shobnall, on the grounds that part of it was built on the canal company's property. It was also said that the T&M were abstracting water from the Shobnall Brook, formerly conveyed under the canal, so that the Bond End Branch should not have it.[5]

Requests for a connection between the Bond End Canal and the T&M were refused in 1787. The Burton Co. attempted to force the issue in 1790, by employing a group of men to cut through the ground that separated the two canals during the hours of darkness. The T&M resorted to law and the cut was filled in.[6]

The Burton Company then brought pressure on the T&M by promoting their own canal, between the river and the Coventry Canal at Fradley Junction. Faced with direct competition, the T&M decided to build the Shobnall link. Despite strong

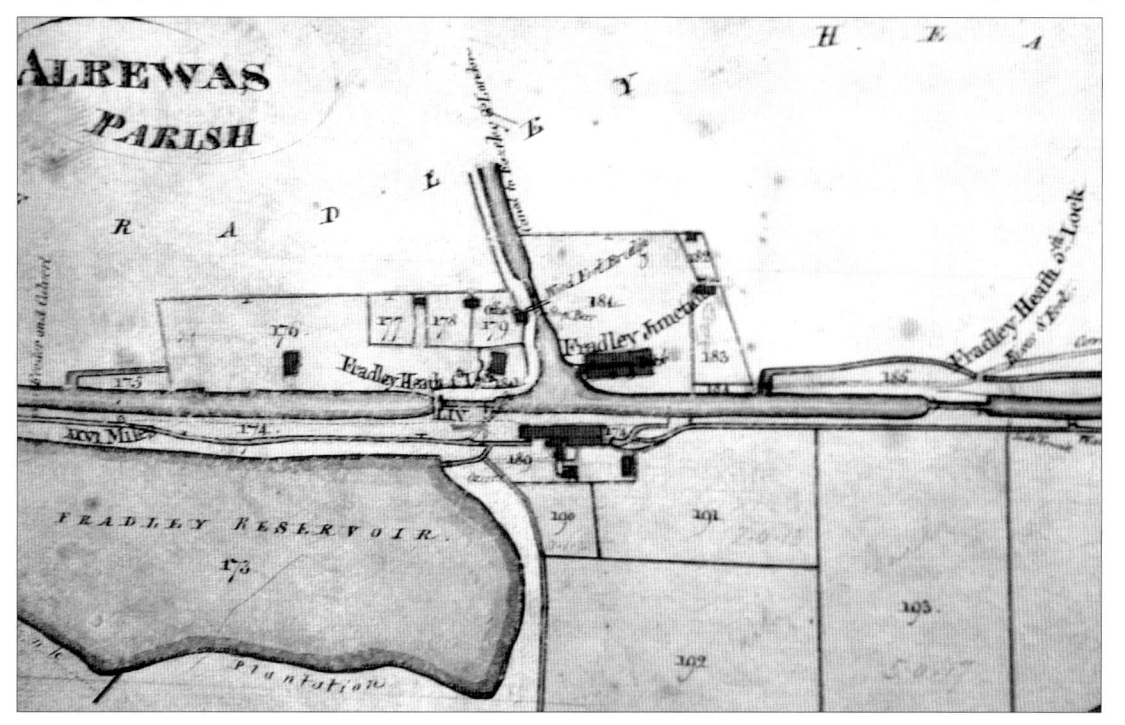

The wharf, Fradley Junction as shown on the 1816 T&M plan. Above Junction Lock, the canal turns off towards Coventry and London. The section as far as Whittington Brook was built by the T&M and later sold to the Coventry Canal Company. There is a dry dock to the right of the junction, opposite a range of buildings comprising the Swan public house, stables, wharf and warehouse. NATIONAL WATERWAYS MUSEUM

The canal entered the River Trent below Alrewas River, or Trent, Lock and left it again above Wychnor Lock. As can be seen from this plan, boats entered Alrewas millstream immediately below the lock and the main river fifty yards beyond, which made navigation difficult when the river was running fast. (The view downstream from Alrewas Lock can be seen on page 185.) COURTESY THE WATERWAYS ARCHIVE

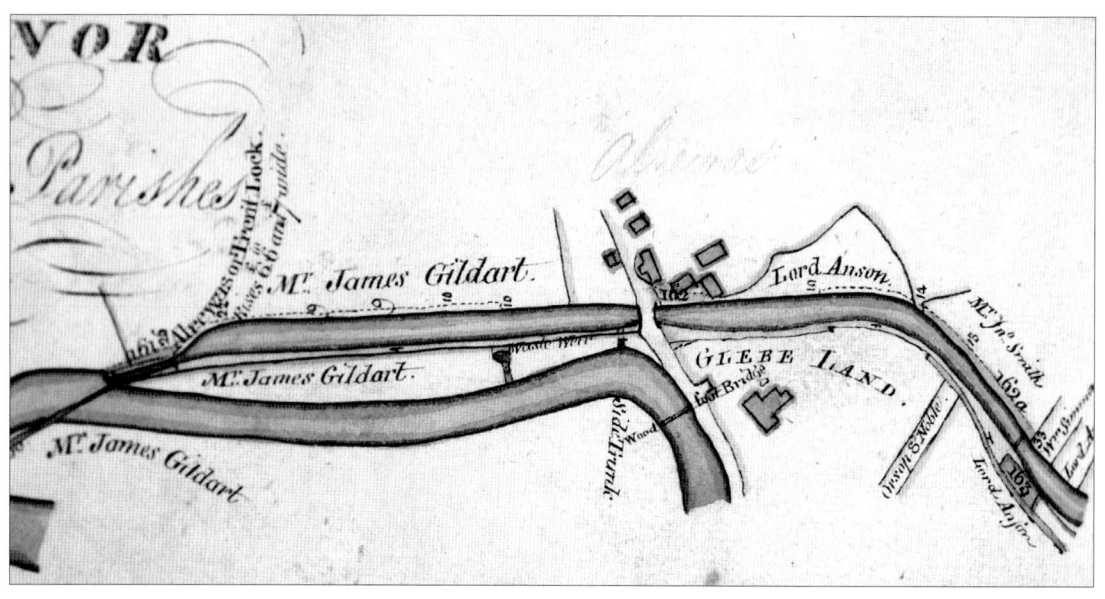

A spoon dredger at Steam Mill Bridge, Alrewas. A perforated spoon was pushed into the mud with the aid of a hand winch and 2 cwt of spoil was raised by a crane to be tipped into the boat. It was unloaded by hand from the boat and the job was paid by piece-work, i.e. by the amount of spoil dredged. WATERWAY IMAGES COLLECTION

opposition from local interests, an Act was finally passed on 2nd June 1795, in which year the Burton Co. owned eighteen narrow boats. In 1779, 452 tons of flints entered the canal at Burton, compared to 3,233 tons at Shardlow. The more efficient and dependable T&M route gradually displaced traffic on the river and the Burton Boat Co. disposed of its canal boats in 1805. Their flyboat services and their Shobnall Wharf were taken over by Pickfords. A few barges continued to operate on the Upper Trent Navigation and the Bond End Canal, which remained independent from the T&M. In 1850, the T&M entered into negotiations to lease the Bond End Canal and the Upper Trent Navigation but there is no evidence that they did, in fact, do so.

Whereas the T&M skirted Burton on Trent and its main wharf at Horninglow was over a mile from the town, the Bond End Canal ran close to the heart of Burton, making it advantageous for canal carriers to establish depots thereon. Among these were the various Tunley partnerships, with a depot at Lichfield Street. This was subsequently taken over by the Bridgewater Trustees and used by their subsidiary, the Anderton Company. William Tunley was their wharfinger in 1851. The Burton depot of the Grand Junction Canal's carrying department was on the River Trent.

A small amount of local traffic passed between the Trent and the Bond End Canal until the Midland Railway bought the latter in 1872 and built a railway along much of its length. They had already, in 1847, made a rail/canal interchange basin at its junction with the main line.

The canal was opened between Great Haywood and Weston Cliff in September 1770 and a regular twice weekly service was started. Applications for the carriage of goods were to be made to Hugh Henshall & Co. or to Joseph Smith, wharfinger at Gainsborough. The canal and river were adjacent at Weston and it appears that goods were transshipped here over the towpath until the last five miles of canal was completed to Derwentmouth.

On the 12th November 1771, the canal was opened to Stone and two boats laden with flint and clay arrived there. The Potteries were reached in October 1772 and, by that time, Henshalls had twenty-seven boats and other users eleven. Henshalls also employed ten Trent boats between Shardlow and Gainsborough. Shardlow soon became a major inland port and many of the early carriers were based here. The canal carrying families of Sutton, Soresby and Cowlishaw owned much of the land.

In 1795, the journey from London to the Potteries via Gainsborough and a sea passage took 14 to 20 days. The rates of carriage between the Potteries and Gainsborough were:

Perishable goods..........................23s 10d per ton
Unperishable goods ....17s 3d per ton
Bulky goods.................................32s 10d per ton to 35s 10d per ton[7]

Of particular interest in this early period is the

firm of Hugh Henshall & Co., run by several of the proprietors of the canal and, in effect, the canal company's carrying arm, sharing the same offices at Stone. The firm was set up to get business onto the canal during its early days and its activities were to be reduced in the years to come. At this time, canal companies were legally prevented from acting as carriers and many of them circumvented this restriction by setting up nominee carriers. This was the only way they could control competition, because a canal company could not alter its toll charges to one carrier but had to apply any alteration to all users of the waterway. It could, however, alter the carriage rates of its nominee carrier.

Canal companies often encountered combinations between carriers which could raise charges to a level detrimental both to traders (of whom the larger were often among the canal proprietors) and to the level of traffic, thus affecting the canal company's toll income. In the years to come, they might need to make independent carriers their agents, so as to control rate cutting in breach of the canal companies' agreements with the railways.

In the years 1783-84, freight charges were reduced for iron, lead, copper, timber, glassmakers' sand, clay, flint, pottery ware, slates, corn, malt, cheese and salt. Henshalls turnover, which had been £19,671 in 1778, rose to £54,579 in 1784. In the early 1790s, by which time the canal was open throughout, Henshalls controlled almost all of the trade between the canal and the River Trent and employed seventy-five vessels.[8] In 1795, they had sixty-five boats, although they appear to have sold their Trent craft to the Gainsborough Boat Company in the previous year. The Gainsborough Boat Co. ceased to trade in about 1812.

Also trading on the canal from its opening was the Cavendish Bridge Boat Company which, by 1780, had warehouses and property on both sides of the canal near the turnpike at Shardlow extending down to the Trent, and a fleet of twenty boats trading to Manchester and Birmingham. Its short life was brought to an end by the bankruptcy, in January 1781, of one of its partners, John Webster of Derby. Six Trent boats and ten narrow boats were offered for sale. Canal carrying, like any other business, could be a precarious undertaking in the days when it was mostly carried out by individuals and partnerships.

Joseph Smith, whom we have mentioned as a Gainsborough wharfinger, became a carrier based at Horninglow Wharf, Burton on Trent. He advertised in the *Universal British Directory* in 1793 and had thirteen boats by 1795. Smith carried between the Trent and both the Potteries and Birmingham, and was prominent in carrying from the Potteries to London via Gainsborough, in competition with the route via Coventry and the Grand Junction Canal. He was also a flint and salt merchant. His wharf in the Potteries was at Shelton Bridge. In 1816, he was in partnership with Spilsbury & Co., with a wharf and basin at Willington.

Among the carriers based at Cavendish Bridge, which was only some 600 yards distant from Shardlow Port, was William Crosby. Unlike most of the Cavendish Bridge carriers, he appears not to have transferred his operations from the Bridge to Shardlow, although it is quite likely that he

Bond End Basin, Burton-on-Trent in 1973, taken from the bridge at the junction with the T&M main line. WATERWAY IMAGES COLLECTION

Bond End Canal Basin looking towards the junction bridge. Railway interchange sidings ran along both sides of the basin. WATERWAY IMAGES COLLECTION

THE MILL AND CANAL WHARF, GREAT HAYWOOD.

The junction with the Staffordshire & Worcestershire Canal (through the towpath bridge to the left) at Great Haywood. Boats to and from Preston Brook or Manchester used this route to South Staffordshire and Birmingham until 1923. JOHN RYAN COLLECTION

transshipped at least some goods overland, the distance being short, rather than send his canal boats down to Derwentmouth and then up again to Cavendish Bridge. Speed was of the essence in the carriage of high value goods. Crosby, who was operating in 1774, built up a substantial carrying business between Birmingham, Lancashire and the East Midlands, and also traded in London porter and timber from his Cavendish Bridge warehouse. He was bankrupted in 1781.

Of the canals connecting with the eastern end of the T&M, the first to be completed was the Staffordshire & Worcestershire Canal on 28th May 1772. Running from the River Severn at Stourport to a junction with the T&M at Great Haywood, it was finished shortly before the T&M reached the

Great Haywood Lock circa 1906. The T&M type of top gate paddle, with the spindle extended to the end of the balance beam, is clearly shown. BASIL JEUDA COLLECTION

CANAL BRIDGE, TRENT LANE, GREAT HAYWOOD

THE CANAL, MEAFORD, STONE.

A north bound horse drawn boat climbing Meaford Locks near Stone circa 1906. The original line of the canal below the top lock, which is beyond the bridge in the distance, curved away behind the trees to the left. It incorporated staircase locks that were replaced by the Road Lock, ahead of the boat, and House Lock, through which it has just passed, rejoining the present line just above the Bottom Lock. BASIL JEUDA COLLECTION

Potteries from the east and thus afforded almost immediate competition for pottery materials with the Trent route. Cornish, Devon and Dorset china and ball clay, and china stone, was transshipped at Bristol Channel and Severn ports into river vessels which brought materials to Stourport, where they were transferred to narrow boats to complete the journey to the Potteries.

In 1772-3, Emery, York & Co. were despatching potters' clay from Stourport, transshipping to Soresby's boats at Haywood Junction. In 1806, Henshall was carrying Wedgwood's crates to Stourport but there is no mention of any return loads of clay. The Stourport carrier J. & G. Ames was important in the clay trade via the Severn route. In 1822, he relaid part of his wharf at Stourport with stone flags for the storage of clay. Mathew Heath also had arrangements to store clay at Stourport, brought up river from Lydney, where there was a special warehouse at the dock to store china clay, which formed a return load for large schooners trading in Lydney coal to south Cornwall.

In 1831, the Weston Salt Company recorded a payment to Heath & Co., the Stourport carriers, for

The Canal Wharf, Stone.   Photo. by P.C. Dutton.

Hugh Henshall's Stafford Street Wharf at Stone around 1910, with the gas works in the background and a North Staffordshire Railway spoon dredger alongside. Prior to the First World War, it was said that there could be as many as fifteen coal boats at a time alongside this wharf. BASIL JEUDA COLLECTION

Stubbs' Mill at Stone, originally Hugh Henshall's warehouse, seen in 1978. WATERWAY IMAGES COLLECTION

Agnes at Aston near Stone circa 1912. She is a boat of the type used on the River Severn and adjoining canals, and is carrying small timber from the Wyre Forest for making pottery crates. NEIL PARKHOUSE COLLECTION

Severn freight, wharfage and weighing Cornwall stone. In 1834, the Weston Company were supplying Colton Mill near Rugeley with that commodity via the Severn route, using a wharf at Brindley's Bank.[9]

The potters' materials and ware trade via the Severn was destined for a relatively early demise, as Bristol declined in importance as a port relative to Liverpool, which latter was in any case preferred by the potters, many of whom used, or were in partnership with, Liverpool merchants. The standing of William Bentley, Wedgwood's partner, as a Liverpool merchant was such that the City of Liverpool and the corporate body of merchants subscribed the funds to secure the passage of the

ON THE CANAL, ASTON-STONE.

A peaceful scene on the canal at Aston-by-Stone around 1905, looking back towards the bridge from which the previous picture was taken.
NEIL PARKHOUSE COLLECTION

T&M Act through Parliament. In return, Wedgwood arranged with Bentley to send his ware via Liverpool. William Adams had his own warehouse in Liverpool and acted as a merchant for several pottery manufacturers.[10]

The decline of the Bristol route was speeded by the unreliable state of navigation on the Severn. The fact that, before long, most exported ware went through Liverpool meant that there was always a supply of boats at the various Mersey canal terminals for return loads of raw materials. By the end of the 19th century, the transport of potter's raw materials and ware via Stourport had ended.[11]

The Staffs & Worcs provided, from September 1772, a connection with the Birmingham Canal to Wolverhampton and Birmingham. Ware consignments to these and other provincial towns were of less than boatload quantities and formed part of the mixed cargo of general merchandise flyboats. As such, they were particularly vulnerable to railway competition from 1838 onwards. By contrast, ware for export and the London market made up full boatloads and the carriers could hold their own against the railways. In 1806, barrels of copper coins from the Soho Mint at Birmingham were being sent by canal to Etruria.

Two other important commodities used the S&W route to the Potteries. One was wood from the Wyre Forest, loaded into boats at Bewdley and used for making Pottery crates. This trade survived until the start of the First World War.[12] This type of openwork wooden crate was later superseded by crates made of wire mesh, known as 'tanks'. The second was firebricks for lining the pottery kilns, loaded on the summit of the Stourbridge Canal and boated to the Potteries until 1951.

An important connection with the T&M was the route to London via the Coventry Canal, joining the T&M at Fradley Junction. In May 1777, the Coventry Canal was opened, with the exception of Fazeley aqueduct, to get round which the early carriers had to transship to road wagons. A through water route awaited the completion of the Oxford Canal to Oxford in 1790. Pickfords began to use this route for London traffic from the start of their canal services, when they took over Henshalls' London stock and trade in 1785, transshipping at Coventry or Braunston to road wagons when the canal reached these points. Express carriers considered the all water route via Oxford and the Thames to be too slow and unreliable.

The first indication that pottery materials might have passed this way comes in a letter[13] requesting a quotation for tolls on flints. It seems unlikely that the carriage of Newhaven or Gravesend flints via the Thames and Oxford would have been competitive with the Gainsborough route and the reference may be to chalkpit flints, loaded on the Thames where it passed close to the flint-rich Chiltern Hills. Flints were already being carried on the Thames for

A view of Braunston Wharf looking south circa 1930. Braunston was an important transshipment point on the Lancashire to London route. It survives in use today as part of a large marina, which has been dug out to the left of the bridge. Running across the background is the ex-L&NWR railway line from Weedon to Daventry, which closed finally in 1963 and the viaduct seen in the centre, which spanned the A45 road, has since been removed. Modern apartments surround the marina. TOM FOXON COLLECTION

building purposes. Moore owned the Shirleywich salt works and would have been interested in flints as a return load for his boats carrying salt to, among other places, Oxford and Reading.

The completion throughout of the Grand Junction Canal in 1805, opening up an all inland water route between the Potteries and London, completely changed the competitive picture. It not only competed with the Gainsborough route for ware to London but the imbalance of traffic, there being much more going to London than in the other direction, led to a great demand by all the general carriers for flints to provide back loading as far as the Potteries. By 1830, records show large quantities of flints being stored and transshipped at City Road Basin, on the Regent's Canal, and others at Bulls Bridge.

Competition with the coastal route was fierce. In 1828, the Grand Junction Canal reported that, *'preferential tolls were already in existence on goods for places north of the Trent so as to divert traffic from the coastal to the inland route'*.[14] The introduction of steamships in the 1830s further intensified sea competition with the inland route. Appeals from the carriers to the canal companies for lower tolls fell, with the exception of the Grand Junction, on deaf ears. A further initiative from the Grand Junction itself in 1838 was similarly disregarded. Pickfords made an experimental run with a steam boat in September 1836 but the results were inconclusive and it was not followed up. In later years, some Grand Junction and Fellows, Morton horsedrawn flyboats to and from the T&M canal were attached to steamers for the part of their journey between London and Braunston.

The last canal to join the eastern end of the T&M was the Derby Canal, completed on 30th June 1796, providing an alternative route to a part of the Trent whose navigational difficulties were causing delays. This letter is from the Butterley Company, whose iron works were on the Cromford Canal:

'I am sorry and ashamed the execution of your order should have been so long delayed. The difficult and tedious passage for our Narrow Boats up the Trent has almost solely occasioned it and I have waited for alternate opportunities of sending it through ... till wearied by continual disappointments I am grown as impatient for its being sent off as you can possibly be to receive it - you may depend on its being sent off tomorrow ... it will reach Shobnall by Friday or Saturday. We shall shortly have a communication with the Grand Trunk Canal by Derby, when our Narrow Boats can with ease go to Burton and your

A length of the T&M Canal at Manor Park, near Middlewich circa 1910. JOHN RYAN COLLECTION

Runcorn Big Pool, Bridgewater Canal, circa 1905. The Big Pool was a natural lake which James Brindley was able to take advantage of when building the canal, although the original cut was later by-passed, creating a small island on which a boatyard was established. The Big Pool was long used as a dumping ground for old boats, as here with several abandoned Mersey flats. The Big Pool has today largely been filled in, the area being bisected by the A533 Bridgewater Expressway dual carriageway. NEIL PARKHOUSE COLLECTION

A solitary motor car on Middlewich Road, Elworth, near Sandbach, overtakes a horse boat on the parallel T&M Canal circa 1930. The view is looking north, whilst the road is today the A533 and named Booth Lane. NEIL PARKHOUSE COLLECTION

Wheelock Wharf and warehouse, which served the nearby town of Sandbach, was once an important traffic centre on the canal. Here, the canal has been dewatered after inserting stop planks beneath the bridge, probably for maintenance of the aqueduct over the River Wheelock, behind the camera. GRAHAM HOVEY

further orders ... shall be executed on the shortest notice.'[15]

A commodity that went to the Potteries via the Derby Canal was chert. Large blocks were used as millstones and made to revolve round and upon a floor made of smaller blocks, grinding up calcined flint and at the same time grinding away the chert stones. Derbyshire output in 1896 was 3,699 tons.

The western end of the canal was completed in May 1777, to a junction with the Bridgewater Canal at Preston Brook. A substantial inland port grew up here, at the point of transshipment between the narrow boats using the T&M and the estuarial flats of the Duke of Bridgewater that conveyed goods to and from Liverpool. By 1785, there were clay sheds, warehouses and a salt office for the Chester, Frodsham and Potteries transshipment trade, although some of the Chester traffic was transshipped between canal and road wagons at Wheelock. T&M traffic for Manchester could remain in narrow boats throughout. In the eighteen months from 4th July 1777, Henshall paid tolls and charges of £2,479 to the Duke. In May 1784, the Duke agreed lower tolls in return for a reduction on his coal to Middlewich.

There was an immediate fall in the River Weaver's Winsford tonnage, reflecting the North Staffordshire trade which, before the opening of the canal, had been transshipped there between river flats and road transport. In the five years ending 5th April 1778, clay shipped to Winsford averaged 2,336 tons per annum and flintstones averaged 357 tons per annum. In the next five years, Winsford clay had fallen to 467 tons per annum and flints to 210 tons per annum. Between 12th February 1778 and 14th December 1782, the Duke's boats carried 21,745 crates of pottery from Preston Brook to Liverpool. The Weaver Trustees were to fight to regain this traffic.

The opening of the western end of the canal did not immediately affect clay traffic through Shardlow. It is interesting to note that flint traffic from Preston Brook declined from 758 tons in 1777 to 171 tons in 1779, while flints from Shardlow increased from 2,516 tons to 3,233 tons in the same period. The Trent route had at that time an obvious distance advantage for flints from Gravesend and Newhaven. In 1785, it was claimed that two thirds of the whole tonnage between Liverpool and the Potteries consisted of pottery raw materials and ware, and there were complaints of insufficient accommodation for these articles at Preston Brook.

By the time this photograph was taken in the 1930s, Shardlow was no longer a busy inland port. JOHN RYAN COLLECTION

It is perhaps surprising that the Weaver Navigation Trustees did not put forward proposals for regaining their lost trade until some eleven years after the completion of the T&M, when proposals were made for '*quays with communications and other convenience*' to be made at Anderton or Barnton, for transshipping goods between the canal and the Weaver. The plan was not proceeded with but the Trustees decided to repair the road from the canal at Broken Cross to the river at Northwich and transfer goods by this method. The road and a warehouse at Broken Cross had been completed by 1780 and the Weaver Trustees appointed a clerk at Longport, to organise the carriage of ware between there and Liverpool by this route. The trade was not profitable and was given up after four years, the wharf, warehouse and cranes at Broken Cross being put up for sale. Instead, the road from Winsford to Middlewich was repaired and shipments of flints to Winsford continued.

In response to a suggestion in 1788 from the salt proprietors of Middlewich that transshipment facilities should be made between the canal and the river at Anderton or Barnton, plans were laid before the T&M Co. on 5th August 1790. A new basin was made on the river at Anderton, within 44 yards of the canal, and carts were wheeled down the 50 foot drop to the basin. This method was replaced by an inclined plane in 1799. In the 1790s, this connection was used only for salt, not for clay or crates, the first proposals to transship other materials being in 1800, when a party of '*gentlemen concerned in the Pottery trade*' approached the Trustees and '*proposed to carry flint and crates up and down the canal and to reship the same to and from vessels navigating on the River Weaver*'. The younger John Gilbert was certainly involved in this traffic by 1802 as, in January of that year, the firm of Wedgwood & Byerley paid him £133 for '*freight and tonnage on clay from Anderton*'.[16]

Henshall & Co. seem to have coexisted amicably with the other carriers until a crisis arose in 1782, which appears to have been an attempt by the Bridgewater interest to secure a large share of Henshalls' carrying trade to themselves. The elder John Gilbert, who was both agent to the Duke of Bridgewater and one of the Trent & Mersey proprietors, set up a competing business on the Stourport route, in partnership with Jonathan Worthington, who was a considerable road carrier between Manchester and Bristol. Not unnaturally, the Duke's traffic went to his Head Steward's firm. Worthington & Gilbert shared a warehouse at Manchester with Henshalls, so any preferential treatment given to Worthingtons could hardly go unnoticed. The warehouse at Manchester (Castlefield) used by Henshall and Worthington was later known as the Grocer's Warehouse. It was claimed that Worthingtons' boats were unloaded in two hours, whereas those belonging to Henshall could wait two days. The Duke allowed

The T&M Canal in the Potteries, from a circa 1910 picture postcard. Even in the pre-First World War industrial age, ironic images of the Potteries such as this were a common theme and speaks volumes in regards to the conditions in which people in the area then lived. JOHN RYAN COLLECTION

Worthingtons to use his clerks and, in respect of the Liverpool trade, which was transshipped from the Duke's flats to narrow boats at Preston Brook, he ordered his agent to deliver all unconsigned goods to Worthington.

The rumour, obviously detrimental to Henshalls' trade, was spread that they intended to withdraw from the Manchester to Stourport (for Bristol) route. Wedgwood, furious that the Duke was treating the T&M like a branch of his own canal, was determined to break the dominance of the Gower/Bridgewater interest in the company's affairs. He and others countered by preparing to support a new carrier between Liverpool and Preston Brook to compete with the Duke (who had a monopoly on this traffic), which would reduce the charges on all goods from 3s 4d per ton to 2s 4d per ton. It would use river boats slightly smaller than the Duke's (i.e. narrow enough to be able to go through Preston Brook, Saltisford and Barnton tunnels) so that cheese and salt could be carried between Middlewich and Liverpool without transshipment.

A number of complaints against the Duke were presented by Caister, the T&M's chief agent at Manchester, in a letter of 13th September 1783, objecting to the partiality shown by '*his Grace's people*' towards Worthington. On being shown this letter, the Duke demanded Caister's dismissal and, on 7th January 1784, he threatened to dispose of his shares in the T&M if his demand was not met. Undeterred, the T&M committee uncovered '*partialities*' shown to Worthington & Gilbert at Liverpool and Preston Brook, claiming that goods which should have been delivered to their boats had been given to their rivals.

In 1785, the T&M committee had a large majority in favour of '*a proposition to give up trading as a company and … sell all their boats and let their warehouses*'. In September 1786, they proposed a reduction in freight charges for clay and flint from Liverpool to Longport to 9s 6d per ton; to Etruria 9s 10d per ton and to Stoke 10s 3d per ton, including tolls, wharfage and all other expenses. They also proposed the erection of additional cranes and the appointment of an agent at these wharves.

The quarrel was still continuing in 1788, with more complaints that goods supposed to be forwarded by Henshall were being delivered to '*other persons*' but the Wedgwood party had broken the power of the Bridgewater and Gilbert faction on the T&M committee and a compromise seems to have been reached based on belated recognition of their common interests. The Duke became more co-operative in his dealings with the T&M and did not carry out his threat to sell his shares. The Trent & Mersey neither gave up their carrying concern nor implemented their proposal for a new company to handle their trade between Preston Brook and Liverpool. Thomas Gilbert had ceased to be Chairman of the committee in 1785 and, although he and John Gilbert retained their shares in the canal, they ceased to play any active part in its management. In 1794, the nine storey Staffordshire Warehouse was built at Castlefield, to which Henshalls soon moved.[17]

In December 1786, Henshalls sold their London stock and handed over their London trade to the firm of T. & M. Pickford of Manchester, who were the largest road carriers in the Manchester and London trade and wanted to transfer their traffic to the canal. In 1812, they disposed of their Stourport and West Midland trade to the Stourport carriers, Heath, Tyler & Danks. It appears that most of the merchandise traffic to the Potteries came to be handled by Kenworthy & Co.[18] and thenceforward Henshalls concentrated their remaining craft on the Pottery materials trade. Returning now to competition with the Weaver; in 1807, the Weaver Trustees proposed to improve access between their waterway and the tidal Mersey by the construction of the Weston Canal. The T&M threatened to oppose this in Parliament and the Weaver Navigation Trustees bought off this opposition by agreeing to relinquish their rights to transship clay, flints and ware - but not coal, salt or limestone - at Anderton. This limitation was repealed in 1825[19] and the way was now open for a period of intense competition.

It was this that encouraged the firm of Alexander Reid to enter the Potteries carrying trade in February 1829. In 1829-30, the Weaver Navigation Trustees had greatly enlarged the basins at Anderton and had built two new entrances. In 1832, a new inclined plane was built for the transshipment of coal, salt and other goods, and the Weaver toll on pottery goods was halved. In 1835, Reid was authorised to construct his own rails at Anderton for transshipping timber and, in 1836, he changed the name of the firm to the Anderton Carrying Company. In 1837, the Anderton Co. entered the general merchandise trade and also, having acquired the Macclesfield Canal carrier Swanwick & Co. in October 1838, started carrying to Macclesfield and entered the Burton ale trade. Within seven years, they had built up an extensive trade between Liverpool and the Potteries via the Weaver. The encroachment made on the Bridgewater Trustees' trade via Preston Brook was assisted by complaints of delays, exposure and rough handling at Runcorn and Liverpool.

The Bridgewater, however, were convinced that the Anderton Company's entry into the merchandise trade was financed by its profits on clay and ware, and was undercutting the Bridgewater's carriers. In December 1837, they engineered an agreement with Henshalls to effect, jointly, a reduction on the rates of freight from Liverpool to Etruria, which had previously been equal whether by Preston Brook or Anderton. The plan depended on inducing coasters to use Runcorn rather than Liverpool, enabling transshipment direct into narrow boats and cutting out the costs of carriage by flats from Liverpool. The Trustees were to reduce by 10d per ton and Henshalls by 10d per ton, plus 1d per crate on ware. The original common rate was 9s per ton on clay from Liverpool to Etruria.

The Anderton Company countered by reducing carriage on clay by 10d per ton. Henshalls were unable to continue their reduction on the Liverpool portion of the trade, which gave the Anderton

A pre First World War view of the River Trent sluice immediately above Wychnor Lock, the top paddles of which are visible above the right hand end of the sluice. The lock is in front and to the right of the cottage, which was replaced by the present house not long after this photograph was taken. WATERWAY IMAGES COLLECTION

An 1880s view of Old Quay Dock, Runcorn, where the Runcorn & Latchford Canal section of the Mersey & Irwell Navigation entered the Mersey Estuary above Runcorn Gap, upstream from the Bridgewater Canal Docks. Boats from the T&M would have used the Mersey & Irwell to access works on that navigation and to get to Warrington. Most of the structures in this view were cleared for the construction of the Manchester Ship Canal in the 1880s; this section opened in 1893. Part of the dock survived the upheaval for a while as an isolated pool but most of the land area was eventually taken over by the MSC's extensive boatyards, lock gate making workshops and maintenance facilities. A pair of horse narrow boats lie by the entrance lock opposite an interesting hopper bottomed dredging boat – this is a clear view of the mechanism for opening the bottom of its two holds to discharge its load onto the river bed. The building in the left background was a steam mill. NEIL PARKHOUSE COLLECTION

Co. the advantage of being 10d below the carriers via Preston Brook, as the Bridgewater had never undertaken to reduce on the rates between Liverpool and Preston Brook. Presumably, the hope of attracting more coasters to Runcorn was unfulfilled in the short term and, by April 1839, the Bridgewater were negotiating with the Anderton Company for a restoration of clay rates to the level existing before the reductions.

By the end of 1841, the Anderton Company had gained a complete monopoly of the Congleton and Macclesfield trades, in addition to which they carried twice as many crates per week as Henshall. One of their principal customers was William Davenport, who not only owned a pottery at Longport but also all the land there through which the T&M ran, including the freehold of the canal wharves.

Henshalls had by now become specialists in the carriage of ware, advertising in 1822 that, from the Potteries, they carried only ware.[20] The Bridgewater Trustees countered by establishing Thos Jackson in the Macclesfield trade in October 1839 and granting him a drawback on their tolls. In November 1841, the Bridgewater started to send their own boats from Preston Brook to the Potteries (their wharf at Shelton may date back to this date) and along the Peak Forest and Macclesfield canals. This was an emergency measure designed to save their general goods trade (groceries, wine, spirits, etc) from annihilation. Kenworthy, a carrier to the Potteries from Preston Brook and later one of the Bridgewater Trustees' commission agents, had just withdrawn from this traffic, leaving nearly the whole of the groceries trade to the Anderton Company.

In order to stabilise freight rates, the Bridgewater Trustees appointed a number of commission agents. These carriers hired their boats and equipment to the Trustees but continued to operate them for a commission on freight rates fixed by the Trustees, who met agreed expenses such as tolls.

In Macclesfield and in the Potteries, endeavours were made to solicit a traffic, not only in groceries but in iron and Manchester goods, by undercutting the Anderton Company. The Trustee's action primed the pump of independent enterprise. Suttons engaged an additional Potteries agent and reduced rates to compete with the Anderton Co., whilst Pickfords adopted the Anderton Company's charges in the Macclesfield and North Staffordshire trade. This enabled the Bridgewater Trustees to withdraw from the North Staffordshire carrying trade on 15th December 1841, after little more than a month, and in 1842, the revived Macclesfield trade was handed over to Pickfords.[21]

It may be noted from the above events that Hugh Henshall & Co., the carrying arm of the T&M, was able to do little to assist in the fight against competition from the Weaver route, with its attendant loss of tolls to the T&M, and appears by this time to have given up all its trade except for pottery raw materials and ware. The battle had to be taken up by the Bridgewater Trustees, who were from then on to exercise a considerable influence over the Trent & Mersey's trade, on the routing of which via Preston Brook their own toll and lighterage income depended.

Having fought against a direct link to the Weaver for many years, in 1831, the Trent & Mersey investigated a line for a flight of locks to the Weaver. They purchased land above Acton Bridge and, in 1832, installed a tramway for Staffordshire coal down to the river and a crane to transship heavy goods. The T&M expected that Staffordshire coal could be sold to the Weaver salt works and feared a possible connection between the Ellesmere & Chester's Middlewich Branch and the Weaver, by which this traffic could be diverted. In the event, the coal trade was a failure but the tramway was used for rock salt. Apart from their hopes for the coal trade, if there was no escaping the leakage of traffic to the Weaver, the T&M obviously saw the benefits of an extra 3 1/2 miles of tolls on their waters, being the distance from Anderton to Acton Bridge, Acton Bridge being only 3 miles from their junction with the Bridgewater at Preston Brook. The Acton Bridge connection unfortunately did not last long under the fierce competition of the Weaver Trustees, who wanted that 3 1/2 miles of tolls and carriage for themselves.

The Macclesfield Canal had been completed in 1831. Joining the T&M at Hall Green, it connected with the Peak Forest and Ashton canals to provide a shorter route to Manchester. It had no effect on the trade in pottery raw materials, although some ware to Manchester used it. The Anderton Company established a depot in Ducie Street Basin at Manchester but its effect on other traffic will be discussed elsewhere. In the same year, the Cromford & High Peak Railway, connecting the Cromford and Peak Forest canals, also opened and was later to have a severe effect on the merchandise traffic between Manchester and the Trent.

Of more importance to the Potteries trade was the Middlewich Branch of the Ellesmere & Chester Canal. This terminated 110 yards from the T&M, who constructed the short Wardle Branch, with one lock, to connect the two waterways, thus enabling them to charge tolls sufficiently high to deter the Trent & Mersey's traffic from proceeding to and from Liverpool by the Ellesmere & Chester. These high tolls also discouraged the diversion of traffic between Birmingham and Manchester to the Birmingham & Liverpool Junction Canal, opened in 1835. All pottery raw material and ware was charged the maximum bar toll of 10 1/2 d per ton.

We have seen the Trent & Mersey Canal develop from a virtual monopoly position in 1770, apart from the Burton Boat Company's Upper Trent Navigation, to a waterway facing considerable competitive pressure by 1840. This arose not only from the construction of competing canals and in the toll reductions and provision of transshipment facilities by the Weaver Trustees but from competition between the T&M's carrying arm, Hugh Henshall & Co., and Worthington & Gilbert and the Anderton Carrying Company. At the same time, cooperation was taking place. The Bridgewater and the T&M acted in concert to repel the threat from the Weaver and parts of Henshall's carrying trade were handed over to Pickfords and Heath, Tyler, Danks & Co., firms with the connections and ability to develop these respective trades to the benefit of the T&M toll income.

Toll revenue, which had been £23,152 in 1784, had risen to £123,707 in 1815 but carrying profit declined sharply from 1791 onwards. It had fallen from £5,084 in 1791 to £2,409 in 1815, reflecting the

The top pair of Staircase Locks on the old line at Runcorn and Toll Office circa 1905, with Anderton Company narrow boats **Millicent** *and* **America** *working up.* NEIL PARKHOUSE COLLECTION

Wardle Junction, Middlewich, looking south, circa 1930. Here the short Wardle Branch of the T&M Canal heads off to the right for less than one furlong to Wardle Lock, at the head of which it makes an end on junction with the Shropshire Union Canal. The bridge has a date stone reading 'Wardle Canal 1829' and the T&M was empowered to charge an extra compensation toll on traffic using this short branch. The bridge carries Booth Lane (now the A533) over the branch canal. BASIL JEUDA COLLECTION

Cheddleton Wharf circa 1909, with an NSR maintenance boat on the left. The building just to the right of the bridge is Cheddleton Silk Mill and to its right, with the roof ventilator, is Cheddleton Brewery. BASIL JEUDA COLLECTION

gradual contraction and increasing specialisation of Henshalls. In the absence of any definite information, we might presume that the T&M had found, as were so many canal companies to find in the future, that carrying, while sometimes necessary for policy reasons, was usually best left to independent carriers. Many of these had a wide ranging organisation, commercial contacts and carrying experience often predating their entry into water transport and most of them seem to have been able to keep a tighter control on costs than the canal companies.

By 1820, the annual dividend on T&M shares was 75% a rate which was maintained until 1831, when the Grand Junction Railway, connecting the Liverpool & Manchester Railway with Birmingham

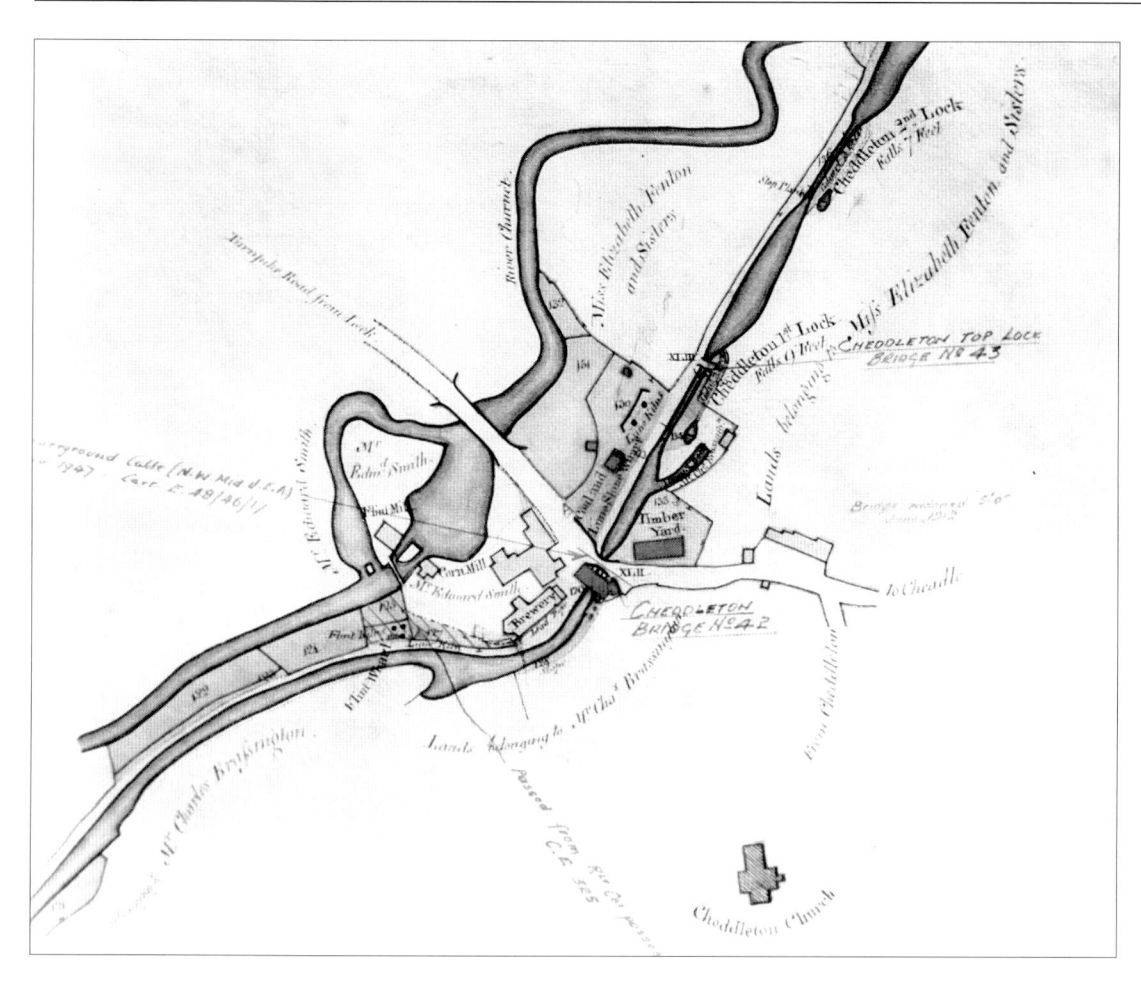

A plan of Cheddleton from the Caldon Canal Estate Plan of 1816 but with later notations. BASIL JEUDA COLLECTION

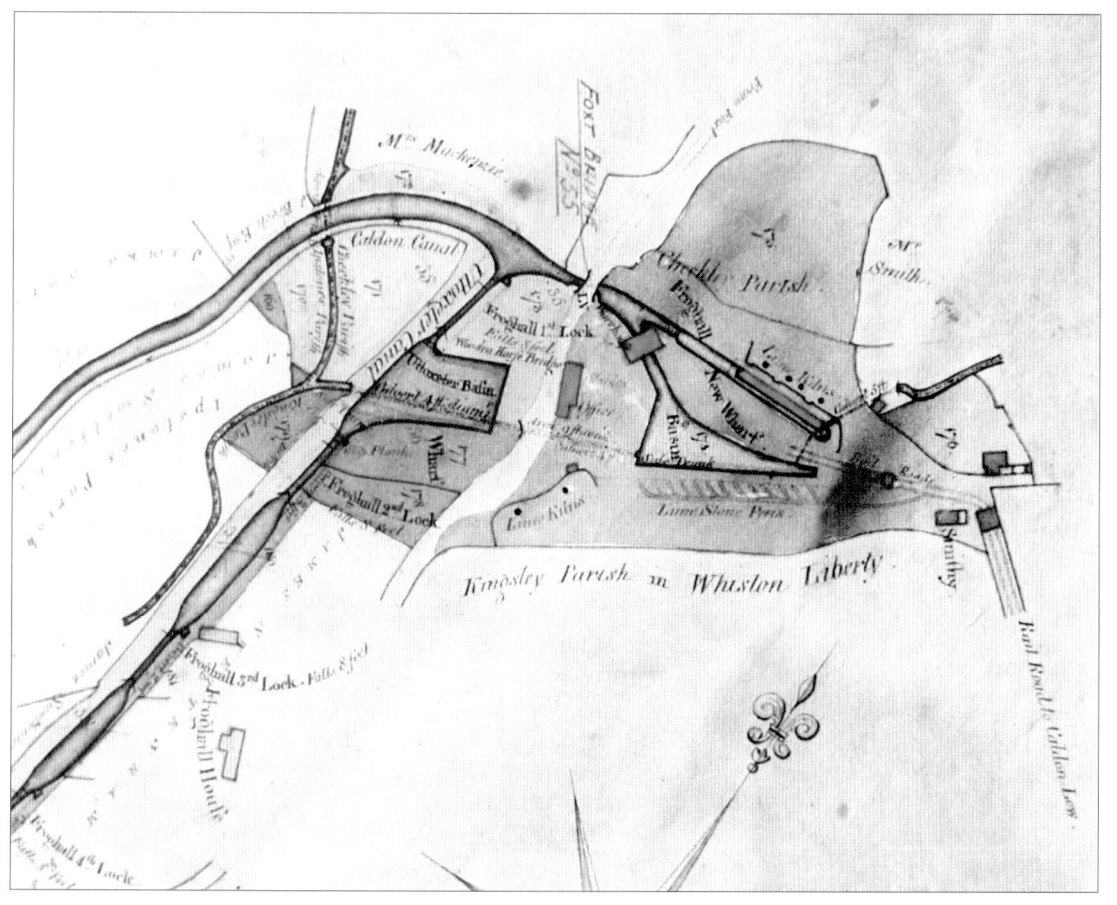

A plan of the Caldon Canal at Froghall, again from the Estate Plan of 1816. The original wharf of 1778 is at the top centre left, by the notation 'Caldon Canal'. The New Wharf of 1785 is to the right, the construction of which involved extending the canal by just over 500 yards, through Foxt Bridge, later Bridge No. 55. The new basin was built because it allowed better access for the tramway or waggonway coming down from Caldon Low Quarries. This was replaced by a new rail road in 1804, of which the base of the incline coming down from the quarries can be seen on the right. Also shown is the Uttoxeter Canal of 1811, which climbed through four locks to join the Caldon Canal just to the left (west) of Foxt Bridge. This canal was closed in January 1849 and much of its bed hereabouts used for the Froghall Junction Branch of the NSR. BASIL JEUDA COLLECTION

The canal at Barlaston, between Stoke on Trent and Stone, looking north in the 1930s. The public house is the Plume of Feathers (Prop. Alfred E. Wood), which is still open today but has been completely rebuilt from the building seen here. Bridge No. 103 carries Station Road over the canal. JOHN RYAN COLLECTION

and there with the London & Birmingham Railway, was first proposed. In 1832, just before the authorisation of that line, there were toll reductions of up to one third and in 1834 there were more selective reductions.

In 1836, 70,000 tons of clay, 30,000 tons of flints and 4,000 tons of other pottery raw materials are said to have entered the canal from Liverpool and the shipment traffic of ware was 51,000 tons. The ware trade to London amounted to 12,000 tons and that to Birmingham and the west of England 6,000 tons. However, these latter figures should be treated with caution, as there is no mention of the substantial flint traffic from London via Fradley nor of any traffic to and from the Trent.[22]

NOTES TO CHAPTER THREE
1. Wedgewood Archives 1805, quoted in Thomas J., *The Rise and Fall of the Staffordshire Potteries*, Adams & Dart, 1971
2. Shill, Ray, *Working Boat*, Heartland, 2001, p39 and *London Gazette*, 12th and 26th July 1803
3. *Derby Mercury*, 31st August 1759
4. Thomas J., op cit, p87
5. SRO D 603/N/6/8. Documents relating to a dispute between Lord Paget and the Trent & Mersey Canal
6. For more detailed information on the Upper Trent Navigation and Bond End Canal, their wharves and carriers, see a future volume by Shill, Ray in the *Working Boats* series.
7. *Staffordshire Advertiser*, 21st March 1795
8. Lindsay J., op cit
9. SRO D240/E(i)/4/9, Weston Salt Accounts 1830-37
10. Thomas J., op cit
11. SRO D3900/2, Haywood permits, 1901
12. McDougall D., 'Bound for Bewdley', *Waterways World* magazine, June 1995, p42 and Rolt L.T.C., *Worcestershire*, Robert Hale, 1949
13. PRO RAIL 855/107, 17 April 1798
14. Turnbull G., *Traffic and Transport*, Allen & Unwin, 1979, p96
15. DRO, D503/12/1, Letterbook, Outram to Gorton & Thompsom, 21st Feb. 1798
16. Lead, Peter., *Agents of Revolution*, Keele 1989, p105
17. Lindsay J., op. cit., p88-91 and Lead, P., op. cit., p80-81
18. Kenworthys were still carrying between Liverpool, Manchester and Huddersfield in 1849, in which year they became commission agents for the Bridgewater Trustees. They had become independent carriers on the Grand Junction Railway in 1838, restricted to through traffic between Lancashire and London but had been forced to give up their railway business by 1852
19. 6 Geo iv c29
20. *Pigot's Directory*, 1822-23
21. Mather F.C., *After the Canal Duke*, 1970
22. Ward J., *The Borough of Stoke on Trent*, 1843, p389

CHAPTER FOUR
THE POTTERIES TRADE AFTER 1840

The opening of the Liverpool & Manchester Railway in 1830, followed quickly by proposals for the Grand Junction Railway (GJR) and other lines, did not immediately stir the Trent & Mersey Canal Company into action. Admittedly, it had carried out some improvements, including the duplication of the single bore Harecastle Tunnel and of most of the locks between Wheelock and Kidsgrove but its commercial policy was the subject of complaint by its neighbour, the Bridgewater Trustees. They complained that high charges on the Wardle Branch prevented the joint reductions in tolls necessary to win back the South Staffordshire and Welsh trade, diverted to Ellesmere Port after the opening of the Birmingham & Liverpool Junction Canal (B&LJ). In 1842, the T&M finally made reductions at Wardle but only for timber, bricks and tiles.

The T&M and Bridgewater did, however, reorganise the way the South Staffordshire iron trade was handled and reduced tolls on it. This affected the Pottery trade, because the Shropshire Union Railways & Canal Company (SUR&C), who now owned the Ellesmere & Chester and the B&LJ, retaliated by cutting freight charges on pottery material from Ellesmere Port via the Middlewich Branch. The Ellesmere & Chester had become carriers in 1837 and had opened a dock at Ellesmere Port in 1843. Before this, they had only been able to deal with traffic barged to and from Liverpool but now that they had a dock which could accommodate coasters, the way was open to compete in the potters materials traffic. In 1844, the Bridgewater Trustees leased from the Ellesmere & Chester, at two years notice, the whole of their Mersey flats and steam tugs, as well as the dock, wharves and warehouses at Ellesmere Port, plus accommodation at Liverpool. This agreement was not supposed to prejudice traffic to north and south Staffordshire by the Ellesmere Port route but the Trustees at least got some income from the E&C's competing route. The SUR&C took over the E&C and B&LJ and their carrying departments in 1845 but was itself then leased by the L&NWR in 1847.

The GJR opened in July 1837 and there was an almost immediate leakage of ware traffic, which was carted from the Potteries to the GJR station at Witmore (opened for goods on 30th November 1840) and there put on train. A number of canal carrying firms became carriers by railway, including Pickfords, Kenworthy, Bache, Crowley, Robins and George Appleby of Longport although, initially, usually only part of their traffic was transferred to the iron road. This mainly affected the merchandise trade, in particular the London trade and the movement of ware in less than boatload quantities.

Ellesmere Port circa 1907. The buildings on the left were used for dealing with general merchandise traffic. The Shropshire Union operated fly-boat services over the whole of its own system, to South Staffordshire and to the Potteries. BASIL JEUDA COLLECTION

*A lovely view of the Salt Union Ltd's horse boat **Ireland** heading north through Trentham, on the southern outskirts of Stoke, circa 1908. After delivering salt these boats took whatever back loading was available, which in this instance appears to have been a light load of timber. The delightfully ornate bridge which it is about to pass under did not survive the demands of modern road traffic and the A5035 Longton Road which crosses over is now a dual carriageway. However, the houses either side with the distinctive half-timbered gables, which look quite recently built, still remain. BASIL JEUDA COLLECTION*

As early as 1842, Suttons, a major carrier on the canal, advertised a service from Etruria to London, Yorkshire and Hull by transshipment from boat to the Birmingham & Derby Junction Railway at Derby,[1] Suttons had by this date taken over the London trade of Kenworthy & Co.

Railway competition in the T&M heartland arrived in 1846, when authority was sought to build four lines. These were to run from a junction with the Manchester & Birmingham Railway at Macclesfield, to a junction with the Trent Valley Railway at Colwich, with a branch from Harecastle to Crewe and another from Stone to Norton Bridge on the GJR; and from North Rode via Uttoxeter and Willington to Burton on Trent, the junction with the Birmingham & Derby Railway. These lines were to form the North Staffordshire Railway (NSR). On 12th July 1845, an agreement was signed between the railway promoters and the canal company to purchase their shares at the then current price of £450. The current dividend of 30% was to be maintained until the opening of the whole line and then to be reduced to 22%. The railway lease was to date from 15th January 1847 and canal shares were then to be exchanged for 5% railway preference shares. The profits thereafter were to be divided in proportion to capital, until canal shareholders had received a total of £30 per share.[2]

The Trent & Mersey thus became a railway owned canal. Or did it? Some commentators suggest that the NSR was a canal owned railway! J. Thomas in *The Rise of the Staffordshire Potteries* poses the question '*Did the Trent & Mersey Canal create the NSR?*' Phillips, a former NSR manager, '*considered the NSR is a canal owned railway not vice versa*'.[3] Savage considered that the T&M converted itself into a railway.[4]

The NSR took a rather more vigorous attitude to the management of the T&M than had obtained for many years. On 1st July 1847, the Navigation Committee reported that it had imposed a limitation of one month on carriers' credit and had, in an arrangement with the Staffs & Worcs Canal, reduced tolls on the South Staffordshire trade between Haywood Junction and Preston Brook to $^1/_2$d per ton-mile. There had been a general tightening up of discipline, with the reintroduction of strict indexing of boats and their gauging by day and night. Traffic was to be allowed to pass at all hours. The last few remaining boats of the Hugh Henshall fleet, whose decline had resulted in a rise in freight rates, became the nucleus of the North Staffordshire Railway &

A scene at Preston Brook, close to the junction between the T&M and the Bridgewater Canal, probably circa 1920. This was a large inland port where goods to or from Liverpool were transshipped between Mersey flats and narrow boats. At one time boats ran from here to all parts of the canal network. Goods were also stored here and forwarded in small consignments on regular fly-boat services. The warehouses seen on pages 14 and 115 may be glimpsed beyond the bridge. The boat in the left foreground belongs to Noah Webb of Brierley Hill, near Dudley. It is more likely that the presence of the photographer, rather than the activity on the waterway below, has attracted the small crowd of interested onlookers to the bridge. WATERWAY IMAGES COLLECTION

the finished product, 63,376 tons of ware was carried by canal and 33,818 tons by rail. The railways had, in particular, made huge inroads into the trade in ware to London and the return carriage of flints. Birkenhead, a railway inspired port, attracted a considerable traffic in ware due to its superior facilities.

The flint traffic via Gainsborough also suffered from railway competition. On 31st March 1853, the NSR complained of the small profit on their salt and flint trade between the Potteries and Gainsborough, and gave notice to discontinue operations on the River Trent from 1st May. Their Nottingham agent, Daniel Brown, continued to carry on his own account, becoming an agent of the Bridgewater Trustees at the end of that year. The Shardlow carrier, Suttons, had given up in 1851. In 1855, the Bridgewater Trustees abandoned their Hull and Gainsborough agencies, and disposed of their Trent boats, while retaining control of freight charges to Derby and Nottingham through their agents. In 1856, 1,683 ton of flints, 216 tons of earthenware and 11,014 tons of salt moved between the Trent and the canal.

Soresby & Flack were the only other major T&M carrier to operate on the River Trent. Having sold most of their stock to the Grand Junction Canal in 1848, they disposed of their last eight Trent boats and two canal boats to Joshua Fellows & Co. in 1861. Their clerk, George Cowlishaw, became Fellows'

first agent at Shardlow.

By the 1890s, the use of Shardlow as a transshipment port seems to have ceased, transfer between narrow boats and river craft taking place at Nottingham, where the Trent Navigation company had opened a depot by 1881. This enabled the canal boats to transship directly into a larger type of barge known as Lower Trent boats, which could go to Hull. The former system of transshipment into Upper Trent boats at Shardlow meant that Hull traffic had to undergo a second transshipment at Newark or Gainsborough into Lower Trent boats. As a result, Shardlow's population fell from 1,306 in 1841 to 842 in 1891.

The trade in pottery materials and ware on the Trent continued to decline. Germany raised her import duties on manufactured goods to protectionist levels in 1879 and raised them again in 1885. They were moderated in the early 1890s but the upward trend was resumed in the 1900s. The bad state of the Trent Navigation at that time was a cause for concern. By 1906, German import duties had almost killed the ware traffic from the Potteries to Hull.[8] Ware to Russia had also declined. From the early 1930s, the River Trent carriers started to forward goods to the Potteries by road from their waterheads at Nottingham.

The opening to goods traffic of the Birmingham & Gloucester Railway, in October 1840, severely affected the viability of the route to the Potteries via

*The Bunn family was well known on the canals. Here, on 2nd August 1923, Edwin Bunn poses on **Swiftsure**, whilst the rest of the family occupy the stern space of **Saxon** behind. Both boats belonged to Potter & Son of Runcorn. BASIL JEUDA COLLECTION*

The Potteries Trade After 1840

the River Severn. Combined with the poor state of the river and the relative decline of Bristol as a port, while Liverpool was growing in importance, the trade in pottery materials and ware via Stourport rapidly declined. There was an attempt to revive the trade in ball clay around 1860, when two steamships started to trade between Poole and Worcester. However, the experiment failed because of the bad state of the Severn below Tewkesbury.

The inflexible charges on the T&M and Coventry canals had contributed to the loss of Birmingham and London traffic between 1833 and 1849, and it was not until after the latter date that there were attempts to revive the London trade. The departure of the earlier major carriers, leaving the GJC as the only big carrier, led to a perception among the manufacturers and merchants of the Potteries that existing rates were too high. This prompted the formation of new carriers. The Mellor family had been corn and flint millers for many years, and members of the family had interests in the manufacture of Parian ware and as earthenware, cement and plaster merchants.[9] Mellor, Colsell & Co., general carriers of Stoke on Trent, commenced trading to London on 1st February 1856, with premises at No. 7 Wharf at Paddington Basin. Their intention to carry flints was initially frustrated by high tolls but eventually they established a trade in ware to London and flints back. Because the route to London involved five separate canal companies, six if going beyond Paddington, the negotiation of competitive tolls was difficult. The Oxford Canal Co. was particularly obdurate, arguing that toll reductions on their canal would benefit the Grand Junction's carrying business at their expense. In May 1832, the Oxford had actually raised the tolls on flints from 1s 5 1/2d to 2s 2d per ton.[10]

Mellor's son, George, who had a flint mill at Sandon by 1851, established himself as a china and earthenware merchant, and also as G. & J. Mellor, a grinder of potters materials, with canalside mills at Fenton Road (Stoke), Etruria and Newport. The Mellor family's involvement with milling goes back to the 15th century. The partnership with Colsell seems to have dissolved in 1872. By 1879, Mellor was having to send his ware to London by rail and route his flints via Runcorn but seems to have re-established his London canal traffic later. In the 1880s, he was involved with flint traffic from Harefield, on the Grand Junction Canal, to Stoke. By 1884, he had moved his London depot to City Road Basin. He was still advertising as a general carrier in 1893, his London offices and depot now being at 10 South Wharf, Paddington, the move there perhaps being in response to the high Regent's Canal tolls on ware. He disposed of his London stock in 1895-96. His last directory entry as a carrier appears in 1912, when he had an office at 24 Glebe Street, Stoke. On retirement from general carrying, the firm still seems to have carried their own materials and had one boat left in the early 1950s. Mellor used a wharf at Lytton Street, Stoke, adjacent to his Fenton Road mill.

Another carrier on this route was John Walley, who also was engaged in the ware and flint trade as well as being a carrier of cement. Walley was born in Burslem about 1804 and, by 1842, was working as a canal clerk at Shelton Bridge. In 1851, he was an agent and wharfinger at Middleport, and a few years later he set up as a canal carrier. Edward Walley, another member of the family, had a pottery at Burslem and James Walley, of Tunstall, was a china dealer. John died in 1871 and his third son, John Edward, took over the business. He was in partnership with Colsell for a short while, apparently only two years, advertising as Colsell, Walley & Co., flyboats to London and all parts, from Copeland Street Wharf. Under John Edward, the firm developed their interests as flint merchants. In 1895, Walley, who had brought 832 tons of ware to London in sixty-four boats the previous year, was in dispute with

Potter & Son's boat **Swan** *at Mersey, Weaver's Burslem Wharf in the mid 1940s. Behind can be seen part of the Anderton Company warehouse, the terminal basin and the Furlong Flint Mill, with many potteries in the distance.* BASIL JEUDA COLLECTION

the Regent's Canal Co. over the charging of higher tolls for ware than for Birmingham goods. The Regent's refused to amend its preferential charging policies. By 1896, Walley was an agent for Coles, Shadbolt & Co., cement manufacturers of Harefield on the Grand Junction canal. Shadbolt's chalkpits contained large quantities of flints, which Walley took to the Potteries.[11]

John Edward was succeeded in 1904 by his son, Albert Leonard, who developed a branch of the business for the acquisition of flints in Essex known as the West Thurrock Flint Co. Like Mellors, Walleys gave up the general carrying trade but continued to carry pottery materials from the Mersey in a small way until the 1950s.[12]

The firm of Potter & Son, merchants and shipbrokers of Runcorn, were also involved in the London flint trade by 1875. Potter's involvement with canal carrying had begun in 1821, in partnership with another Runcorn concern, forming the firm of Simpson & Potter. Simpson was later to be a partner in Simpson, Davies & Co. Potter's boats were still trading on the London route in 1892,[13] and they were substantial carriers from Runcorn and Weston Point until 1958. In July 1937, Potters and the Weaver Navigation jointly applied for a special toll on china clay to Kettlebrook on the Coventry Canal, where there was a works making ceramic insulators.[14]

Around the end of the 19th century the sales of North Staffordshire ware in London had become subject to fierce competition from ware imported from the Continent. The manufacturers compelled the railways to reduce freights below the lowest economical canal rate of £1 per ton [15] and the end of the ware traffic made it uneconomical for the T&M carriers to send boats onto the Grand Junction for flints. The flint trade from Harefield was contracted to S. Barlow (Tamworth), as a return load for his boats carrying Warwickshire coal to the London area. Coles, Shadbolt also carried flints in their own boats in the years prior to the First World War, often subcontracting this flint traffic to owner boatmen from the Coventry and Oxford canals. One of these, Mr Joseph Skinner of Oxford, recalled taking flints up the Caldon Canal and recollected how shallow it was. The flint traffic from Harefield continued at least until the 1930s. The Anderton Company later made a shortlived attempt to revive the ware traffic to London, applying for a credit account for Coventry Canal tolls in May 1931.

In 1851, the NSR sought parliamentary authority to amalgamate with the London & North Western Railway. The bill was opposed by the Bridgewater Trustees, the Grand Junction, Coventry and Leicestershire & Northamptonshire Union (L&NU) canals, and a number of traders. The two railway companies offered to sell or lease the T&M to the

*The empty narrow boat **Three Sisters** descending Napton Locks on the Oxford Canal. Before the Grand Junction Canal was completed, all the heavy trade between Lancashire and London had to use this route, although lighter goods were usually transshipped to road wagons at Braunston. Even after the opening of competing railways, Staffordshire salt was still sent to destinations on the Oxford Canal and the River Thames, the boats sometimes returning with Oxfordshire flints from the Chiltern Hills.* NEIL PARKHOUSE COLLECTION

The Docks, Ellesmere Port.

L&NU who turned down the proposal, as did the Grand Junction and Coventry canals. The L&NU stated that the T&M tolls were exorbitant and the Grand Junction and Coventry refused to withdraw their opposition to the amalgamation unless the T&M tolls and dues were revised. The bill was defeated.[16] The two railway companies set up a joint traffic committee to consider matters of mutual interest. In January 1853, the minutes recorded the L&NWR as being against any rises in canal tolls and freights. Two months later, the L&NWR deferred both consideration of lower rail rates on potters' materials and ware to and from Liverpool, and also consideration of a canal trade via Ellesmere Port. In 1852, its subsidiary, the Shropshire Union Railways & Canal Company, had given the Bridgewater Trustees notice to quit the premises at Ellesmere Port leased by them in 1844. In December of the

A busy scene at Ellesmere Port circa 1900. This was the Mersey terminal of the Shropshire Union Canal whose route competed with the T&M to both north and south Staffordshire. Centre left is the three masted schooner **Enterprise**, *owned in Anglesey, which broke up on Hayle Bar in Cornwall in February 1904, having grounded there the previous September.* NEIL PARKHOUSE COLLECTION

The SUC at Ellesmere Port, looking from Powell's Bridge towards the docks around 1905. A Wolverhampton Corrugated Iron Company steam flat takes centre stage but the second boat on the right is loaded with pottery ware. BASIL JEUDA COLLECTION

*Weaver Navigation steam hopper barge **Whale**, approaching Winnington Bridge towing a wide boat around 1905. BASIL JEUDA COLLECTION*

same year, Miller, the NSR Railway & Canal Goods Superintendent, was to confer with his opposite number on the L&NWR, Huish, to consider whether any of the canal tolls and charges could be raised without loss of trade. In October 1866, there was a pending suit by the Shropshire Union, leased by the L&NWR in 1847, over the Wardle bar tolls.[17] The prohibitive tolls at Wardle remained and were not reduced until the Railway & Canal Traffic Act of 1888. These tolls did not, however, prevent the Shropshire Union from entering the Potteries trade, in which it was well established by 1867.

In March 1857, the Potteries Chamber of Commerce opposed a bill to amalgamate the Bridgewater Canal with the NSR. It was feared that the result would be monopoly control of transport to the Mersey. However, the Bridgewater Trustees were unable to provide accounts of the net earnings of their navigations and the bill was abandoned. In April of the same year, proposals for a one third reduction on pottery raw materials and ware were refused against a background of increasing canal tonnage. In the autumn of 1857, there was a slump in trade, largely caused by bank failures in the United States and the raising of the Bank of England's discount rate to 10%. This led to cuts in railway rates. In October 1858, the L&NWR quarrelled with the NSR and began a survey of a line from Whitmore or Madeley into the Potteries. This proposal was welcomed by the potters, who saw in it a way of escaping the heavy NSR freight charges between Stoke and Crewe. The two railways were, however, soon reconciled and in 1859 promoted another bill to authorise their amalgamation, which was defeated.

In 1862, the potters again challenged the high level of freight charges on the T&M, claiming that the NSR, both as a railway and a canal proprietor, was making their raw materials unnecessarily expensive. Further plans for building new railways into the Potteries were made, from Silverdale to Wellington and to Market Drayton, both on the GWR. There was also a scheme for a canal from the Weaver to the Potteries to carry 130-ton flats. In 1863, the NSR responded to these threats by a reduction in canal tolls on potters' materials of one farthing per ton. The Bridgewater Trustees reduced the freights charged by their subsidiary, the Anderton Company, by 10d per ton and their charges between Runcorn and Preston Brook from 2s 4d per ton to 2s 2d per ton. Under an act of 1864, the NSR extended their Silverdale Branch to Madeley and Market Drayton.[18] In 1863, trade on the canal had risen to its highest amount so far, 1,652,530 tons. Toll receipts, however, were only £93,132, as against the 1857 figure of £102,809 for 1,557,551 tons. NSR railway traffic had risen from 1,011,883 tons in 1857 to 1,423,004 tons in 1863. There were more toll reductions in 1866, the year of another banking crisis.

In 1865, steam tugs were introduced at Preston Brook Tunnel, followed by their use in Barnton and Saltersford tunnels also.

In the 1870s, the T&M and its ally, the Bridgewater, faced a new threat posed by the Weaver Navigation Trustees, who were improving facilities at Anderton and had, in 1866, obtained an act which resulted in the deepening of the river and enlargement of the locks. The Weaver Navigation Trustees were assisted by the formation, in 1864, of the Weaver & Mersey Carrying Company, formed by the owners of several salt businesses at Winsford to speed up traffic and cut costs. The carrying company's first steam flat was launched in 1866 and others followed. They could carry 180 tons of cargo and tow six to eight loaded barges. Compared with the 60 ton payloads which could reach Preston Brook by the Bridgewater route, the Weaver flats could reach Anderton with loads of over twice that amount and small coasters could now come this far up the river. The first of

The Potteries Trade After 1840

these arrived at Anderton in 1870 to load coal for Dublin. Evidently, the T&M had managed to start an export trade in North Staffordshire coal even if they could not sell it to the Weaver salt works.

To meet this threatening situation, a canal traffic committee was set up, consisting of representatives of the NSR, the Bridgewater and the Shropshire Union. This met at intervals between 1867 and 1875, mainly to fix freight charges between North Staffordshire and Liverpool, although the Weaver Carrying Company, by 1870, also competed in the South Staffordshire trade, charging 9s per ton as against the NSR's 10s per ton. In 1867, NSR freights for potters' materials between the Mersey and the Potteries were reduced by 6d per ton. On 29th April 1870, the following rates were agreed from Liverpool (via Ellesmere Port or Preston Brook):

	Pottery materials	Flints and cherts
Tunstall	5s 9d	5s 4d
Longport and Burslem	5s 11d	5s 5d
Etruria	6s 2d	5s 7d
Stoke	6s 5d	5s 9d

The Bridgewater Trustees allowed the NSR a further toll discount of 2d per ton on all pottery materials that they carried, whilst reciprocally, the NSR allowed a toll discount of 1.5d per ton on all pottery materials carried by the Bridgewater-owned Anderton Company.

A price war was now on. A few days later, on 10th May 1870, it was reported that the Weaver Navigation Trustees were taking further action to divert traffic to their route, including reductions in their rates. The T&M therefore agreed to further reductions on freights on pottery materials of 6d per ton. On 19th August, the NSR decided to charge the full parliamentary toll on all traffic interchanged at Anderton.

Still pursuing their goal of cheaper transport, the Potteries Chamber of Commerce and the iron

Potter & Son's Speedwell at Wardle Junction, Middlewich in the mid 1940s. BASIL JEUDA COLLECTION

The south end of Barnton Tunnel circa 1910. Nearest the camera is an empty coal boat, Nellie, returning to the Bridgewater Collieries. Abreast and in front of her are two loaded crate boats bound for Runcorn. NEIL PARKHOUSE COLLECTION

Delamere Dock, Weston Point circa 1890. Narrow boats from the Midlands and elsewhere were able to access this dock directly following the opening of the Anderton Lift in 1876.
BASIL JEUDA COLLECTION

The lock giving access from Weston Point Docks to the Manchester Ship Canal. BASIL JEUDA COLLECTION

traders representatives set up the Traders (North Staffs) Carrying Co. Ltd, with the aim of carrying raw materials and manufactured goods between North Staffordshire and the Mersey via the Weaver route. Its prospectus was examined and approved by the Chamber on 13th March 1871, by which time the company had absorbed the business of Joseph Davies, the originator of that phase of competition on the Weaver route. The company had accommodation at Anderton and Tunstall, and offered to guarantee 30,000 tons of pottery materials and 15,000 tons of manufactured goods by the Weaver route, considerably more than was then being sent.

These amounts did not materialise and the company was shortlived but the pressure on rates was having an adverse effect on the NSR, who complained that the railway revenue was not benefiting to the extent of tolls lost on the canal.[19] The Traders (North Staffs) Carrying Co. went into receivership in April 1874, when its assets included a wharf in Liverpool docks, wharves and warehouses at Weston Point, Anderton, Tunstall, Burslem, Etruria, Shelton and Stoke, as well as general offices at Glebe Streeet, Stoke, canal boats, horses, wagons and a steam flat.

The expectation of this much traffic was enough to cause the Weaver Trustees to consider building a boat-carrying connection at Anderton and a bill was prepared for the 1872 session. This took the form of an hydraulic lift, costing £48,000 and opened in July 1875.[20] The NSR was invited to participate in financing the lift as a joint venture but declined. A charge of 1s per boat plus 1d per ton was allowed but, by 1886, the lift was free to those who had paid Weaver tolls. It was the threat of the lift that probably persuaded the Bridgewater to put steam tugs on its canal. Surprisingly, there was no proposal that the NSR might provide steam towage over the 16.5 mile of level waterway between Preston Brook and Middlewich.

A total of 17,028 tons of goods used the lift in 1876, rising to an all time maximum of 213,771 tons in 1914. However, the other transshipment arrangements at Anderton were still in situ in 1897, the OS map of that year showing much the same facilities as were in place twenty years earlier. It is not possible to state how much traffic continued to use the old facilities and for how long but traders stored goods, particularly ware, grain and iron, at

The Potteries Trade After 1840

A circa 1900 view of the Anderton Lift, showing two salt chutes and a boat waiting to ascend the lift. The lift is seen here in its original form, when it was still hydraulically operated. BASIL JEUDA COLLECTION

Anderton for later shipment and it would have been just as convenient to use the existing buildings and machinery for this type of traffic. The same applies to traffic to and from Liverpool, which still had to be transshipped between flats and narrow boats, there being no particular reason to send the boats down the lift to perform this operation.

The lift's main benefit was to enable narrow boats to make the journey between Weston Point Docks and the narrow canal system without transshipment. It would be wrong to assume that the lift, which in its original form was often out of action, itself attracted all the traffic between the T&M and the Weaver immediately it was opened. The years between the opening of the lift and 1914 were very busy for water traffic, with the result that the Anderton area must have been heavily congested and the pressure on its facilities enormous.

As originally built, one tank of the lift rose while the other descended. When the lift was rebuilt in 1908 and converted to electric operation, the tanks could rise and fall independently, thus speeding up

A later view of the Anderton Lift, after conversion to electrical operation completed in 1908. To support the heavy new electrical machinery, a new lift superstructure was built over the top of the original one. The timber clad projection from the building on the left covers a hoist. The volume of traffic and saving of charges for use of the lift meant that hoists, rails and chutes were used for some years after the lift was built. NEIL PARKHOUSE COLLECTION

The Newcastle Canal slowly being overtaken by nature at Trent Vale, Stoke in the 1920s. Closure of the canal was sanctioned by Act of Parliament in 1921 and it was abandoned completely in 1935. It was subsequently filled it. Trent Vale was about midway along the 4 mile route, which was level all the way so there were no locks along it. Commercially, however, it was a failure. This was Bridge No. 12 and there was also a wharf here. JOHN RYAN COLLECTION

transit.

There was a further proposal in 1872 for an amalgamation of the NSR and L&NWR, again strongly opposed by the Potteries Chamber of Commerce. They argued that such an amalgamation would remove the fear of rival lines being constructed, always a salutary pressure on transport charges, and that Staffordshire already suffered because of lack of competition between canal and railways. It was feared that the L&NWR would not have the same interest as the NSR in keeping the canal open and would force as much traffic as possible on their railway. The Chamber of Commerce stated that some of the most important manufactories and mills had been built beside the canal, and that water transport was essential to the Potteries.

J. Allport, Traffic Manager of the Midland Railway, gave evidence to the Select Committee on Railway Companies Amalgamation on 2nd May 1872, to the effect that the T&M had 90% of the traffic in china clay from Runcorn to the Potteries and that there was a return trade in salt via Runcorn to Cornwall. He suggested nationalisation of the canals but doubted whether competition with rail could be maintained except for short distances and special traffic. The northern end of the T&M was

An Edwardian view of a rural stretch of the canal at Little Leigh, north west of Barnton, site of two breaches into the Weaver Valley (to the right) in recent years. JOHN RYAN COLLECTION

clearly a canal to which this last remark applied. Relative to other sections of canal, its trade held up remarkably well.

In 1872, the Bridgewater Trustees disposed of their canals to the Bridgewater Navigation Company (BNC), who decided to withdraw from their involvement in the carrying trade. The Anderton Carrying Company was sold to a partnership between William Boddington, the Bridgewater's agent at Liverpool, and Edward Pamphilon, the NSR's Goods & Canal Manager. Pamphilon had been the NSR's agent at Stoke wharf in 1851. The new company traded as 'The Anderton Company'. The agreement was finalised on 29th February 1876 and came into effect on the following day, 1st March. The stock was transferred at valuation, the Bridgewater to retain ownership until full payment had been made on an instalment basis.

The Anderton Company thus acquired sixty-nine narrowboats valued at £4,881 and sixty-seven hauling horses at £1,295. The value of these horses was much less than that of the cartage horses, forty-four of which were valued at £2,165. Carts and wagons were valued at £750. Tenancies included wharves at Port Vale and Tunstall, as well as the tenancies of the Bridgewater's own premises

A smart British Waterways boat at Lock No. 50, at the top of the Lawton Treble Locks flight around 1960. The original circa 1776 lock built by James Brindley is on the left, with the later circa 1830 lock, built under the supervision of Thomas Telford to help speed up traffic, on the right. The original lock has been filled in at some time since the date of this view.
BASIL JEUDA COLLECTION

*George Radford waits with Potter & Son's motor boat **Sunshine**, whilst his butty rises in Lock No. 57 at Hassall Green in 1957. **Sunshine** had joined Potters fleet from the Anderton Co. in 1948 and was to be sold for conversion to a houseboat a year after this photograph was taken.*
GORDON BRIGGS

Bethune tied outside the pub at Broken Cross, Northwich. The date is sometime after June 1934, when Mersey, Weaver's had bought her from A. &A. Peate, the mill owners of Maesbury, who had taken over a number of Shropshire Union craft when the latter ceased carrying at the beginning of the 1920s. BASIL JEUDA COLLECTION

(originally bought with the Anderton Carrying Co. in 1848) at Stoke and Etruria. The Bridgewater retained the former Anderton Carrying Co. depot at Anderton. The Anderton Company remained an agent of the BNC and freight, toll, dock, towage and transshipment rates were scheduled for its traffics and for services provided by the BNC. The agreement was for a term of four years, thereafter subject to six months notice but the Navigation Company reserved the right to terminate if the business was not conducted to the satisfaction of their General Manager. The name of the Bridgewater Navigation Company was to be painted on one side of the boats and displayed at the various wharves, so that the continuing interest of the Bridgewater Navigation Company in the North Staffordshire trade was perpetuated. Later on, the boats carried the slogan 'Bridgewater Navigation Route' below the Anderton Company's name. Pamphilon retired from the business on 31st March 1892.

In 1879, the Anderton Company carried 4,994 tons between Liverpool and the Potteries via Preston Brook at 9s 10d per ton, 22,492 tons between Anderton and the Potteries at 5s 3d per ton, and 17,492 tons between Liverpool and Anderton at 6s 1d per ton. In 1884, 118,102 tons of pottery materials and 36,759 tons of ware were dealt with at Runcorn.

In 1894, the NSR entered into an agreement to sell all its boats, horses, lorries and wharf working plant to the Anderton Company, leasing to it Stoke Basin, Etruria Basin and Navigation Road Wharf, Burslem. If the NSR subsequently required the Anderton Company to provide public wharfage, they were also to provide suitable accommodation. The stock was taken over on valuation and the wharves were leased for three years and then at six months' notice for £400 per annum. As much traffic as possible was to go via Runcorn, the NSR to assist them to obtain such traffic. A joint agent at Runcorn was to be appointed to attend to NSR and Anderton Company business, his salary to be shared on a 50/50 basis and the appointment to be made alternately by each concern, the first appointment being made by the NSR. The agreement, witnessed by Richard Edge of Shelton, Carrier's Agent, was to come into effect on 1st January 1895.[20] In 1896 the Anderton Company was incorporated into a new limited company, The Anderton Company Limited under the chairmanship of Henry Boddington, William Boddington's son. The Boddington family continued to own and manage the company until it was sold to the Mersey, Weaver & Ship Canal Carrying Company in 1953.

The Anderton Company's manager, James Malkin, died in 1894 at the age of 65. Richard Edge, who witnessed the Agreement, was related to him by marriage and could have been managing the company at that time. The term 'Agent' seems to have been applied to all the Anderton Company's managers regardless of rank.

Another important event in 1894 was the opening of the Manchester Ship Canal (MSC), which, for the first time, enabled north western narrow boats to work cargo alongside deep sea ships. The MSC purchased the Bridgewater Navigation Company and it also resulted in an agreement that was beneficial to the T&M traders. In return for special charges on the MSC between the Weaver and the Mersey via Weston Mersey lock, the Weaver agreed to special charges for traffic to and from the T&M and the Weaver, via the lift, to any point on the Weaver within one mile. This distance included the Bridgewater Department's Anderton wharves. Goods landed at these were to be charged as through traffic. Another concession made in the same year was to allow vessels up to 400 tons, carrying pottery raw materials, to use the MSC free of dues up as far as Runcorn if they were too late for the tide.[21]

In 1896, the railways reclassified china clay from Class 'C' to 'B', thereby reducing their rates on that commodity. The Bridgewater Department reduced its carriage rates on ware between Runcorn and Liverpool by 2d per ton (to 4s 3.7d), carrying 36,823 tons as against 28,759 at 4s 3.9d per ton the previous year. The Bridgewater were still carrying on the Weaver Navigation, with 8,857 crates from Anderton to Liverpool in 1896 (5s 6.3d), having managed to increase traffic on that route from 6,177 crates in 1895 without reducing their rate. The Bridgewater's (formerly Anderton Carrying Co.) depot at Anderton handled 10,872 tons in 1896.

Between 1896 and 1900, decreased traffic via the Bridgewater route was reported, blamed on reduced manufacture of heavy earthenware for America and some diversion of china stone to Weston Point. In that period, the Bridgewater's earthenware traffic from Anderton and Runcorn fell by 23.46% from 45,600 crates to 34,900 crates at a rate, by both routes, of 5s 6d. There was also a reduction of 29% in pottery materials from Runcorn Docks from 107,700 tons to 76,500 tons. In 1897, 5,103 tons of clay from Runcorn was routed via the Runcorn & Weston Canal and the Weaver. Liverpool to Preston Brook (for the Potteries) traffic increased from 60,959 tons to 61,061 tons with a reduction in the lighterage rate from 3s 5d to 3s 2.8d per ton.[22]

The Anderton Company Ltd now emerged as the largest carrier between the Mersey and North Staffordshire. Twenty-two boats from the NSR were added to the sixty-nine taken over from the BNC and to the steady stream of boats that the company had been building since it gained its independence. At its peak, the company had nearly 200 narrow boats in service, making it not only the largest trader to the Potteries but the second largest carrier in the north west. Its agreements with the NSR, BNC and the Shropshire Union put it into a very strong position and it might have been thought very difficult to challenge. The Weaver, however, was not going to lie down under arrangements clearly designed to concentrate traffic via the Bridgewater route (apart, that is, from the Shropshire Union's rather smaller trade via Ellesmere Port). In 1894, the Mersey, Weaver & Ship Canal Carrying Co. appeared on the scene.

The origins of the Mersey, Weaver Co. arose from the involvement of the Weaver and T&M salt works in general carrying. They did this to provide back loads for their flats and boats, and some of the salt owners were also merchants of pottery materials. The Weston Salt Works on the T&M was one of those heavily involved in this activity. When the Salt Union, a cartel incorporating most of the Cheshire salt producers and including others from Staffordshire, Worcestershire, Teeside and Ireland, was formed, it inherited the Weaver & Mersey Carrying Co. and about eighty narrow boats. In 1894, the Salt Union set up subsidiaries to conduct the general carrying business it had taken on. One of these was the Mersey, Weaver & Ship Canal Carrying Company, which carried not only raw materials and ware for the pottery industry but was also involved in the South Staffordshire trade and carried on the Bridgewater and Manchester Ship canals. The MSC

Bethune again, alongside Mersey, Weaver horse boat *Mersey* (which had joined their fleet in about 1905) at Runcorn Locks in the mid to late 1930s. BASIL JEUDA COLLECTION

The Legin Tunnel, Harecastle.

The north end of the Harecastle Tunnels at Kidsgrove in the 1920s. The steerer of the laden horse boat has placed his tow line round the fore-stud so as to pull the fore-end round the sharp turn. Boats had needed to be 'legged' through Brindley's original smaller bore tunnel on the right but this was closed to traffic in 1914, when subsidence caused parts of the roof to become too low for even loaded boats to pass through.
BASIL JEUDA COLLECTION

had acquired the Bridgewater Navigations in 1887, the former BNC waterways now being known as the Bridgewater Department. The Bridgewater Department was soon complaining about competition from Mersey, Weaver, who competed for the bigger consignments by using large vessels on the MSC instead of the smaller flats on the Bridgewater Canal, and there had been a substantial transfer of traffic from the Bridgewater's Runcorn Docks to Weston Point. The year 1895 was a bad one for trade but there had been a massive leap in tonnage through the Anderton Lift, from 84,434 tons in 1894 to 129,187 tons in 1896.[23]

Mersey, Weaver's activities had become so damaging to the established interests on the T&M that a pooling agreement between the Shropshire Union, the Anderton Company and the Mersey, Weaver Company was made in 1905, which was renewed in 1912.

Initially, Mersey, Weaver used public wharves in the Potteries but they had taken over the Anderton Company's Port Vale Wharf by 1912, as well as the former Shropshire Union wharf at Wharf Road, Stoke, and had also set up a wharf on the premises of the former Atlas Foundry at Tunstall. When the Shropshire Union closed its carrying department in 1921, they took over that company's wharf at Navigation Road, Burslem and subsequently built a new wharf and warehouses, known as Weaver Wharf, at Belmont Road, Etruria. They also had a transshipment depot at Anderton and a warehouse at Northwich. The company's trading position was secured by its connections with the salt and chemical manufacturers, and by its agencies for the supply of salt, borax and bentonite clay.

In 1935, the Salt Union sold Mersey, Weaver to its manager Charles Shirley. The Shirley family's interests included the merchanting and milling of pottery materials, and they owned the Etruria Bone & Flint Mill. The family were also prominent in local politics in the 'Five Towns'. The Salt Union itself had continued to participate in the trade in pottery materials under its own name. In November 1926, it was involved in a dispute with the Weaver Navigation over cleaning china stone.[24] It would be wrong to suggest, as some writers have claimed, that Mersey, Weaver was a specialist in the carriage of basic pottery materials. Their December 1925 monthly total of 281 tons of china clay from Weston Point to Anderton for the Potteries must be compared with a weekly consumption of 150 tons by one large potworks. In fact, that month's total of clay, china stone, flints and bone ash, 765 tons, represents only thirty-five boatloads or 1.4 boats per working day, whereas they carried 1,300 tons of general goods to Anderton (for transshipment to Staffordshire), Northwich and Winsford. Potter & Sons carried a total of 2,373 tons of basic pottery materials from Weston Point in the same period, more than three times as much.

The Potteries Trade After 1840

In 1902, the Anderton Company's crate traffic via Anderton had fallen to 146 tons (Runcorn 30,411 tons) A report of that year states that the Bridgewater were trying to close this depot and none were sent by that route from 1903. Anderton Company operations on the Weaver were thereafter confined to the carriage of pottery materials from Weston Point Docks.

In 1905, the Anderton Company's up traffic via Preston Brook was 29,934 tons, in addition to 32,303 tons of ware down. It must be remembered that the company also had traffic that did not pass onto the Bridgewater system, so its total tonnage was larger.

We must return now to the Shropshire Union. In 1867, it had been included in the Traffic Committee set up by the NSR and Bridgewater to control rates and charge but its access to the Trent & Mersey was still hindered by the high bar tolls at Wardle Junction, Middlewich and, in 1870, it had only twenty-four boats trading to the Potteries. By 1872, it had established wharves at Stoke (Wharf Street, later Copeland Street) and Tunstall.

In May 1874, pooling discussions between the NSR and SU became the North Staffordshire Conference, operative by 1890 and including the Bridgewater Navigation Company. Its principal object was the exclusion of private carriers. After the enforced reduction of the 10 $^1/_2$ d per ton Wardle bar toll on all the main commodities in the potteries trade and also on ware was made in 1892 (as a result of the Railway and Traffic Canal Act 1888), the Shropshire Union expanded rapidly, with additional wharves at Etruria, and Burslem (Navigation Road). It also shared a wharf at Middleport with the L&NW and Midland railways, and had a depot at Longton on the canal company's Lane End tramroad. The opening of the Manchester Ship Canal in 1894 led to a major expansion of its facilities at Ellesmere Port and a large increase of traffic to the Potteries.

The SU fleet was subsidised by the L&NWR. During the First World War, the government subsidised all canal carriers but this came to an end on 31st August 1920. Faced with the loss of the wartime subsidy, the prospect of a trade union claim for higher wages and an eight hour day, and with rising costs generally, the Shropshire Union decided to give up its carrying fleet from 31st August 1921. The impending grouping of railways, whereby the L&NWR and the NSR were to be included in the London, Midland & Scottish Railway, almost certainly had a major influence on this decision. The Anderton and Mersey, Weaver companies, and another T&M carrier, Joseph Rayner of Runcorn, bought some of these boats, a few others going to owner boatmen in the potteries trade. The SU wharves at Navigation Road were taken over by Mersey, Weaver.

In February 1886, the NSR announced that maintenance of the canal was to become separate from that of the railway and a canal engineer was appointed. Dredging was carried out and, by 1906, boats could carry 28 tons between the Potteries and Runcorn compared to 21 tons in 1886.

A year later, notice was given of a bill to improve

*Loading J. & G. Meakin's **Alice** with crates of ware, at their Eagle Pottery on the Caldon Canal at Hanley circa 1950. This is a rare instance of mechanical handling of canal traffic in the Potteries. Meakins ran a fleet of three boats, the last of which ceased operating in 1953, carrying export loads of pottery to Weston Point Docks or Runcorn and returning with potters' materials.* BASIL JEUDA COLLECTION

The British Waterways boat seen on page 83 meets a couple of pleasure craft between the top of Lawton Treble Locks and Hall's Turnover Lock, on its way to the Potteries circa 1960. GORDON BRIGGS

the Trent Navigation and widen the T&M between Derwentmouth and Burton on Trent. This was never done. An Act obtained in 1891 (54 & 55 Vict c 34) authorised the widening and straight-ening of the T&M between the Potteries and Preston Brook. The towpath in Harecastle Tunnel was to be removed, thus allowing its use by wider boats, and the NSR was to provide steam tugs for compulsory towage through the tunnel. The thirty-five locks were to be replaced by twenty-one larger ones, each 135 foot by 15 foot by 6 foot, which could accommodate a steam barge carrying 40 tons and towing a dumb barge of 50 to 80 tons tons burden.

Traders opposed this scheme believing that it was only intended to prevent the construction of the Birmingham & Liverpool Ship Canal, proposed in 1885. The locks at the north end of Harecastle Tunnel had been duplicated, the volume of traffic, between 170 and 180 boats daily, being more than a single lock could handle without serious delay. Calculations show that it would have taken thirteen hours to handle this number of boats through a single lock, even if everything ran completely smoothly all day and every day, which of course it never did.

The Railway & Canal Traffic Act 1888 set up the Railway & Canal Commission and allowed the Board of Trade to establish a uniform classification of merchandise, to be applied to all railways and canals. The new maximum rates were authorised by a series of Railway (Rates & Charges) Acts in 1891 and 1892, and the new rates had to be in the rate books on 1st January 1893. Companies were free to adjust and vary their rates within the statutory maxima, as long as no undue preference was shown.

Lamprey leaves the top of Lawton Treble Locks with the Turnover Lock ahead en route to the Potteries in the early 1960s. The steerer is Reg Barnet. GORDON BRIGGS

Site of the former Brindley's Bank flint wharf. The wharf was located just beyond the present day seat. Flints and china stone were brought here by canal and transshipped to craft on the River Trent, to be taken to Colton Mill at Rugeley. TOM FOXON COLLECTION

As the companies were unable to do all the necessary alterations to their rate books by this date, they decided, for the time being, to raise their rates to the maximum permitted by the Board of Trade. The result came as a rude shock to the public and there was a major outcry. Parliament was appealed to and a further Railway & Canal Traffic Act was passed in 1894, requiring the companies to justify any increase in rates before a court if a trader made a complaint to the Railway & Canal Commission. This meant the companies could not easily raise rates and they were therefore reluctant to lower them. They were now practically tied to the rates existing in 1892, being inhibited from lowering a rate experimentally, because they would have difficulty in raising it again if the experiment proved unprofitable.[25]

The T&M therefore entered into an agreement with the North Staffordshire traders, that all tolls were to remain at the rates authorised by the canal's enabling Act (6 Geo III ch 96).[26] The 1894 Act was also to lead to labour troubles, the difficulty in varying charges preventing the raising of wages.

The consequences of the Railway & Canal Traffic Act 1888 were costly for the NSR. Legal expenses in respect of the canal alone had been nearly £3,500 and much time and labour. The new schedule of tolls would result in a *'serious diminution of the receipts of the Canal'*. The canal's income was said to be insufficient to meet the 5% interest guaranteed on its preference shares.

Under these circumstances it was considered necessary to stop, *'for the time being'*, the improvements that had been contemplated. The work to be undertaken would now be limited to the *'maintenance of a sufficient waterway and to the most simple and essential repairs'*. The enlargement of the canal between Anderton and Middlewich had been carried out in 1891 at a cost of £322,000, allowing barges of 60 tons capacity to travel from the Mersey as far as Middlewich. This required specially built craft and the facility seems to have been little used. When the Croxton aqueduct was rebuilt, it was made only 8 feet 2 inches wide.[27] As we have seen, the NSR carrying department was discontinued in 1895, almost certainly in response to the restrictions imposed by the 1894 Act.

No such restrictions were imposed on independent canal carriers. In 1894, the NSR was authorised to provide, and make a charge for, mechanical haulage (other than by steam) through Harecastle Tunnel. Predictably, the North Staffordshire Chamber of Commerce and other traders opposed this, because it would mean that they would have to use the company tugs and not be allowed to use their own horses or leggers. An electric tug was not put into operation through the second tunnel at Harecastle until 30th November 1914 - in the event, a decision that was forced by subsidence in the original tunnel making it unnavigable.

The 1888 and 1894 Railway & Canal Traffic Acts had not brought traders the rate reductions they had hoped for. Their unrest over transport costs led to proposals for a system of nationally owned large dimension waterways and the Royal Commission on Canals & Inland Navigation in the UK was set up in 1906 to consider this. Its lengthy deliberations led to no action being taken. The country's transport network remained one where an inflexible system of charging by value of the goods, and rate agreements between the canal and railway companies and between carriers, prevented any competition in the real sense and was said to keep the cost of transport unnecessarily high. On the other hand, it could be argued that without these agreements, unrestricted rate cutting would soon have placed the companies and carriers in a precarious financial position. Even with them, we have seen the T&M unable to meet all the payments on its preference shares, while canal carriers had to impose strict economies and their boatmen worked long hours for low wages, often having to provide, at their own expense, such essential items as ropes.

A foretaste of things to come was the introduction of a motor lorry export service between the Potteries and Liverpool in 1906 but it would not be until the availability of mechanised road transport on a substantial scale after the 1914-1918 war that traders could enjoy the benefits of competition, and even that was to be curtailed by the Road Traffic Act 1930.

In 1905, it was said that the amount of ware shipped via Runcorn was 50,000 to 60,000 tons annually. Traffic fell slightly from 1903 to 1913 but by no large amount. It was to be the First World War and its aftermath that started the T&M on a severe decline in tonnage carried and began the process of turning it, eventually, from a vital artery of commerce into a linear pleasure park. The working history of the canal from 1913 to 1970 will be discussed later.

NOTES TO CHAPTER FOUR

1. *North Staffordshire Mercury*, 18th March 1842
2. PRO RAIL 532/4, NSR Report, 23rd September 1846
3. BW GLOS, BW 22.86, Evans J., 'History of the Railway owned Canals during the period of Control (WWI)', p36
4. Savage C., *An Economic History of Transport*, London 1967
5. Hayman A., 'Involvement in the North and South Staffordshire trades and places beyond by the Bridgewater Trustees, the Bridgewater Navigation Company and the Manchester Ship Canal (Bridgewater Department)'; also Mather F.C., *After the Canal Duke*, Manchester, 1970
6. PRO RAIL 532/4, Extrapolation from quarterly figures in NSR Report 1848
7. Poole B., *The Commerce of Liverpool*, 1854
8. Royal Commission on Canals, 1906
9. *Slater's Directory*, 1862
10. SRO 240/E/(1)/4/4, Weston Salt Accounts, 1830-37
11. I am indebted to Mr C. Jones for allowing me to use the results of his research into Mellors' and Walleys' trade
12. Faulkner A., 'Two Carriers to Stoke', *Waterways World* magazine, June 2001
13. BW GLOS, BW 72.568, Light boats through Fradley
14. BW GLOS, Not catalogued, Coventry Canal letter book
15. Royal Commission on Canals, 1906
16. Lindsay J., op cit, p124-5
17. PRO RAIL 532/27, L&NWR/NSR Joint Committee
18. Lindsay J., op cit, pp132-3
19. Hadfield & Biddle, *The Canals of North West England*, David & Charles, 1966, p225
20. For a detailed description of the lift see Carden D., *The Anderton Boat Lift*, Black Dwarf 2000; Hadfield & Biddle, op cit; Lindsey J., op cit and Murray S. M., 'The Anderton Lift' (unpublished dissertation), Chester, 1990
21. PRO RAIL 532/68
22. Manchester City Archives, Bridgewater Tolls & Freight 1895-1922
23. BW GLOS, WM 101.75, MSC (Bridgewater Department) Rates, Charges and Agreements.
24. BW GLOS, BW 27.81
25. Savage C., op cit
26. BW GLOS, WM101.75
27. Royal Commission on Canals, Minutes of Evidence Pt II 1906, NSR Report pp83-4

The footbridge over the canal near Barnton, circa 1904. It remains today. JOHN RYAN COLLECTION

BARNTON NEW BRIDGE.

CHAPTER FIVE
THE IRON AND COAL TRADES

Iron

It should be noted that the term 'iron', when used in canal and railway traffic records, includes pig iron, bar iron and steel, and manufactured iron and steel articles such as boilers, tanks and tubes. Smaller iron articles were described as goods. There were various classifications, which decided the rate the traffic was to be charged at, according to the value of the iron.

The North Staffordshire coalfield contained large deposits of blackband ironstone. There were many iron ore pits alongside the canal and the ore was used both in the local ironworks and shipped to those elsewhere.

The Caldon Canal ran through a band of ore known as Froghall haematite, whose iron content averaged out at about 50%. The ore contained about 20% lime in some form or another, making it easy to smelt. It was in great demand with the South Staffordshire iron masters, who used it to help with the smelting of poorer quality ores. Commercial production appears to have started in 1854 and in the years 1856-1869, an average of 415,964 tons were dispatched per year, about half of which went by canal from the dozen or so wharves between Consall Forge and Froghall. An average boatload of 22 tons gives a yearly passage of nearly 10,000 ironstone boats, agreeing with the recollections of old folk of about thirty ironstone boats per day.[1] In 1857, Mathew's Corbyn Hall Furnaces near Kingswinford received 3,060 tons of Froghall haematite by canal (about one third of which was carried by Price & Sons, Brierley Hill) and the nearby Oak Farm Furnaces 12,657.25 tons.[2]

Between 1869 and 1881, production fell to an average of 42,280 tons, suggesting that the canal traffic fell to less than five boats daily. The 1861 Census returns record fifteen boats engaged in this ironstone traffic, all hailing from Birmingham or the Black Country. One of these mines, the Cherry Eye, produced a red ironstone, towards the end of its life, used mainly for paint making. This was

The loading wharf for Cherry Eye ironstone mine on the Caldon Canal near Consall, a view thought to be just prior to the First World War. The wharf was at the base of an incline, leading down from the mine which comprised several levels connected by a tramway. The ironstone was a deep red and was used mainly for paint making; the mine ceased operating in 1923.
BASIL JEUDA COLLECTION

A 1912 view of Burnell's Iron Works, Ellesmere Port, which was established in 1879. It was one of two iron works attracted here by the cheap land and the good transport links with Staffordshire and the Midlands, the other being the Wolverhampton Corrugated Iron Company (founded 1857), who moved their manufacturing here also to a site alongside the SU Canal and close to Burnells in 1904. Both companies made extensive use of the waterway. The WCIC works was taken over by John Summers & Sons Ltd of Shotton in 1917. Burnell's remained independent until Nationalisation of the steel industry in 1951 but was then taken over by Summers in 1956. The works was closed in 1963, having become too antiquated to compete with more modern sites. The Wolverhampton Corrugated Iron Co. works was immediately behind the photographer. BASIL JEUDA COLLECTION

carried to Froghall by boat and crushed in a mill by the station. The mine finally closed in 1923, when the mill owner found he could obtain Spanish haematite more cheaply than the local product.[3]

In the Harecastle area, ironstone from Goldenhill was brought by tramway (partly relaid in 1827) to Williamson's Wharf to the south of Bridge No. 130. There were eight tips here in 1847 and tramroad sidings alongside a basin. Thomas Peake worked coal and ironstone at his tileries from 1856 to 1891, loaded to boat at his Tunstall Wharf. Ironstone deposits at Burslem were brought to the Burslem Arm by tramway. In the 1830s, much Burslem ironstone was being raised, calcined on the spot and sent to South Staffordshire. Burslem ironstone working reached its peak in 1856 but declined from the 1870s.

There were ironstone deposits at Hanley, loaded onto canal boats at Earl Granville's Wharf (and later by a chute in the towpath side basin at Shelton iron works). There were other tips at Nelson Place Bridge (No. 10), on the east side of Bucknall Road Bridge (No. 12) and to the east of Ivy House Wharf. Of the last three, only the latter was in use in 1894.[4]

There were also facilities for loading ironstone into boats at Kidsgrove, there being seven tips belonging to Mr Kinnersley, and also at the terminus of the Newcastle Canal. Another source of ironstone was Brereton Colliery, located on Cannock Chase, but having its coal and ore brought by tramroad to the T&M at Brereton near Rugeley. Brereton was one of the last mines to send ironstone by canal, still despatching quantities to Grazebrook Iron Works on the Dudley Canal in April 1923.

The blackband ore was richer than the Black Country ores and there was a substantial trade in ore between North and South Staffordshire, supplemented by ore brought in from other districts for mixing, notably the red haematite from Cumberland brought by coastal vessel to Ellesmere Port, Weston Point and Runcorn. From the late 1850s, Cumberland became a net importer of ore and only small amounts of haematite left Cumberland, for specialised use. A trade in Cumberland and Scottish pig iron grew up between those parts and the Staffordshire iron districts. Foreign ores, particularly from Spain and Ireland, were also imported into Staffordshire.

Gibbons' Corbyns Hall New Furnaces, on the Stourbridge Extension Canal, received 2,689 tons of ironstone from the Potteries in 1857; 1,105 tons of this was carried by Price & Sons, who also carried 323 tons of pig iron from the works to Manchester. This carrier was also engaged in the fluxing limestone trade between Froghall and South Staffordshire. In the same year, '*a few boats*' of North Staffordshire ironstone were brought to the nearby Foster's Shut End Furnaces. The fact that Shut End was mainly supplied with local ores suggests that the 'few boats' contained Froghall haematite for mixing.[5]

In 1832, in anticipation of railway competition, tolls on most goods had been reduced from $1^1/2$d to 1d per ton per mile. On 17th May 1834, ironstone was reduced to $^3/_4$d per ton-mile but the earlier toll was restored on 12th November 1836. On 1st June 1840, calcined iron ore was reduced to $^3/_4$d and uncalcined iron ore to $^1/_2$d per ton-mile. In the six months ending 6th April 1848, 21,894 tons of ironstone were sent from the Potteries to the Black Country. There was a further toll reduction from January 1865, when pig iron was reduced from 1d to $^3/_4$d and calcined ore $^3/_4$d to $^5/_8$d per ton-mile. In 1867, tolls on finished iron from places between Stoke and Harecastle to Preston Brook were reduced to $^3/_4$d per ton-mile and this concession was extended to Haywood and Fradley (iron from South Staffordshire) by the end of that year.[6]

As early as 1866, the Black Country produced only 50% of the ironstone consumed by the local iron trade and pig iron brought in from Cumberland, Scotland and Wales, as well as imported ores, became more prominent among cargoes of canal boats from the Mersey ports. Ten years earlier, the Shelton Bar iron works was receiving pig iron from Runcorn, the toll on this being reduced from 2s 11d per ton to 2s 3d per ton on 27th December 1856. These works were not on the canalside at this date, so the traffic would have been delivered to Earl Granville's Wharf for transshipment. Shelton sent iron to Preston Brook for Liverpool by the Anderton Company. In 1875, 28,000 tons of various ores were imported through Runcorn, about half of which came from Irish ports.

Derbyshire ironstone, pig iron and manufactured iron (tubes, etc) from the ironworks at Butterley on the Cromford Canal and Stanton on the Erewash Canal entered the T&M at Swarkestone, and was sent mainly to South Staffordshire. It made a journey of 19 miles on the T&M, between Swarkestone and Fradley junctions, being then routed via the Coventry Canal and the Wyrley & Essington line of the Birmingham Canal Navigations. On 25th January 1846, most goods carried the entire distance between Swarkestone and Fradley Junction had their toll reduced to $^1/_2$d per ton but iron was excluded from this concession. Carriers in this trade included W. Fletcher, who brought Stanton pig iron to iron works at Moxley, Leabroook and Walsall, and S. Sharp, who served the Church Lane, Birchills and Walsall District ironworks. This trade finished in 1919.[7]

In earlier days, Scandinavian pig iron had entered the canal at Shardlow and Staffordshire iron had been exported from there. There were iron warehouses here and Daniel & Co., a London firm of iron merchants, maintained an agent here in the 1820s.

A rather distressed photograph of Shelton Bar Iron Works from the canal circa 1912.
BASIL JEUDA COLLECTION

Tipping molten slag alongside the canal at Shelton around 1910. BASIL JEUDA COLLECTION

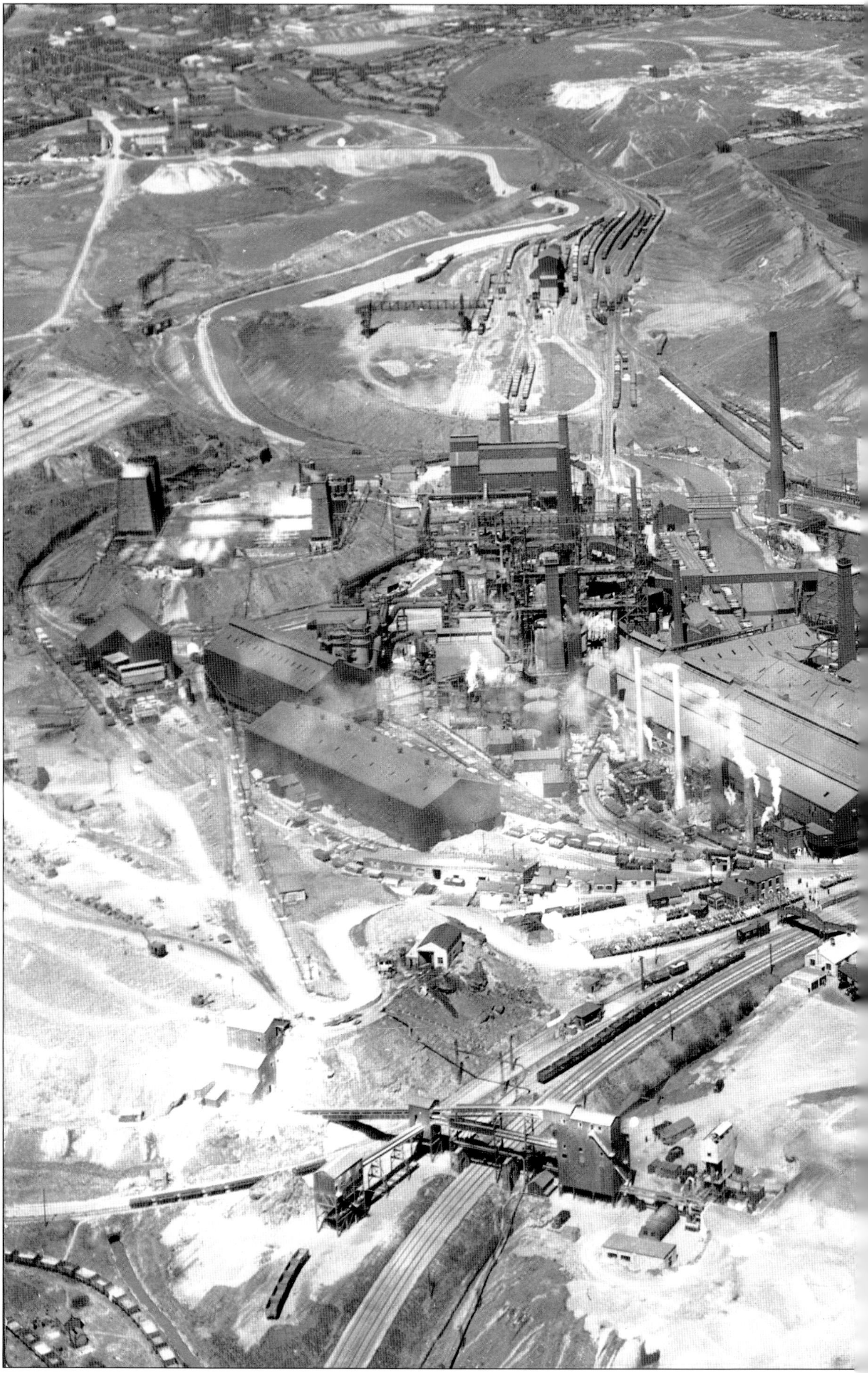

The Iron and Coal Trades

An aerial view of the Shelton Iron, Steel & Coal Company's works, looking north-east towards Congleton in the late 1940s. The T&M Canal can be seen coming in on the right, into the 1864 canal diversion, and it then winds through the works and past the blast furnaces. The waterway then turns sharp left, under the private railway line from Grange Branch Sidings into the works. It then passes the power station and makes an 'S' bend before, in the top left corner of the photograph, the Burslem Canal departs to the left. The Wedgwood Works appear in the angle of the railway and the canal diversion, in the centre right foreground. COURTESY THE POTTERIES MUSEUM & ART GALLERY, STOKE-ON-TRENT

Shelton Iron Works seen from the Caldon Canal in the 1960s. Courtesy The Potteries Museum & Art Gallery, Stoke-on-Trent

Also used in iron making were cinders, the toll on these between Preston Brook and Haywood Junction being reduced from 1/2d to 1/3d per ton-mile on 28th May 1856.

The carrying department of the Shropshire Union Canal was a prominent carrier of ore from North Staffordshire. The production of iron in this region was insignificant until well into the 19th century; in 1839, for instance, there were seven furnaces producing 18,200 tons of pig iron. Production rose to 130,000 tons in 1856 and to a peak in 1870, when thirty furnaces at nine iron works produced 303,878 tons of pig.

There was an iron works at Goldenhill, under which ran a branch canal whose functions were described in 1826: '*The Harecastle Tunnel of the Grand Trunk Canal runs under this Estate; by which means, as well as by a cross canal which has been driven at immense Expence beyond the Furnace, the mines are not only laid dry to a depth of from 45 to 75 yards but Coals, Ironstone and Limestone are conveyed to the Furnace and manufactured iron carried to Market at very light Expence.*'[8]

The local legend that the original section of this lateral tunnel was built by John Gilbert is confirmed by the name of Gilbert's Hole. It is thought that the iron works were probably commissioned in 1815, after John Gilbert's death in 1795. The branch tunnel to Goldenhill Iron Works was unsafe by 1820 and its use was discontinued after the opening of the new Harecastle Tunnel. Robert Heath's Goldendale Iron Works, at the south end of Harecastle Tunnel, were opened in 1840, using Goldenhill ironstone brought down by a tramway relaid by Robert Williamson in 1827. Robert Williamson, of Longport, was a nephew of Hugh Henshall and owned six boats in 1795. The tramway was first used for bringing calcined ironstone to the canal for shipment to South Staffordshire and Wales.

Adjacent was Ravensdale Iron Works, with Ravensdale Forge lower down at the junction of the long arm to Chatterley Iron Works. The Atlas Iron Foundry was adjacent to Tunstall Wharf. Ravensdale was owned by Richard Heath & Sons, who also owned ironworks at Biddulph and Norton, and they were carriers on the canal by 1838. A number of Ravensdale Iron Works boats were sold to the Shropshire Union in 1913.

In 1841, Earl Granville had blown in three blast furnaces at Hanley, connected by tramway to the canal at Etruria. In 1852, this became the Shelton Bar Iron Company and a forge and rolling mill were added. The works was extended to a canalside location in 1858 and, in 1860, was producing 50,000 tons of pig iron. As the Shelton Iron, Steel & Coal Company, it produced its first steel in 1888. The concern was acquired by John Summers & Company of Shotton, in Flintshire, in 1919, at which time it included five coal mines and three furnaces, producing 2,000,000 tons of coal, 215,000 tons of pig iron and 200,000 tons of steel.

Granville's Wharf had been built over by extensions to the works by the end of the 19th century. Earl Granville still owned boats in 1881, carrying iron, coal and sand but the entire complex was connected to the railway system and the canal trade in iron and its raw materials was badly affected thereby. One of the company's directors was Lord Faringdon, who was also Chairman of the Great Central Railway, to which, by 1916, much of the former iron trade to London had been lost.[9] Small amounts of iron were being sent from Shelton Iron & Steel Works to customers on the BCN in the 1930s.

To the west of Newcastle-under-Lyme but separated from the T&M by a high ridge, lay rich coal seams overlaid by iron bearing clays. These are known to have been exploited by the Romans, whilst blast furnaces were established in Silverdale and Apedale by the mid 17th century. In 1770, the first coke fired furnace in Apedale was built and in 1783, the Apedale Iron Works were rented by the South Staffordshire firm of Parker.

Sir Nigel Gresley owned large deposits of coal and ironstone at Apedale. The mines and ironworks were served by Sir Nigel Gresley's Canal, running three miles to a basin on the Liverpool Road, leading to the town of Newcastle-under-Lyme. By this means he acquired control of the coal trade in the town. Iron, however, had to be taken out of the district from the terminal basin by road.

In 1795, the Newcastle-under-Lyme Canal (the Lower Canal) was built from a junction with the main line of the T&M at Stoke to the outskirts of the town. Two years later, the town council approved the Newcastle Junction Canal, (the Upper Canal) to join Gresley's Canal and the Lower Canal, a link which was to include a railway a quarter of a mile long to overcome the difference in levels between the two. When the Apedale furnaces were offered for sale in 1818, the advertisement stated that they were connected to the T&M Canal by a 200 yard long inclined plane. Such a link would be considered essential to send pig iron to foundries and puddling furnaces for working up the finished product. There was also a market for coal and the ironstone could be sold in South Staffordshire. That the inclined plane actually existed is still a matter of argument among historians. If it did not, traffic would have had to be carted the quarter mile between the two canals, not necessarily a problem as the heavy traffic was downhill. However, the precarious financial position of the Newcastle Canal indicates that it had little traffic at this time.

The transport problems of the area would have been alleviated had the Commercial Canal, proposed in 1796, come to fruition. It would have connected Sir Nigel Gresley's Canal to the Chester Canal at Nantwich and to the terminus of the Ashby de la Zouch canal via Cheadle and Uttoxeter.

Silverdale Iron Works circa 1860, with the blast furnaces to the left. BASIL JEUDA COLLECTION

Burley Bridge at Chesterton, north east of Newcastle-under-Lyme, on Sir Nigel Gresley's Canal circa 1910. This three mile canal was authorised in 1775 and closed in the late 1850s. BASIL JEUDA COLLECTION

Preston Brook Tunnel south end circa 1910. BASIL JEUDA COLLECTION

Meanwhile, Walter Sneyd had opened the first iron works at Silverdale in 1791, whose only outlet to the outside world was a tramway, built in 1805, to the Newcastle to Nantwich turnpike at Madeley Heath. The 1798 Act for the Newcastle Junction Canal included provisions for railroads to connect Brook Lane Basin with Silverdale but these were never constructed.

There was another abortive plan in 1806, to connect Sir Nigel Gresley's Canal at Apedale with the Chester Canal at Nantwich, this time by a tramroad. The desire to make this connection arose out of the 18th century trade in Apedale coal to Nantwich, Middlewich and other Cheshire salt refining centres. Two tons of coal were needed to make three tons of fine salt. The trade had declined by the time improvements to the River Weaver and the 1779 opening of the Chester Canal enabled waterborne Lancashire coal to compete. The tramway, had it been built, would have had a rail connection to Silverdale and thence to the Lower Canal at Brook Lane, and would have been a neat solution to the district's transport problems.[10]

In 1826, the Apedale furnaces, which had a weekly make of 60 tons of iron, were being worked by William Firmstone, who also had iron works in South Staffordshire. In 1837, the Grand Junction Railway opened between Stafford and Crewe, and

Barnton Tunnel south end, from a postcard sent in 1919. Barnton was said to be the largest village in England and was home to many watermen. NEIL PARKHOUSE COLLECTION

The Iron and Coal Trades

SALTERSFORD TUNNEL, BARNTON.

Saltersford Tunnel south end circa 1904, with the tunnel tug about to enter with a northbound tow. The photograph was taken from close to the small dock below Barnton village, where the tugs lay overnight. They were coal fired and unable to complete a tow from the southern end of Barnton Tunnel to the northern end of Saltersford without the fire being stoked and the amount of smoke the tug is emitting indicates that the atmosphere once inside would have been very noxious. NEIL PARKHOUSE COLLECTION

Thomas Firmstone built a 1½ mile mineral railway from his Leycett pits to Madeley station. Its aim was to supply the railway company with coke and to convey iron to Birmingham and Manchester.[11]

In 1849, construction started on the NSR line between Stoke and Newcastle. It was intended that this line should extend to Sneyd's works at Silverdale but delays in building it caused Sneyd to build a private line, the Silverdale & Newcastle Railway (S&NR), in 1849-50, mostly on his own land, from his iron works to Pool Dam at Newcastle. In 1853, the Newcastle Canal Company built the Canal Extension Railway between Brook Lane Wharf and the S&NR at Pool Dam. Until 1881, working was restricted to horses. It had taken fifty-eight years to connect Silverdale with the canal but, by this time, the canal was being surrounded by the NSR and this, no doubt, prompted its owners to sell out to the NSR in 1864. A sizeable interchange grew up at Brook Lane and the Lower Canal enjoyed a few years of prosperity. In 1894, there were sidings, a 2-ton crane and mineral chutes here but the canal was cut back to Trent Vale in 1921.

The fact that Apedale may never have had a railway connection between the Upper and Lower canals, and that the railway connection between Silverdale and the Newcastle Canal was not made until 1853, does not necessarily mean, in the absence of these connections, that trade was not exchanged between these works and mines and the Newcastle

BOOTHEN CHURCH AND BRIDGE, STOKE-ON-TRENT.

A stretch of the Newcastle Canal at Boothen, Stoke around 1906. A swing bridge and a footbridge can be seen in the distance. JOHN RYAN COLLECTION

Barton swing aqueduct carrying the Leigh Branch of the Bridgewater Canal over the Manchester Ship Canal, looking towards Manchester. The unidentified locomotive in the foreground of this circa 1906 view is one of the MSC's fleet, which worked on the company's extensive railway network. The slightly ragged masonry immediately ahead of the locomotive, on what had been the northern bank of the River Irwell, is the remains of the abutment of the original aqueduct, engineered by James Brindley and John Gilbert for the Duke of Bridgewater in the early 1760s. BASIL JEUDA COLLECTION

Canal. At this time, and even much later, there were ample instances where intermediate road cartage was used for short distances to provide a connection between a canal and a railway, or between a works and a canal.[12]

On the Caldon Canal, the Norton Iron Works near Ford Green were established by Robert Heath and were in production by 1866. He also operated Norton Colliery as part of a fully integrated works. A short branch canal was built from Foxley, which brought Froghall limestone and ironstone to the works.[13]

Outside the Potteries were furnaces at Kidsgrove, Lawton and Vale Royal,[14] and ironworks at Wheelock and Rugeley. The Wheelock Iron & Salt Co. had their own boats. On the eastern section of the canal were also ironworks at Wychnor, reached by an arm from Wychnor Lock, and at Clay Mills.

In its early days, the canal had a monopoly of the carriage of South Staffordshire iron to Liverpool and Manchester, carrying, in the year ending 30th June 1836, 7,000 tons of Black Country iron. The development of transshipment facilities to the River Weaver at Anderton around 1800 drew off a little of the Liverpool traffic and the Macclesfield Canal, opened in 1831, offered a route to Manchester

A similar period view along the length of Barton aqueduct, with empty boats passing through bound for collieries on the Leigh Branch. Notice the horse walking over the high level cantilevered towpath at the far end of the span; it is said that some refused to pass over such a structure high above the waterways and accordingly had a coal sack unceremoniously placed over their heads. BASIL JEUDA COLLECTION

The Iron and Coal Trades

Bolton's Iron Works at Froghall, on the left, with the new Brass Works on the right, shortly after completion in 1911. The Caldon Canal runs on the higher level just behind and Froghall Wharf is marked by the smoke in the right distance. BASIL JEUDA COLLECTION

that was thirteen miles shorter than that of the T&M. By the end of 1837, the Macclesfield had abstracted nearly all the iron trade from South Staffordshire to Manchester, much to the annoyance of the Bridgewater, which retaliated by encouraging Welsh and Scottish iron into the Manchester trade. The T&M was already losing toll income between Hall Green and Preston Brook to the Macclesfield, and the Bridgewater's action caused a further loss.

At the time, much of the iron was carried in boats belonging to ironmasters, apart from small consignments borne by the general carriers. Henshall & Co., in their early days, had carried iron in boatload quantities. In 1797. it was reported that *'Henshall & Co's boat No. 2 is coming up the locks with 20 tons pig iron the steerer says he knows they have too much on the boat … the steerer intimated to him* [Brookes, the lock-keeper] *that he was carrying a considerable weight for which he should have nothing.'*[15]

It was the large export iron traffic to Liverpool which was most lucrative to the T&M and Bridgewater canals, and which they fought hardest to protect. The opening of the Birmingham & Liverpool Junction Canal (B&LJ) in 1835, reduced the mileage between South Staffordshire and Liverpool by twenty-three miles and the lockage by thirty locks. It was also a more convenient canal to work, with only one short tunnel (which was provided with a towpath) and more easily worked locks. Some South Staffordshire iron was immediately

diverted via Ellesmere Port or Chester, one of the largest carriers to move being Shipton & Co. of Wolverhampton. Shiptons returned to the Preston Brook route on being made commission agents for the Bridgewater Trustees in 1849. The Ellesmere Port route provided dangerous competition to the T&M, particularly when the Ellesmere & Chester and the B&LJ became carriers in 1837. In 1838, it carried 38,758 tons of South Staffordshire iron.

The distance to Manchester via the Middlewich Branch was six miles shorter than via Haywood but still seven miles longer than the Macclesfield route. Traffic to Manchester via the Middlewich

An empty boat heading north at Meaford circa 1903. BASIL JEUDA COLLECTION

A boat approaching Hunt's Lock on the River Weaver circa 1908. It is a Bridgewater-style 6 planker but it has a tidemark part way up and looks to have rot and open joints in the planking towards the top. It is probably an old 'knacker' being used as a Weaver maintenance boat, hence the all male crew and the 'cock' or 'cog' boat being towed behind.
BASIL JEUDA COLLECTION

*British Waterways boats waiting to unload coal at Seddon's Salt Works, Middlewich in the late 1950s. Butty **Alsager** is one of the boats converted from LM&SR day boats by British Waterways between 1955 and 1957.* WATERWAY IMAGES COLLECTION

branch was hampered by the 9 1/2d toll at Wardle, applying to both iron and ironstone. Nevertheless, 10,370 tons of iron to Manchester used the branch in 1838, although mainly from North Wales. The two companies became the Shropshire Union Railways & Canal Co. in 1845.

The loss of iron traffic to the Ellesmere Port route was met by a reduction in T&M tolls on wrought iron, from 22nd May 1843, to 1/2d per ton-mile and re-organisation of the way it was handled, the ironmasters to carry from South Staffordshire to Etruria and Henshall's thence to Preston Brook. The Ellesmere & Chester retaliated by entering the trade in pottery materials. In 1845-46, the Preston Brook route was recovering traffic from Ellesmere Port.

In a move to recover some of this lost trade to the Bridgewater route, the Bridgewater Trustees, in September 1841, took the initiative by entering into an agreement with the Grand Junction Railway to carry South Staffordshire iron by rail to transshipment points at Preston Brook or at Walton on the Trustees' Mersey & Irwell Navigation, from which places it was to be forwarded to Liverpool or Manchester in the Trustee's flats. Had this agreement come to fruition, it might have deprived the T&M of much of its remaining iron traffic. However, there were problems with the lack of a suitable transshipping point at the South Staffordshire end.[16] Some traffic began to pass in 1843 but the scheme had little effect. The 1847 absorption of the Grand Junction Railway by the London & North Western Railway put an end to it entirely, although the sidings at Preston Brook remained. The Trustees' next move, in 1849, was to make an agreement with Shipton & Co., of Wolverhampton, to surrender their iron trade between South Staffordshire and Lancashire to the Trustees, in exchange for being appointed their Midland agents. This ensured that Shiptons' traffic was routed via the T&M and Preston Brook. At the same time, they bought the Wolverhampton based part of the North Staffordshire Railway fleet (which, it will be remembered, had only been operating for two years) and leased for seven years the T&M tolls between Preston Brook and Fradley Junction. Tolls on traffic originating east of Haywood Junction were excluded.

The forty-six boats bought from the NSR and the thirty-five from Shiptons created a fleet large enough to influence the trade, which also included iron traffic from South Staffordshire to Hull. Shiptons were required to provide extra boats as required, at an agreed rate to Preston Brook. The Trustees' grip on the South Staffordshire trade was further tightened by agreements with James Fellows of Tipton, for six years from July 1850, and with Price & Sons of Brierley Hill, for five years from October 1851. Joseph Whitehouse of West Bromwich was added to the list in 1856. In 1853, the Trustees had fifty-six boats in the South Staffordshire and Preston Brook trade and fifty-three in the South Staffordshire and Trent trade.

On 15th May 1852, the Trustees entered into an agreement with the Shrewsbury & Birmingham Railway (S&BR), by which they withdrew from their 'light' trade between Birmingham, South Staffordshire and Lancashire, in exchange for being appointed the South Staffordshire collection and delivery agents for the S&BR. Earlier, in the second half of 1852 and most of 1853, the iron industry had a boom period and the Trustees had to divert some of their iron trade to the S&BR due to a shortage of boats.

The 1852 agreement was replaced by a more comprehensive agreement of 30th April 1853,

Anson and *Keppel* *approaching Hassall Green Bottom Lock (No. 58) around 1962, with the bridge carrying the still under construction M6 motorway in the background. Mrs Leah Tolley is steering the butty, while daughter Rose waits by the paddle gear.* GORDON BRIGGS

which included the Great Western Railway (GWR). It was a condition that Liverpool traffic was to be taken across the Mersey from Birkenhead in the Bridgewater's flats and the Manchester traffic was to be transshipped to the Bridgewater at Norton (part of the Preston Brook complex). The Norton Branch line was opened on 19th October 1853. The agreement never worked as planned. The S&BR and its associated companies on the Birkenhead route, under the influence at that time of the L&NWR, declined to execute the agreement, refusing wagons containing Bridgewater traffic and delaying their flats at Birkenhead. The Birkenhead Railway fixed rates between Chester and Norton at so high a level as to prohibit working of a transshipment trade through that place.[17]

The T&M must have been annoyed by the withdrawal of the 'Preston Flys' but they were to return even before the amalgamation of the Shrewsbury & Birmingham and Great Western railways in 1854, which soon destroyed the 1853 agreement. Amid much acrimonious argument, the GWR alleged that the Trustees were diverting traffic, allocated by the agreement to the railway, to their own services, having reinstated the flyboat services to the North.[18]

The Shropshire Union was leased by the L&NWR in 1847. Its carrying department was actively supported by the L&NWR and there was a policy of excluding, as far as possible, all other carriers on its route.

Throughout the 1850s, in the iron trade between the Midlands and Scotland, the canals were helped by vigorous coastal shipping rates that were in competition with the L&NWR, keeping the through canal/sea rate competitive. The acute competition between 1837 and 1854, the Bridgewater Trustees South Staffordshire trade having shown a loss of £7,560 in 1852 and £13,650 in 1853, now led to an attempt to control rates by the Northern Alliance Conference, meetings of which took place between 1854 and 1856. The Great Western, London & North Western, South Staffordshire and Midland railways all took part, along with the Shropshire Union and the Bridgewater Trustees.

One traffic considered was that in Cumberland iron ore brought by coaster to Runcorn, Ellesmere Port, Garston and Saltney. The canal carriers were allowed 8s $5^{1}/4$d per ton for haulage and tolls as far as Autherley, the junction of the Shropshire Union and Staffs & Worcs (S&W) canals. To this was added the S&W toll of $4^{1}/2$d plus a BCN toll of $6^{3}/4$d. The total rate (to Iron Districts 1, 2 and 3)[19] was 9s $4^{1}/2$d per ton, as against a railway rate of 9s 10d. However, to Districts 4 and 5, the railway and canal rates were identical. These agreements seem to have put an end to competition by price between the T&M and the Shropshire Union routes but of course the SU remained the fastest route and competition on service and facilities could still take place.[20]

Although the proposed amalgamation of the

Willow Wren Canal Transport Services boat **Snipe** *tied up opposite Seddon's, Middlewich works awaiting unloading.* **Snipe** *had been built for Fellows, Morton & Clayton as* **Kildare** *in 1913, passing to Willow Wren via Black Country carrier Ernest Thomas.* WATERWAYS IMAGES COLLECTION

Raddle or Iron Ore Wharf, Ellesmere Port around 1908. Ore from the Cumberland iron mines was delivered here from the ports of Ulverston and Whitehaven, and was then taken by narrow boats up the SU Canal to the iron works of the Midlands. The large buildings dominating the background were flour mills and that to the right a grain elevator alongside the Manchester Ship Canal. BASIL JEUDA COLLECTION

L&NWR and the NSR in 1853 had been refused, the two railways had effectively merged for financial purposes by means of a revenue pool from the beginning of that year, and the end of competition between the two railways was extended to their canals, the Trent & Mersey and the Shropshire Union.[21] From 1850, the railways made substantial inroads into the Black Country trade in ore, pig and manufactured iron, aided in their access to the canalside iron works by a growing number of rail/canal transshipment basins on the BCN. In 1853, the NSR announced its intention to transfer iron traffic from the canal to the railway and ordered 200 new wagons. This probably related to arrangements with the L&NWR, whereby the NSR was allowed to carry mineral traffic over the Stour Valley Railway.[22] This required the completion of Bushbury Junction, reported finished on 2nd June 1853.

In 1857, the Trustees reduced their direct carrying to and from South Staffordshire and relied more on commission agents. Their trade between Wolverhampton and Liverpool in that year was 40,891 tons.

The Black Country iron industry had reached its peak in 1863, its decline thereafter largely accounting for the decline of iron carriage by canal. The area's manufacturing industry increasingly came to rely on steel brought in from other parts of the country, notably, South Wales.

In 1874, the Bridgewater Navigation Company gave up their carrying business between South Staffordshire and the North West, selling their remaining thirty-four boats to Fellows, Morton & Co. Frederick Morton had been one of the Bridgewater's agents. The Bridgewater reserved the right to see that the business was managed to their satisfaction, and were still a party to the carrying business in regard to dock charges at Runcorn and barging of through traffic between Liverpool, Preston Brook and Ellesmere Port. The Bridgewater route via Preston Brook was protected by a payment of 3d per ton to the BNC on the first 6,000 tons per year on all traffic via Ellesmere Port, over and above the present weight of traffic (6,500 tons) sent by Fellows, Morton & Co. via Ellesmere Port, and 6d per ton on all traffic in excess of 12,500 tons sent by that route. In practice, most of Fellows, Morton's traffic was routed via Haywood Junction, the Trent & Mersey Canal and Preston Brook, and continued to be so even after the toll reductions at Wardle in the early 1890s. Their Ellesmere Port traffic was mainly in commodities that either arrived there by ship, such as ore or grain, or, like flour, were manufactured there.

In 1876, a witness before the Factory & Workshops Commission stated that many of the boats going up the Trent & Mersey Canal had the name of Messrs Foster '*the great ironmasters*' on them.[23] It was at one time the practice for stocks of iron to be held at Preston Brook, Anderton and Ellesmere Port awaiting shipment orders. In 1895, 6,631 tons of iron were held in stock at Preston Brook, declining to 2,284 tons in 1897 and nothing in 1898.[24]

In 1905, the T&M was estimated to carry about 25,000 tons of iron annually (about half of which

A northbound loaded horse boat in the Big Lock Pound at Broken Cross in the early 1950s. AUTHOR'S COLLECTION

came from South Staffordshire) and 10,000 tons of iron ore.[25]

S&W toll records for Great Haywood for the period 1898-1910 show little ore and iron going to South Staffordshire by that route. There are small quantities of iron blooms, recorded as part cargo of boats carrying other commodities, and only occasional loads of ore. Records for the outward iron traffic from South Staffordshire for that period are not available but we have the evidence given to the 1906 Royal Commission that it was about 12,500 tons annually. After the First World War, all that was left of the T&M iron trade was a little iron from Shelton for export and to works such as the District Iron Co. at Smethwick or Bayliss' at Wolverhampton.

With the 1923 railway grouping, which brought both the T&M and Shropshire Union under the ownership of the London, Midland & Scottish Railway Co (LM&SR), such iron traffic to and from Lancashire as remained was routed via the SU, and either Ellesmere Port or the Middlewich Branch and Wardle Junction. During the Second World War, with the canals under government control, the Preston Brook, Weaver and Ellesmere Port routes were used indiscriminately. In 1948, the Bridgewater severed its remaining links with Fellows, Morton & Clayton and closed Preston Brook. When FMC sold its boats to the British Transport Commission later that year, all the remaining iron traffic, almost entirely composed of steel tubes and nuts and bolts, was routed via the Shropshire Union, the Middlewich Branch and the Weaver.

A loaded coal boat leaving Hartford Lock on the River Weaver, bound for Winsford. This lock was removed and the river channel here straightened during the modernisation of the navigation which was completed in the 1890s. Notice how the horse towing line has been lead through the tall towing mast, just visible at the right margin, to keep it clear of obstructions and the water on its long span to the river towpath. BASIL JEUDA COLLECTION

*The Dickenson & Henshall narrow boat **Cheshire** at Weston-on-Trent, near the eastern end of the canal, around 1930, bound for the collieries.* SHARDLOW HERITAGE CENTRE

A circa 1850 engraving of typical Staffordshire colliers with some of the tools of their trade. NEIL PARKHOUSE COLLECTION

221.—Staffordshire Colliers.

Coal

The Trent & Mersey Canal passed through the North Staffordshire coalfield between Kidsgrove and Hem Heath, and its Caldon Branch likewise between Etruria Junction and the end of the Norton Green Branch, and again between Consall and Froghall. Places where coal from this field were loaded to canal boats included (north to south): Rigby's Wharf (below Lock 46); Kidsgrove (at a number of wharves on the main line and Hall Green Branch); side tunnels from Harecastle Tunnel; at the south end of Harecastle Tunnel; at Peake's Bridge, Tunstall; on the Burslem Branch (on the site later to become the Shropshire Union Wharf); south of the junction with the Burslem Branch; at Earl Granvilles Wharf, Etruria; at Stoke New Wharf and at Sideway.

On the Caldon Canal and its branches, coal was loaded at a number of wharves between Bridge No's 5 and 11 in Hanley; to the east of Ivy House Wharf; at Primes Drawbridge; at Red Hills Bridge (No. 16); on the Foxley Branch; near Downfield Bridge (No. 19); from the Cockshead Colliery at Norton Green; on the Norton Green Branch; at a number of wharves around Consall; and at Froghall.

In 1760, while the canal was still being planned, a partnership between Thomas Gilbert, Hugh Henshall, Robert Williamson and John Brindley (a younger brother of James) had purchased the Goldenhill Estate at Harecastle. This led to the proposal that the canal, originally planned to terminate at Longport, should be extended to the south side of Harecastle Hill, so that the coal

Roach and *Howard* ready to depart from Sideway on 25th June 1962, loaded with coal from Florence Colliery. *Cypress* and *Aberystwyth* await loading in the background. WATERWAY IMAGES COLLECTION

measures could be worked in the same fashion as was pioneered at Worsley. In 1781, John Gilbert bought the Clough Hall Estate at Kidsgrove. These purchases together were to constitute the beginning of large scale coal mining operations adjacent to the T&M Canal.[26] In both these instances, lateral tunnels were driven from Brindley's Harecastle Tunnel into the various collieries and coal was brought out by small boats. At first, the practice was simply to knock a hole in the tunnel lining and construct a lateral boat level, so the colliery undertakers were constantly making payments to the canal company for repair work.

Gilbert owned boats and his son, also John, extended the family carrying business, using them to supply Kidsgrove slack to the lime burners at Froghall. Kidsgrove coal was also supplied to his salt works at Marston. The *Staffordshire Advertiser* reported, on 21st March 1795, that '*Some of the better quality coal* [Cockshead and Harecastle] *is conveyed very considerable distances even to Oxford. Prices at the pits 5s to 6s per ton of 21cwt.*'

An early carrier to the south was the Buckingham Company who, in 1791, were recorded as carrying coal from Harecastle and Hanley to the Coventry Canal. Boatloads at this time were only between 19 and 22 tons.

Another coal owner and carrier was John Sparrow, Clerk to the T&M, a partner with William Adams and Benjamin Godwin in the Cockshead Colliery on the Norton Branch. In 1788, he was delivering coal to Wedgwood's Etruria Works by canal at 6s 6d per ton. Some coal was delivered to the works by road, whilst John Gilbert also supplied Wedgwood with canal borne coal. Josiah Spode, whose pottery was at Stoke, leased coal mines at Lane Delph in 1802 for twenty-one years. His works also received coal by canal and road.

Not all this coal was used for firing the kilns. Wedgwood applied steam power to his milling and grinding mills in 1784, and steam was later used to mechanise throwers' and turners' wheels, flatware and hollowware pressing, and tile making. In 1852, the firm of Wm Boulton & Co. was established in Stoke, to make tile presses and the steam engines to operate them. The coalfields on the western outskirts of the Potteries in Apedale and Silverdale have been described in connection with the iron trade. The North Staffordshire coalfield contained a variety of grades of coal. The potters liked the Great Row seam, while the Crabtree seam was suitable for coking. Gas coal was raised at Harecastle. In 1836, 30,000 tons of North Staffordshire coal was sent by canal to London. Coal was also loaded at Hal 'o Lee Wharf on the Macclesfield Canal, close to its junction with the T&M, and this coal may have

Containers of coal being transshipped to boat at Little Eaton Wharf on the Derby Canal around 1905. The Little Eaton Gangway was a horse operated tramroad, built as an extension of the canal, which ran for around 7 miles from collieries at Denby. Gangs of four horses hauled trains of eight laden coal waggons down to the wharf. As can be seen, the body of a laden waggon was lifted off the chassis into the boat, in an early example of containerisation. BASIL JEUDA COLLECTION

entered into the T&M trade.

Coal and ironstone were brought to Brereton Colliery Basin, near Rugeley, by a tramway built by Lord Shrewsbury in 1815-16. It was converted to edge rails in the 1880s and steam haulage was then used. The basin was closed in 1924. Hayes Colliery was, at an earlier date, connected to the canal by a tramroad through the streets of Rugeley.

Coal also entered the T&M from the Bridgewater Collieries around Worsley, travelling as far as the salt works near Wincham, as well as from the Staffs & Worcs Canal at Haywood, from the Coventry Canal at Fradley and from the Derby Canal at Swarkestone.

Most coal traffic on the T&M travelled short distances to domestic coal wharves and waterside works. The quantities required for earthenware manufacture were prodigious, the amount of coal burnt in the kilns being six times the weight of clay used. Many of the potters' mills converted from water power to steam engines. Gas works, of which there were many with wharves on the canal, also

*Another view of the Little Eaton Gangway and wharf. Some of this coal passed onto the T&M. This was the last crane to remain in use; at one stage there had been three. The tramroad closed in 1908. Both narrow boats in view belong to Derby-based operators, T. Walker and, on the left, F. &R.H. Johnson's **Harry**.* BASIL JEUDA COLLECTION

required coal. Stone Gas Works, built in 1878, was one receiving coal from collieries in the Potteries. In the 1880s, it was carried by the Sproston family, coal merchants and carriers of Haywood, Sandon and Stone. Herbert Sproston recalled that, at one coal loading point in the Potteries, the canal was so shallow that the coal had to be barrowed across planks into the boat. The largest gas works, at Etruria, had coal by canal, unloaded between Locks 38 and 39 until it was relocated away from the waterside. Fenton Gas Works was separated from the canal by Whieldon Road and had a tramway to the towpath. There was an electricity power station at Eastwood on the Caldon Canal and a wharf was built for a waterworks at Brindley's Bank in 1904. Joules Brewery, Stone, also once had two boats for the supply of coal.[27]

The sale of North Staffordshire coal to Manchester and Stockport could not compete with the local Worsley coals until the Macclesfield Canal was opened but, in 1836, 25,000 tons were sent to those towns. As late as the 1940s and 1950s, coal was still being sent from Sideway Colliery to mills at Marple (carried by John Green of Macclesfield) and at Miles Platting on the Rochdale Canal (carried by the Mersey, Weaver & Ship Canal Carrying Company).

There were three pits connected to the T&M at Brereton - Brickkiln, Hayes and Brereton Coppice. By 1818, large quantities of coal were being carried to Lichfield and beyond by canal.[28] In 1877, customers included: Banbury Cooperative Society; Birmingham Wagon Company; Albion Iron Works, Rugeley; Sprostons, Haywood; J. Smith, Barton Turn Wharf; Staton & Co. (plaster works); E. John's pottery, Armitage; Moorcroft, Handsacre; Weston Salt Works; Joules Brewery, Stone; W. Walker; and the Mersey Wheel & Axle Company. Coal was also sent to Alrewas, King's Bromley and Whittington (Coventry Canal) wharves.[29]

Before the 1870s, all Brereton coal was disposed of by landsale at Rugeley or by canal but in 1881, after construction of the Brereton Colliery Railway, only 90,000 tons of coal from Brereton was being sent by canal, against 200,000 tons by rail. In 1892, the Hayes Colliery Company employed four steerers on short distance work, most traffic being handled by independent carriers. Some of the Brereton coal went to wharves and works on the BCN, for instance W. Charles carried to Wednesbury and J. Perry to the Cape Arm.[30]

Coal from the Black Country and Warwickshire mines entered the T&M at Fradley, carried by a variety of small carriers, Bowaters being the largest. They served King's Bromley Wharf from West Cannock and Roway collieries, and also took coal to the Lichfield Creameries near King's Bromley. T. & S. Element took coal from Wednesbury to Burton.[31]

As indicated above, one of the coal merchants and carriers on the eastern part of the canal was the Sproston family of Haywood, who had their own wharves at Rugeley, Sandon and Stone. Also at the eastern end of the canal, James Sutton, a major

*Another view of the boats loading at Sideway on 25th June 1962, with **Cypress** and **Aberystwyth** nearest the photographer. The winding gear of Florence Colliery, named after the Duke of Sutherland's daughter, is in the background. Sinking of the pit commenced in 1874. After nearly 100 years of operation, it was merged with Hem Heath Colliery in 1974, to become the enlarged Trentham Colliery, a new so-called 'super pit', but this subsequently closed in 1990. Much in this view, including the tips but excepting the cottages, main line railway and the canal with its 'new' concrete banks has since disappeared.* WATERWAY IMAGES COLLECTION

*British Waterways' ex-Fellows, Morton & Clayton motor boat **Roach**, loaded with aluminium ingots for Wolverhampton, above Wardle Lock at Middlewich on 11th July 1962. Built as part of the T&M's Wardle Canal, the original ground paddles remain but the top gate paddle has been removed and a Shropshire Union gate strapping post has been substituted for the T&M pattern. The towline hangs down in the lock, which is starting to fill, having been used to pull the butty in.* WATERWAY IMAGES COLLECTION

The all water route via Oxford and the Thames was of limited value, being indirect and hampered by navigational problems on the river, as reported in the *Staffordshire Advertiser* of 9th May 1795: '*A few days ago a barge laden with nails and crates of Staffordshire goods belonging to Mr Hammack, Bargemaster, sunk at Sandford lock near Oxford.*'

Some idea of the explosive growth of the trade between the north and London can be gleaned from some Coventry Canal records. For the six months from March to August 1803, Pickfords paid tolls of £808. The Grand Junction Canal from Braunston to London was completed in 1805 and, in 1807, the payment for the same period was £2,171. Pickfords dominated the London trade, having fifty flyboat licences on the Coventry Canal, as against the fifteen licences of their largest competitor, Bache & Co.

Henshalls later disposed of their Stourport trade to Heath, Tyler, Danks & Co., who were specialists in carrying on the River Severn. In later competition with the Weaver, the Shropshire Union and the railways, the T&M was slow to defend its position and the initiative had to be taken by the Bridgewater, who were fortunate in having an able and energetic management at that time. The Bridgewater condemned the T&M for its reluctance to lower tolls, particularly the high Wardle toll. The Bridgewater's interests did not wholly coincide with those of the T&M, as witness their unsuccessful attempts to have South Staffordshire traffic sent by rail to Walton (on their Mersey & Irwell Navigation) and to Preston Brook but, on the whole, their efforts benefited the T&M and retained on it, for many years, a lot of traffic that would otherwise have been lost.

What has been said earlier of the Bridgewater's attempts to control competition in the South Staffordshire iron trade applies equally to the carriage of general merchandise. Their earlier action to deal with competition from the Weaver has also been described. In that instance, they were particularly concerned with merchandise traffic.

Much of the trade in manufactured goods, groceries, and wines and spirits was carried as 'sundries', in boatloads of mixed cargoes averaging in total weight only 11 tons but containing up to 150 separate consignments. They might also include small parcels of heavier goods, such as slates. From the 1890s, many of these boats were operated as 'flys', travelling day and night with a double crew and relays of horses. They worked to fixed schedules, calling at only a limited number of wharves and space on them from intermediate wharves needed to be booked in advance.

In the early days of the canal, the motor for the merchandise trade was the growing Manchester textiles industry; 'Manchester packs' were exported and sent to inland destinations all over the country. Added to the southbound traffic on the T&M were large quantities of Liverpool groceries, Cheshire cheese and earthenware. The amount of southbound merchandise traffic substantially exceeded the amount of such traffic in the northbound direction,

Preston Brook warehouses looking north from Chester Road bridge, through which the photograph on page 71 was taken. This was the original transshipment area at Preston Brook. On the left, the building in front of the crane was known as the Bell Warehouse, whilst beyond it are the fire engine house and white painted stables. The range of buildings on the right were known as the 'Preston Sheds'. WATERWAY IMAGES COLLECTION

with the result that the merchandise carriers accepted among their cargoes such commodities as grain and flints. By 1840, demand was such that it was sometimes difficult to obtain space on the southbound boats.[3] The boom in trade encouraged the entry of many firms into merchandise carrying. Some were successful and had long lives, whilst others failed to make the grade. In this book, only those of particular interest will be mentioned.[4] The general carriers of the pre-railway period all used the Bridgewater's own flats for traffic between Preston Brook and Liverpool, with the exception of Crocket & Salkeld, who became carriers in 1816 and whose business was taken over by Crowley, Hicklin & Co. in 1830.

One of Pickfords' rate books,[5] unfortunately undated, has survived, giving an insight into the sundries trade on the canal. King's Bromley Wharf served its local area and, together with Fradley and Streethay (Coventry Canal), also served Lichfield. King's Bromley received dry goods, dyers' materials and groceries from Bristol, grain, cheese and groceries from Liverpool, slates from Runcorn, and soap and hardware from Birmingham. Traffic from

Marston*, an Anderton Company horse boat, southbound near Chute (or Soot Hill) Bridge, at Barnton, in the 1930s. The boat is just about to pass Soot Wharf.* BASIL JEUDA COLLECTION

A panoramic view of High Peak Junction circa 1920. The wharf centre left is where goods were transshipped between the Cromford Canal and the Cromford & High Peak Railway. This was part of the through route between Manchester and the east Midlands, completed in 1831 and competing with the Bridgewater/T&M route. On the opposite side is Leawood Pumphouse which was built in 1849 to pump water from the River Derwent into the canal. A volunteer group today maintains the steam beam engine housed inside in pristine working condition. In the right foreground is the aqueduct carrying the canal over the river and running across the centre is the Midland Railway main line to Manchester, which now terminates at Matlock. NEIL PARKHOUSE COLLECTION

Derby included lead and bottles. Lump plaster came from Cuttle Bridge (No. 13) at Swarkestone, and Paris white and ground plaster from Weston Cliff, where it was transshipped from Trent craft that had carried it the short distance from Kings Mill.

There were rates from King's Bromley to London for carriages, passengers, leather and general goods. Trusses of hosiery were sent to Huddersfield and Leeds, while there was a rate to and from Bradford on wool. Rugeley sent cheese, goods and rags, and nearby Armitage despatched cheese, goods and earthenware to Birmingham, whilst both also received hardware. Iron sheet went from Rugeley to several destinations.

Trade passing through the canal between London and Macclesfield included Bengal and Surat cotton, glue, gum, iron liquor, oil and groceries, the boats returning south with cheese, cotton goods, leather and silk.

It is worth noting that Pickfords kept their rate books private, refusing to disclose them to several parliamentary committees.[6]

From its opening in 1831, Pickfords used the Macclesfield route to Manchester but continued to provide a service to Preston Brook. On the completion of the Birmingham & Liverpool Junction Canal, they transferred their Birmingham to Liverpool trade via Ellesmere Port but later returned to the Preston Brook route. Pickfords' tolls to the T&M, paid on 14th March 1840, were £1,902 3s 5d. It is not clear for what period the payment was made but it was dwarfed by a payment made by James Sutton on 7th March of £4,477 13s. Kenworthy & Co., a carrier in the Lancashire to London trade, paid a mere £300 on 17th March, at a time when the firm was on the verge of discontinuing its operations on this route.[7]

Thomas Sutton, who died in 1814, was established at Shardlow by 1775. He built, with his son James, an inn, houses and a salt warehouse between 1792 and 1817. James is said to have started his working life as a boatman and later acquired considerable wealth. He had business interests in coal and salt, and was one of the largest general carriers on the canal, operating both narrow boats and Trent craft. He had a riverside wharf on the Derbyshire bank of the Trent upstream from Cavendish Bridge and used a T&M wharf on the canal at Shardlow. In 1812, he was trading as Sutton, Robinson & Co. and by 1820 as James Sutton & The Shardlow Boat Co. The Shardlow Boat Co. was a local firm of carriers and boatbuilders. Sutton's flyboats operated between Shardlow and Manchester, Preston Brook, Stourport, Wolverhampton and Birmingham, serving the intermediate places on these routes. At Shardlow his canal boats connected with his Trent boats to Gainsborough (for Hull and London), Leicester, Market Harborough and towns on the Trent and its connecting waterways. Sutton had arrangements with other carriers to provide connecting services between Bristol and Stourport, and between Preston Brook and Liverpool. There were also arrangements for serving Yorkshire and *'all parts of the kingdom'*.[8] Sutton's carried all types of goods but westbound shipments from Shardlow were mainly malt, beans, oats, barley, flour, timber and vinegar.

Another major carrier at Shardlow was Soresby & Flack. The Soresbys had been at Cavendish Bridge from some time after 1758, moving to Shardlow on news of the construction of the canal. The canal bisected their land and they owned much wharfage and warehousing. James (1766-1837) took over the carrying business from his father. His sister Elizabeth married James' partner, William Charles Flack, in 1799. Flack had a wharf between Shardlow and Derwentmouth, whilst Soresby worked in conjunction with Pickfords to provide a nationwide service. By 1850, the partnership with Flack had dissolved and the firm traded as James & William Soresby.[9]

The very many general carriers who had emerged in the heyday of canal transport became vastly reduced following the advent of railway competition. Traffic between Manchester and the south was particularly hard hit, halved by 1852 from 19,500 tons in 1839. Pickfords' boats had been withdrawn from the T&M by 1847. Sutton was transshipping his London traffic to rail at Derby in 1842.

In order to divert traffic between Manchester, Hull and London to their route via Selby, the directors of the Manchester & Leeds Railway reduced their rates in June 1841. The T&M at first failed to respond to this challenge and carriers like Sutton and Soresby began to use the route via the Cromford & High Peak Railway (C&HPR). The principal carrier on the C&HPR was German Wheatcroft & Sons, who operated most of the general merchandise trade on that railway using horse-drawn wagons in connection with their fleets of boats based at Manchester and Cromford. This induced a belated lowering of tolls by the Trent & Mersey but irreparable damage to this trade had been done. Trade through Shardlow had fallen to such an extent in 1852 that the T&M halved the rent on Suttons' warehouse there. It will be recalled that both the NSR and the Bridgewater Trustees had withdrawn from the Trent traffic in the 1850s.

Suttons had ceased to act as general carriers by 1860 and a former partner, James Clifford, also of Shardlow, took over some of the stock. Soresby,

Nottingham Road Lock on the Derby Canal circa 1908. NEIL PARKHOUSE COLLECTION

Ellesmere Port about 1908, viewed from the iron ore wharf and with the steam coaster **Clarrie** *unloading its cargo on the right. The buildings over the arches, back centre, were grain warehouses and were designed by Thomas Telford. Sadly, they were badly damaged by a fire in 1970 and subsequently had to be demolished. On their left are the general merchandise warehouses.* NEIL PARKHOUSE COLLECTION

The Mersey, Weaver motor boat **Dane**, *heading for Burslem, at Kidsgrove in the 1950s.* GORDON BRIGGS

however, followed Pickfords in selling most of his business to the Grand Junction Canal's carrying department in 1848. That he retained some craft is evidenced by the fact that he sold eight Trent boats and two canal boats to Joshua Fellows in 1860. Soresby's clerk, George Cowlishaw, became Fellows' agent at Shardlow. Joshua Fellows often returned to Shardlow, meeting the boatmen, valuing and purchasing horses and supervising his business here. His relationship with James Soresby became social, including fishing together, dinner parties that included Joshua's wife, and James's sisters staying with the Fellows. In 1884, Fellows, Morton & Co. were paying £1 5s half yearly land rent to the canal company, probably for the Old Iron Warehouse which they and other carriers were using by then.

The route between South Staffordshire, Birmingham and the Trent had some specialist carriers. In 1808, Redsdale, Walker, Gradsby & Kings left Birmingham twice weekly for Derby, where their boats were met by wagons to and from Chesterfield, Sheffield, Barnsley, Leeds, etc, and by Barrow & Simpsons boats for Nottingham, Grantham, Newark, Lincoln, Gainsborough and Hull, etc.[10] By 1811, they had been taken over by Nathaniel & German Wheatcroft who, in 1815, made the connection with Trent boats at Sandiacre instead of Derby and who, in 1818, were transshipping at Buckland Hollow on the Cromford Canal into their own road wagons to and from Yorkshire.

From 1823, the merchandise side of the business was handled by German Wheatcroft & Son, who were also carriers between the East Midlands and Manchester via the Cromford & High Peak Railway. In 1847, the Cromford side of the business was taken over by the Grand Junction Canal Company and the Manchester establishment by the Manchester, Sheffield & Lincolnshire Railway, owners of the Ashton, Peak Forest and Macclesfield canals.

The general carriers dominating the post 1847 period were the Grand Junction Canal, the Bridgewater Trustees, the Anderton Company, the NSR and James Fellows. The Ellesmere & Chester Canal Co. and several other carriers had traded between Manchester and North Wales via Wardle. The Shropshire Union took over and expanded this trade to include traffic between Ellesmere Port, Chester and the Staffordshire Potteries. These firms were joined, in the 1850s, by James Cockshott (Liverpool and Manchester to Burton and Derby), later Cockshott & Gandy and then J. Gandy.

Fellows, Morton & Clayton boats at the south end of Preston Brook Tunnel in the 1930s. Because boats could not pass in the tunnel there was a timetable to control traffic in each direction. The butty has had its mast moved from the usual position and secured against the cratch. This was done when boats were loaded with lengthy items which needed as much unobstructed hold space as possible. WATERWAY IMAGES COLLECTION

The Anderton Company, Gandy and Fellows were agents of the Bridgewater Trustees and their agreements gave them prescribed spheres of interest. Gandy was a shareholder in Fellows, Morton & Clayton (FMC). The only other general carriers of note on the T&M were Mellor, Colsell & Co. (Liverpool, Manchester and London) and Crowley & Co. (Lancashire, Derby, Stourport and Birmingham). Crowley ceased to carry on the T&M in 1864. In 1894, the Mersey, Weaver & Ship Canal Carrying Co. entered the field.

Attempts by the canal carriers to become railway carriers were unsuccessful and this led to an end to the nationwide services previously provided.[11]

The Anderton Company confined its activities to the Lancashire and Potteries trade, and Cockshott to the Lancashire, Burton and Derby trade. In 1862, James Fellows was still mainly an iron carrier and operated only one advertised service per week, between Lancashire and Tipton. Jos Whitehouse had a weekly service on the same route.

Carriers advertising services to the East Midlands were Daniel Brown, another Bridgewater agent, between the Potteries and the Trent every other day, and Wm Beckett between Preston Brook, the Potteries and Leicester thrice weekly.[12] Brown and Beckett were later taken over by Fellows, Morton. The Grand Junction gave up carrying in 1876, transferring most of its traffic to Fellows, Morton & Co. and, by the end of the century this firm, the Anderton Company, the Shropshire Union and the Mersey, Weaver & Ship Canal Carrying Co. were the main general carriers on the T&M. Fellows, Morton now provided advertised services between Manchester, Preston Brook and South Staffordshire, Nottingham and Leicester, and between the West Midlands and the East Midlands. (Fellows Morton & Co. was incorporated into Fellows Morton & Clayton Ltd on 3rd July 1889). Gandy retained his monopoly of the Preston Brook, Burton and Derby route. Around the turn of the century, John Griffiths of Bedworth near Coventry put on regular merchandise boats between Preston Brook and Coventry, although it appears that they were not actually flys.[13] One of Griffith's customers was Lever Brothers, soap manufacturers of Port Sunlight on the Mersey. In 1913, he was carrying their soap to Coventry and enquiring about soap tolls to Oxford and London.

Although the London flys vanished by the turn of the century, fly boats were operated on shorter routes until 1921 and in a few cases even afterwards. There were flys from Preston Brook to Birmingham in competition with those of the Shropshire Union until 1921, and between Preston Brook or Anderton and the Potteries until the Second World War. Occasional urgent traffic was still worked non-stop on an ad hoc basis, though, the steerers being given a red ticket as authority to pass locks when they were normally closed.

In 1905, Fellows, Morton & Clayton Ltd carried 15,449 tons of Liverpool goods from Preston Brook to South Staffordshire and Birmingham, and 12,082 tons in the reverse direction. To this was added 2,122 tons to and from Manchester, Stockton Quay and Runcorn (Town), whilst 5,218 tons was carried between Lancashire and Nottingham, and 4,614 tons between Lancashire and Leicester. Most of the Leicester and Nottingham traffic was in the eastbound direction.

A rare view of a Mersey flat below Big Lock, Middlewich circa 1900. The flat would have been too wide to negotiate Barnton and Saltersford tunnels further north and so must have gained access via the Anderton Lift from the Weaver Navigation. The milk factory is on the right, although throughout most of the 20th century these buildings have been used for the manufacture of string and related products. The factory has only recently been demolished and housing has been built on its site. NEIL PARKHOUSE COLLECTION

two carriers who specialised in carrying condensed milk from Middlewich to London, Edward Williams of Cliffe Vale, Stoke, who had at least eleven boats in the 1880s, and W.U. Lester & Sons of Copeland Street Wharf, Stoke. The boats of these carriers returned to Stoke with sugar. These cargoes had previously gone by rail. Williams also carried stone, timber, ironstone and grain, while Lester was a merchant of gold, flint, stone and potters' plaster, and carried coal, slack, stone, etc.[26] In the 1890s, Lester was still trading to Derby, London, Shardlow and onto the Trent, and Williams between Middlewich and London.[27] Williams gave up in 1903.

Sugar

The carriage of sugar grew from small consignments in the early years of the canal, to eventually require transport in full boatloads. There were sugar refineries in London, at one of which boats had to load on the tidal Thames, and at Liverpool and boats were also loaded with sugar at Manchester.

The earliest specific reference to sugar in a full boatload between Preston Brook and South Staffordshire is a load of 23 $1/2$ tons passing Haywood on 23rd January 1910. It may be that prior to that date, sugar was usually carried as a part cargo under the general heading of 'goods'. The

A southbound horse boat in Big Lock, Middlewich around 1908. JOHN RYAN COLLECTION

General Merchandise, Foodstuffs and Building Materials

Fellows, Morton & Clayton boats ascending Tyrley Top Lock at Market Drayton around 1905. After the North Staffordshire and London & North Western railways became part of the London, Midland & Scottish Railway in 1923, bringing the T&M and Shropshire Union canals into single ownership, the south Staffordshire trade transferred to the shorter and more convenient SU route. The boats are being 'long lined' up the flight of five locks, the line being long enough to enable a lock to be left between the two boats. Without this, the butty would have had to be bow hauled through the locks. NEIL PARKHOUSE COLLECTION

cargo of the last FMC boat from Preston Brook to Derby on 20th February 1935 included 4 tons 15cwt of sugar.[28]

To give an idea of the total sugar trade from Lancashire to the West Midlands, 20,278 tons passed from Ellesmere Port, Preston Brook and Manchester in 1930, of which 476 tons was to Coventry. 1,231 tons of glucose was sent to the West Midlands from Preston Brook and Manchester in the same year.[29]

From the 1930s, beet sugar was sent from Colwich refinery, on the Trent below Nottingham, to Cadburys' works at Knighton on the Shropshire Union Canal. This passed over the Trent & Mersey between Derwentmouth and Haywood Junction.

Only one reference has been found to the carriage of sugar beet on the T&M. On 29th January 1925, FMC took a cargo from King's Bromley to Derwentmouth (for Colwich).

Other Foodstuffs

Other foodstuffs carried on the T&M included corned beef from Liverpool via Preston Brook to the Potteries, West and East Midlands. It was an important traffic and was usually carried in full boatloads. Other canned goods included Canadian salmon, along with canned meat, fish and fruit. Tea in chests was stored at Preston Brook and carried to the Typhoo Tea Company in Birmingham by FMC, whilst cocoa beans were carried to Cadbury's works at Bournville. Sides of bacon and hams were to be found among flyboat cargoes and potatoes were another regular cargo. The Bridgewater Canal ran through a potato producing area and cargoes from there to the Potteries were supplemented by supplies from Ireland. Other potato movements were mostly local but potatoes were shipped from Middlewich to London in barrels as part of a mixed

Perch negotiating the difficult turn at Wardle Junction into the short Wardle Branch and lock leading to the Shropshire Union's Middlewich Branch in 1957. King's Lock and its adjacent pub are in the background. GORDON BRIGGS

An earlier view in the opposite direction at Wardle Junction, Middlewich in the 1920s. A boat bound for the Shropshire Union Canal passes under the side-bridge while an Anderton Company single motor boat, its designation as a fly-boat shown by the two discs painted on the fore-end, heads for the Potteries. BASIL JEUDA COLLECTION

cargo in the 1830s and there were shipments from Fradley to Birmingham in 1922.

Livestock was also sometimes carried in boats, Bache & Co. loading a sheep at Middlewich on 3rd December 1838 for Lichfield.

Ale

Brewing at Burton on Trent predated the canal and there was a trade to the Baltic from the end of the 17th century. A substantial part of the payment was made in imported barrel staves. Barley and malt were brought from the Eastern Counties and barrel hoops from South Staffordshire. In 1777, Michael Bass, a Manchester road carrier from the 1760s, began brewing and he was soon followed by a number of firms, including Wm Worthington & Son. In 1806, Samuel Alsopp took over the brewery of his uncle, Benjamin Wilson.

The Baltic trade did not long survive the end of the 18th century, the closing of Baltic ports by the French in 1806 causing the brewers to turn to the home market, especially London and Lancashire. After the collapse of Napoleon, the Baltic trade resumed on a smaller scale, until the imposition of prohibitive tariffs in 1822. From 1821, the brewers produced for the Indian market, sending many tons of India Pale Ale to Liverpool. The brewers accepted iron and timber in part payment for ale sold to the Baltic. The iron was sold on to forges including those at Clay Mills and Wychnor

A horse-worked railway was made in 1855-56 from Tooth's London & Colonial Brewery to a canal basin at Horninglow. In 1867, this was replaced by the Midland Railway's Horninglow Branch, the basin being filled in and sidings made on the main line of the canal. There was a 5-ton travelling crane here in 1882 but it had gone by 1888. Bass and Smith received canalborne timber at Horninglow in the 1860s.

In 1878, the Midland Railway made a canal interchange at Shobnall, using the end of the Bond End Canal as a basin. Mann, Crossman & Paulin used it from the beginning. Bass had considered a scheme for a basin on the site of their Klondyke Sidings at Shobnall in the 1870s, together with steam boats on the canal but this came to nothing.

There were two breweries at Stone. In 1780, Francis Joules, a merchant, founded Joules Brewery and the other was Bents, whose main brewery was in Liverpool. During the Second World War, when the Liverpool brewery was damaged by enemy action, Bents supplied their depot at Ashton under Lyne from Stone by canal.

Francis Joules was a boatowner by 1795 and operated flyboats from Stone. Joules developed an export trade to the New World and Australia, via the canal and Liverpool, building a fine ale store on the canal in 1881. They also stored barrels at Stonefield Wharf ready for loading. A former employee, Mr J. Lewis, recollected that both Joules and Messrs Bostock, a firm of Stone shoemakers, did a big business with Melbourne and between them they could almost fill a ship. Joules' sent as many as 400 hogsheads in one vessel and, on one occasion, the ship was sunk in the Bay of Biscay.

When the ale trade by canal became subject to competition, the toll on malt was reduced to $^3/_4$d per ton-mile on 19th November 1832, whilst on 15th January 1842, the toll on ale, except on the Wardle Branch, was reduced to the same figure, only to be raised to 1d per ton-mile on 14th August 1843. The ale toll was reconsidered in 1846 and, from 25th January, was again reduced to ³/₄d per ton-mile, if conveyed the whole distance between Horninglow or Shobnall and Shardlow, Fradley (for the Coventry Canal and London) or Preston Brook. On 30th May, 1848 the NSR minutes recorded an agreement by the Stone ale and shoe manufacturers to use the railway[30] but their use of the canal for some traffic continued until the 1914-18 war.

The brewers sent some ale as part of a boatload but also established stores at canalside warehouses in large towns. Around 1912, there were, for instance, two or three boatloads a week from Burton to Stoke. Alsopp's ale boats from Burton to Bordesley Street Wharf, Birmingham ceased in October 1920.[31]

There were several small, local, canalside breweries, including three on the canal at Copeland Street, Stoke, one at Hanley, one at Wheelock and one at Middlewich.

Wool

Wool was carried in both full boatload and part boatload quantities. It appears, for instance, in Pickfords' rate book as being carried between King's Bromley and Bradford. Wool from London was being sent to Manchester, Rochdale and Yorkshire in 1840, when there were applications by Kenworthy & Co. and Morris, Herbert & Co. for reduced tolls on the BCN section between Fazeley and Whittington Brook.[32] There was also a trade in wool between the T&M and Shrewsbury. A letter from Shrewsbury Wharf dated 31st July 1846, in reply to a complaint from Middlewich that two Shrewsbury boats had refused to take a small consignment of cheese for that place, indicates that the boats were loaded with wool and they were anxious to maintain a good relationship with the wool traders but that, nevertheless, they would investigate to see if the cheese could have been accommodated.[33]

In the 1940s, FMC were still carrying occasional cargoes of wool between London and Manchester and there was also an occasional trade between Liverpool and Stourport, via Anderton and Wardle Junction, in the early 1950s.

Timber and Building Materials

The growth of towns during the Industrial Revolution created an enormous demand for building materials. Home grown timber was supplemented by supplies from the Baltic and later from America. An early timber merchant to use the canal was William Kenwright, who had wharves at Longport, Shelton and Stoke but the Shelton wharf had been taken over by Josiah & T.M. Dimmock by 1837.[34] In 1894, the business was carried on by Bass & Smith. Other timber merchants were Forshaw at Wincham, and Baileys at Stone. Shipton & Co., carriers and timber merchants of Wolverhampton, maintained an agent at Shardlow.

There was also traffic in local timber for example from King's Bromley to Rugeley, and King's Bromley and Handsacre to Bloxwich.

Welsh slates were brought by coaster to Runcorn or directly by canal from quarries near Llangollen. Roofing tiles were produced in the Potteries and at Swarkestone, and there were several brickyards on or near the canal. In 1836, 30,000 tons of bricks and tiles were carried by canal to Manchester. There were extensive deposits of blue brick clay at Etruria. Cement came from the Linley works at Rushall, from

A pair of boats loaded with pottery material moored at Brooks Lane Bridge, above Middlewich Top Lock, in the 1930s. The canal's local maintenance yard is behind the towpath wall close to the stern of the further boat, with the local Inspector's Office bay window overlooking the towpath beyond. To its left can be seen the roof of his company residence, 'Canal House', which faced onto a yard enclosing stables, a saw pit and other buildings associated with local maintenance work.
BASIL JEUDA COLLECTION

A boat loaded with limestone near Cheddleton on the Caldon Canal. BASIL JEUDA COLLECTION

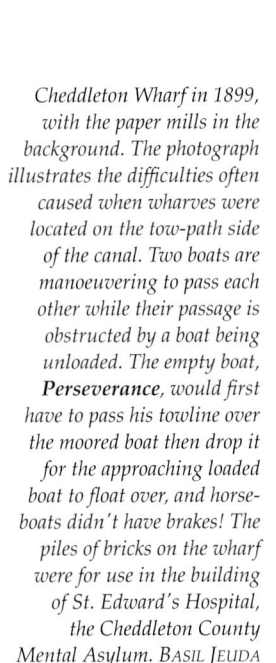

Cheddleton Wharf in 1899, with the paper mills in the background. The photograph illustrates the difficulties often caused when wharves were located on the tow-path side of the canal. Two boats are manoeuvering to pass each other while their passage is obstructed by a boat being unloaded. The empty boat, **Perseverance***, would first have to pass his towline over the moored boat then drop it for the approaching loaded boat to float over, and horse-boats didn't have brakes! The piles of bricks on the wharf were for use in the building of St. Edward's Hospital, the Cheddleton County Mental Asylum. BASIL JEUDA COLLECTION*

Warwickshire and Harefield. The lime trade will be discussed later. By 1849, most roads in Hanley and Shelton had been macadamised, Macclesfield stone being used for this purpose. Granite roadstone was supplied to wharves on the canal from Mountsorrell on the River Soar and from quarries in the Nuneaton area on the Coventry Canal or Rowley Regis on the BCN. Blast furnace slag and potsherds were also used as building or roadmaking materials.

Among the gravel pits on the canal in 1816 were those at Stretton and Brindley's Bank. In addition, sand was loaded at Lawton and at Barton Turn, and also brought off the Coventry and Stafford & Worcester canals.

Paper

Cheddleton paper mill was established in 1797. In 1817, Mintons were buying tissue paper for transfers for the pottery industry from Birmingham and from Fourdrinier, Hunt & Co., who owned Colthrop Mills

Cheddleton Wharf looking west circa 1906. A Brunner Mond boat is moored alongside the wharf on the right and there is an ice-breaking boat tied up on the left. BASIL JEUDA COLLECTION

on the River Kennet. In 1827, Fourdrinier established a paper mill at Ivy House to meet potters' demands for this material. He effectively put the Cheddleton mill out of business, then bought it and built a new mill on the site.[35] Corte & Co., paper dealers of Leicester, maintained an agent at Shardlow.

Non-Ferrous Metals

Copper and lead had been mined in the north east corner of Staffordshire since medieval times but it was not until the end of the 17th century that a successful means of smelting using coal as fuel led to a major upsurge in activity. In the early years of the pottery industry, lead was a popular glaze. Copper was smelted at Alton and most of the refined product sent to Birmingham and Wolverhampton. With the opening of the Caldon Canal, works for making copper wire were established at Froghall. There was also a works at Oakamoor on the Uttoxeter Canal. When it closed the Uttoxeter Canal, the NSR made arrangements with the Cheadle Brass Co. to cart its traffic to the canal at Froghall.[36]

The Cheadle Brass Co. also had a works in Cromford, where calamine (for zinc production) was roasted and zinc sulphate was being sent by canal to Bristol and Birmingham around 1800.[37]

George Vernon's canalside brassworks, a mile south of Stone, was set up in 1794, with supplies of copper and cast brass delivered from Oakamoor from 1811.

In later years, local supplies of raw materials were replaced by imports of copper, lead, zinc,

The lower basin at Froghall around 1910, with Brunner Mond boats loading limestone in the Top Lock of the long closed Uttoxeter Canal on the right. BASIL JEUDA COLLECTION

Froghall top basin around 1904. On the left are narrow gauge railway wagons loaded with limestone from Caldon Low Quarries. The three larger wagons in the foreground are on a standard gauge line, which passes to the right of the covered building housing the Tarmacadam plant. This was supplied with crushed stone via a tub route running from the crushing plant, just out of view on the right, across the trestle bridge. A boat can just be seen being loaded with limestone in the bottom right corner of the picture. BASIL JEUDA COLLECTION

nickel, nickel ore and silicon metal. These arrived at Liverpool and at Manchester Docks and were mainly consigned to Birmingham. Aluminium went to Birmingham and also to an aluminium works at Milton on the Caldon Canal. Some of the finished product from Milton was sent to the West Midlands. Some aluminium, and also nickel scrap, was sent to the West Midlands from Hull.

During the big freeze up of 1916, two boats loaded with copper ingots were stranded below Stone Bottom Lock. The copper was urgently wanted for munitions and so was transferred to lorries. The boatmen carried the half hundredweight ingots across the ice. One of them did not allow for the thinner ice near the lock weir and he really earned the £5 each they were paid for the work.[38]

Shoes

The shoe trade from Stone to Australia was subject to a tariff barrier in 1891. The South African trade prospered until the First World War but had finished by 1920.

Lime and Limestone

The main reason for the building of the Caldon Canal seems to have been to access the large limestone deposits at Cauldon Low, near Froghall. The late 18th century was a period of land improvement and

A limestone boat at Consall Forge in 1912. This is the point where the Caldon Canal departs from the River Churnet, which makes its separate way on down the Churnet Valley beneath the footbridge on the right. BASIL JEUDA COLLECTION

GENERAL MERCHANDISE, FOODSTUFFS AND BUILDING MATERIALS

An aerial view of the British Aluminium Works, alongside the Caldon Canal at Milton circa 1930. The Foxley Branch Canal to Ford Green made its way off to the top left, from where the Caldon Canal makes a sharp right turn by the Foxley Arms public house, top centre. This short waterway, around five furlongs in length, had been abandoned by the time of this view. In the centre of the picture is the British Aluminium Works, originally built in 1888 and used by this date as a rolling mill and foundry. Above this is the works of Midland Tar Distillers, formally Josiah Hardman Ltd, coal tar distillers and manufacturers of tar and ammonia products. A canal boat can be seen at the tar works. STEVE GRUDGINGS COLLECTION

large quantities of limestone were burned to make agricultural lime. Lime was also used in mortar and for limewashing the interior walls of buildings. This versatile mineral was also used as a flux in iron smelting, in the production of alkalis and as roadstone.

Among the Froghall quarry owners were John and Thomas Gilbert, Sampson Whielden and Robert Bill, all involved with the T&M. The quarry owners made an agreement with the T&M to deliver '*good and merchantable limestone to the canal at 7d per ton*'. In 1794, the canal company took between 2,000 and 5,000 tons per month.

The Cheddleton Lime Co., with the same owners as the Cauldon Lime Co., erected kilns on the canal at Cheddleton and Horsebridge. Until 1786, they controlled the only limekilns between Cauldon Low and the Potteries. They owned seven boats in 1795. The Cheddleton Lime Co. ceased trading in 1834 but the kilns were still being used in 1850. Limekilns were soon built at numerous places on the T&M. As early as 1781, John Gilbert was supplying kilns at Etruria and Longport with his own boats.

The younger John Gilbert inherited shares in the Cauldon Lime Co. and the limekilns at Cheddleton and Horsebridge. He extended his interests by erecting two limekilns at Stone in 1796, supplied with his own lime and coal by his own boats.

There were limekilns at the terminus of the Newcastle Canal, at Kidsgrove, Tunstall, Wheelock and Lostock. Burnt lime was reaching Acton Bridge, Cheshire, before 1800, '*having been brought by the Staffordshire Canal in iron boats from the neighbourhood of Leek*'.[39]

By 1812, Cauldon limestone had reached Stafford. Between 1825 and 1830, the quarries were producing between 65,000 and 100,000 tons of limestone per year, nearly all of which travelled on the canal. By 1841, the T&M themselves had taken over the quarrying at Cauldon Low.

Substantial tonnages of limestone were sent to the South Staffordshire iron works until the railway spur from Froghall Junction to Froghall Wharf (sometime between 1857 and 1879) diverted most of this traffic. In 1858, one customer was the Shutt End Furnaces, on the Stourbridge Extension Canal. Northbound traffic was divided fairly evenly between canal and railway.

Typical multi-story canal warehouses, photographed at Leek, terminus of the abandoned 3 mile long Leek Branch, in the late 1950s. The canal was reopened in 1974 but stops abruptly at the Churnet Aqueduct short of Leek, where the site of the basin has been redeveloped.
BASIL JEUDA COLLECTION

The volume of limestone traffic caused the North Staffordshire Railway to build this tippler at Endon Wharf on the Caldon Canal. Stone was brought by rail from Caldon Low Quarries to be tipped into waiting boats.
BASIL JEUDA COLLECTION

The competitive position of Froghall limestone was discussed in a report of 1848,[40] when it was stated that, in the South Staffordshire market, Froghall was in competition with both the local Dudley limestone and with that from Chirk, on the Shropshire Union Canal in Flintshire. Little could be done to compete with the Dudley product, said to take three fifths of the South Staffordshire market. Half the remaining consumption was supplied by Chirk. The Froghall share of the traffic was declining rapidly and there was a stock of 20,000 tons on the wharf at Froghall. It was decided to reduce the charge to customers to the actual cost of the stone, compensating for this by withdrawing the drawback of 10d per ton allowed to the ironmasters on stone carried as a return load for South Staffordshire iron sent to Preston Brook or Shardlow. It was noted that, in the six months ending 25th March 1848, 15,598 tons of iron (on which the drawback on an equal quantity of limestone might have been claimed) was carried against only 3,374 tons of stone. Limestone sent as back carriage in ironmasters' boats was toll free on the Staffs & Worcs Canal. Otherwise, the S&WC toll was 6d per ton. In addition, the NSR proposed to allow a weight of 21cwt to the ton for the South Staffordshire trade only.

It was noted that the North Staffordshire ironmasters enjoyed a drawback of 6d per ton on a quantity of stone equal to the number of tons of iron conveyed 17 miles on the canal and of 8d per ton if conveyed 22 miles. To agriculturalists, there was a drawback of 4d per ton on payment in cash within three months.

Froghall limestone had been almost ousted from the South Staffordshire market by 1851, largely replaced by cheaper Derbyshire limestone brought by the Midland Railway [41] but, after about 1865, Froghall stone entered a new period of prosperity. In 1905, severe railway competition resulted in a large decrease in canal traffic.

In 1893, J. Davenport, who had limekilns at Tunstall, was using both Froghall and Bugsworth limestone and, in 1889, D. Boulton's Red Bull Lime Works was using Bugsworth limestone brought in its own boats, which were also delivering Bugsworth stone to the Potteries.[42]

During the First World War, the demand for limestone exceeded the facilities available at Froghall. The NSR therefore brought the stone by rail to a basin at Endon, where they constructed a machine to tip the wagons' loads into boats. It was still working in 1928.

One of the most important customers for Froghall limestone was Brunner-Mond (later the chemical division of Imperial Chemical Industries). From the 1880s, they operated a fleet of about ten boats to their works at Sandbach. Some limestone was also sent here from the Trevor Hall Quarries, near Langollen, from 1896. Traffic ceased when the works closed in 1920, the tramway connection from the quarries to Froghall basin being closed in the same year.

On the eastern part of the canal, lime was supplied from Breedon, from Crich on the Cromford Canal and from Daw End on the BCN. References to Barrow lime are frequently encountered. Among places where lime was delivered are the little known Bellamoor Wharf, Wolseley Wharf, Lord Harrowby's Wharf at Sandon and the Duke of Sutherland's Wharf at Hem Heath. These served large agricultural estates in the Trent Valley.[43] In 1812, Breedon lime (loaded at Cuttle Wharf, Swarkestone) was advertised for sale as far away as Froghall and Uttoxeter, whilst in 1814, Crich lime penetrated as far west as Harecastle. On the canal east of Stone, in 1816, limekilns included those at Hargate Lane (Willington), Brereton and King's Bromley.

Some gas lime was also carried on the canal.

General Merchandise, Foodstuffs and Building Materials

Bugsworth Basin on the Peak Forest Canal circa 1910. Limestone and lime were loaded to boats here until 1923. NEIL PARKHOUSE COLLECTION

A 2007 view of Bellamoor Wharf, serving the Bellamoor Estate near Rugeley. TOM FOXON COLLECTION

Plaster

For the purposes of canal traffic records, the various products of gypsum are to be found described as plaster. Deposits of gypsum (calcium sulphate) occurred close to the canal in an outcrop between Horninglow and Tatenhill, at Aston on Trent, Fauld and Chartley. Gypsum also occurred on the neighbouring Grantham Canal, River Trent and River Soar.

The large blocks of pure gypsum were called alabaster and used for ornaments or sculpture. Plaster was made from the less pure grades and, among many other uses, was employed in the pottery industry for Plaster of Paris moulds, a process first introduced in 1840. The poorest grades were used in the manufacture of Portland cement, to retard its setting time.

Gypsum, whiting or alabaster from the Chellaston Pit (Messrs Edward Banks) was loaded at Cuttle Bridge Wharf in Swarkestone. There were also lime kilns and a shed under which boats could lie to load in the dry. Some plaster from Fauld Hill and from the Horninglow marl pit was loaded at Horninglow Wharf.

On the T&M there were works at Kings Mills supplied from Humphrey Moore's quarry at Aston, which was connected to the canal by a tramway. The plaster was taken along the canal to Weston Cliff and transshipped across the towpath to Trent craft that took it to Kings Mills. Some of the plaster was sold to Pegg & Ellams, the Derby paint firm. By 1904, the wharf at Aston belonged to Pegg & Harper.

Colton Mill, on the Trent at Rugeley, ground plaster between 1876 and 1896, and had its own wharf on the canal 550 yards away. W.H. Newton was the operator and he also took over a small works on the canal at Shobnall in 1880, later taken over by Staton & Co. There were other works at Clay Mills and Weston (Staffordshire), adjacent to the Weston Salt Works. This was owned by Alabaster Industries Ltd from 1919-63. There was a works, established in 1837 by Newton, below Bagnall Lock, between

The works of the British Alabaster Bowl Company at Weston, a few miles to the north east of Stafford, were established by 1925 on an arm of the T&M Canal adjacent to the site of the former Weston Salt Company, the history of which is covered in the next chapter. This postcard view dates from the late 1920s. The canal arm to the salt works still exists today but nothing remains of the works itself, although its former existence is commemorated in the names of Salt Works Lane, leading down to the canal, and the nearby Salt Works Farm.
BASIL JEUDA COLLECTION

Fradley and Alrewas. In 1868, it was operated by Hargreaves & Craven.

Plaster from Barrow on Soar and Zouch Mills, also on the Soar, was recorded as passing through the Trent & Mersey.

On 27th May 1856, the toll on plaster stone conveyed from Swarkestone to Hall Green, junction with the Macclesfield Canal, was reduced from 3/4 d to 1/2 d per ton-mile. In 1891, empty boats belonging to J. Slater were regularly going to Shobnall from Fradley Junction, together with empty FMC boats from Fradley to Clay Mills and Rugeley. The following year, W. Bishop was recorded as sending an empty boat from Haywood Junction to Shobnall.

From 1916 onwards, there are records of regular boats carrying plaster from Barrow and Zouch Mills, to the paper mills of Smith, Stone & Knight at Saltley and Kings Norton, supplemented by occasional loads from Clay Mills. Initially carried in SSK boats, the traffic was later handled by Fellows Morton & Clayton Ltd.

Oral evidence from the late Mrs Violet Atkins mentions the Anderton Company as carrying 'big stone' (alabaster?) from Burton.[44]

NOTES TO CHAPTER SIX

1. *Aris's Birmingham Gazette*, 21st July 1777
2. Turnbull G.L., *Traffic and Transport*, London, 1979
3. Moss G., *The Middlewich Letters*, Oldham, 1989
4. For details of early carriers see the *Working Boat; Midland Canal Carriers 1770-1845* series, Shill R. & Foxon T., Heartland, 2001
5. PRO RAIL 1133/130
6. Turnbull G.L., op cit
7. PRO RAIL 878/106, Trent & Mersey Canal Account Book
8. Shardlow Working Port website, 1850 Directory entry
9. Ibid
10. *Chapman's Annual Directory*, 1808
11. Turnbull G.R., 'The Railway Revolution and the Carriers 1830-50', *Transport History II*, 1969, pp48-71
12. *Slater's Directory*, 1862
13. Conversations with former Griffith's boatmen, G. Smith and F. Woodhouse
14. Manchester City Archives, M 300, Bridgewater Tolls and Freight 1894-1922
15. PRO RAIL 810/306
16. BW GLOS BW/110 Middlewich cargo receipt book 1838-40
17. *Staffordshire Advertiser*, 16th May 1795
18. BW GLOS, WM 77.51, Wincham Wharf Ledger
19. PRO RAIL 532/7
20. Bridgewater Tolls and Freight
21. BW GLOS, WM 44.125, S&W Haywood Permits 1898-1910
22. BW GLOS BW/109 Fradley Shipping Book 1895-6
23. Moss G., op cit
24. *Staffordshire Advertiser*, 1st July 1827
25. *Pigot's Commercial Directory* for 1818-20
26. Information on condensed milk traffic courtesy of Christopher Jones
27. BW GLOS, BW 72.568
28. Derby City Record Office, Box 12, Derby Canal Permit Book
29. PRO RAIL 810/306
30. PRO RAIL 532/14
31. BW GLOS, BW 1628.96, Coventry Canal Traffic Sheets
32. PRO RAIL 810/14, BCN Minutes, 21st August 1840
33. Moss G., op cit
34. BW GLOS, 213.93
35. Thomas J., op cit
36. PRO RAIL 532/14, 2 December 1848
37. *Victoria County History - Staffordshire*, Vol. 2, p363
38. Bolton J.M., Canal Town, Stone, Wolverhampton, 1981
39. Lead P., op cit, p20
40. PRO RAIL 532/4
41. Mather F.C., op cit, p236
42. BW GLOS, BW 234.96, Stoke Boat Register
43. *Derby Mercury*, 16th April 1812; 21st April 1814; *Staffordshire Advertiser*, 30th April 1814
44. BW GLOS, BW 1628.96 Coventry Canal Traffic Sheets

CHAPTER SEVEN
SALT, CHEMICALS AND LIQUID FUELS

Salt

Salt was an important commodity in the late 18th and early 19th centuries, being used as a preservative, in cheese making, bleaching, for manure, as a glaze in the pottery industry and as an essential ingredient in alkali manufacture. Every canalside town had its salt warehouse, as did the canal ports of Shardlow, Anderton, Preston Brook, Runcorn and Ellesmere Port.

Salt production in Cheshire predated the canal and there was a substantial trade on the River Weaver. The opening of the canal made little inroad into this trade and the 1791 connection between the canal and the Weaver at Anderton helped to retain it for the river.

There were, however, large deposits almost untouched until the opening of the canal. A vast bed of rock salt about forty yards thick stretched from Northwich to Lawton. The first successful borings were made at Lawton just after the canal opened, revealing salt at two levels. A small steam engine was erected to pump brine at Lawton in 1778. It was replaced by a water engine in 1800.

Sir Thomas Broughton (1744-1813) had salt works at Lawton and Middlewich, and warehouses at Paddington and Shardlow. His son and grandson were also involved in the salt trade and were partners in carrying businesses.

In 1820, Morris & Carter operated a salt works at Lawton, sending salt to London, their boats returning with flints to the Potteries. The Lawton works closed in 1927. The elder John Gilbert organised boring through the then floor of Marston Top Mine, near Northwich, in 1780 or 1781 and hit the lower bed some thirty feet down. He worked Marston as part of a partnership and also introduced a steam engine to pump brine and wind rock salt.[1] The Marston works were producing at least 12,000 tons a year at this time, all of which was carried by canal. In 1795, a partnership between Gilbert, Cornelius Bourne and Edward Mason owned seven boats carrying salt from Marston to Runcorn. These boats were also transshipping to the Weaver at Anderton by 1799. Gilbert's son inherited the Marston works and later bought Newton Bank Salt Works at Middlewich. The Gilberts' were able to supply their salt works with coal from their own mines at Kidsgrove.[2]

At Middlewich, John Lowe owned three boats in 1795 and had sent salt in them as far as Manchester since at least 1780. George Chesworth used his three boats to carry salt to Derwentmouth, Harecastle and Anderton in 1795; he had four boats by 1798. There were four salt pits at Middlewich in 1822[3] and six by 1847.

Towards the end of the 1890s, Henry Seddon purchased a salt works on the canal that had been established at Middlewich in 1756. The business was incorporated as Henry Seddon & Sons Ltd in 1907 and took over the Dairy & Domestic Salt Co., which

Salt extraction caused massive ground subsidence. Here in 1894, flats can be seen loading from a tramway connected to a salt works near Northwich. The boats are resting in a 'flash' or water-filled hollow, casued by the ground beneath subsiding due to the pumping of brine and filling with water from the river. BASIL JEUDA COLLECTION

*Henry Seddons' motor boat **Sweden** alongside the River Croco, by Middlewich Gas Works. Coal was barrowed over the river to the gas works via a trestle bridge.* WATERWAY IMAGES COLLECTION

*British Waterways ex-FMC motor narrow boats **Mendip**, steered by Charlie Atkins senior, and young Henry Hollingshead's **Perch** tied at Middlewich Public Wharf, just above the Town Bridge, with Seddons' Salt Works in the background on 5th February 1967.* WATERWAY IMAGES COLLECTION

was also situated alongside the canal at Middlewich, in 1911. Seddons owned their own fleet of boats, carrying salt to Anderton for transshipment to their Weaver flats, and to Manchester and Bolton. There is evidence that Seddon owned boats at an earlier date, one being recorded at Fradley returning empty to Middlewich on 5th December 1892.[4] Seddons supplied all grades of salt but specialised in salt for cheese making and fish preserving. Their fleet was horse-drawn until they bought an ex-Anderton Company motorboat in 1948. One horse pulled two boats on the short journey to Anderton. At Anderton, loose salt was unloaded into barrows by men provided by the Weaver Navigation and tipped down chutes into flats; the use of these chutes was discontinued in 1940. Boats with bagged salt transshipped into flats below the lift.[5]

Other salt producers with their own boats included Ingram, Thompson & Sons, owners of the Lion Salt Works at Marston and the Sunbeam Salt Works at Wincham; Alfred J. Thompson who controlled the Wincham Hall Works; Joseph Rayner of Marston Salt Works, a Runcorn shipowner and canal carrier; and the Cheshire Amalgamated Salt Company of Sandbach, whose boats, in 1879, were trading to Nottingham, Leicester and Derby.

The Anderton Salt Works was connected to the canal by tramroad, as was the Cheshire Amalgamated Salt Works at Wincham.

In Staffordshire, there were two salt works on the T&M at Weston. Production at Shirleywich predated the canal, which served the works by a short branch. Shirleywich was operated by the Moore family for many years, Charles Moore owning eight boats in 1795. In 1852, Moore entered into a partnership with James Sutton, Henry Broughton (who had salt interests in Cheshire and Worcestershire) and William Furnival, formed to exploit a patent for reducing fuel costs. A few months later, Moore was bought out and the British Patent & Rock Salt Company was formed to control the Staffordshire works and others in Cheshire. The company ceased trading in 1859 and the lease was taken over by James Sutton and later by G. Allport. All its production, about 12,000 tons per year, went by canal and it used 16,000 tons of coal annually.

Weaver flats loading salt at Winsford around 1905. BASIL JEUDA COLLECTION

Weston Salt Works commenced production in 1821. It was part of the estate of Earl Talbot that also included the Brereton Collieries. The Weston Salt Co., managed by the Earl's land agent, owned its own boats and also made use of other carriers. There are payments recorded for boat repairs but the company also purchased boatbuilding materials and may have done some boat repairs or building themselves. In later years, their boats were maintained at the Brereton Colliery dock.

For a while, in 1880, both works were under the same management. A railway siding had been put in for the Weston works in 1877, whilst in 1888, it was taken over by the Salt Union. Neither Weston nor Shirleywich was in regular operation after 1893 and both closed in 1901. Both works supplied the Thames Valley, Home Counties, London and Midlands markets.

We have seen that John Gilbert was a merchant and carrier of pottery materials as a sideline to his main interests in coal, salt and limestone. Charles Moore was also involved in the carriage of flints and the Weston Salt Co. was heavily involved as a potteries materials merchant and carrier. These interests were inherited by the Salt Union, who had a large fleet of boats, and passed later to its general cargo subsidiary the Mersey, Weaver & Ship Canal Carrying Co. It may be thought that pottery materials have little connection with the salt trade but they provided useful back loading for the salt masters' boats. The Weston Company benefited in particular from the carriage of flints from south east England, via the inland canal route from London or via Gainsborough. It also received china stone by the Severn route and its books contain costings for the Runcorn route, although little of its salt was

Bulk salt being tipped out of hand carts into a flat at Winsford, again circa 1905. There was little about the work involved in the salt making process that was not arduous and back breaking, whilst much of it was also carried out in conditions that were oppressively hot. BASIL JEUDA COLLECTION

Seddon's Salt Works, Middlewich around 1904.
NEIL PARKHOUSE COLLECTION

sent north of the Potteries. The pottery industry, in its early years, was composed of many small firms, whereas some of the salt masters had access to capital through the wealthy landowners who owned the land on which mineral deposits occurred and in some cases owned the salt works as well.[6]

The T&M tolls on salt were reduced to 1d per ton mile in 1832 and to ³/₄d per ton mile in 1844, except on the Wardle Branch where 9d per ton continued to be charged. A further reduction, to ³/₈d per ton-mile on rock salt between Anderton and Preston Brook was made in 1857. The salt proprietors requested a reduction in tolls on slack coal between Preston Brook and Anderton on 12th May 1857, consequent on a reduction by the Weaver to 4d per ton compared with the T&M toll of 4¹/₂d. A reduction was made on condition that an increased proportion of salt was sent by canal, instead of by the Weaver. On 4th August 1857, the toll on coal from Preston Brook to salt works north of Hawdisher Lane, Wincham, was reduced to ¹/₂d per ton mile. The amount of salt sent through Runcorn had increased from 16,000 tons in 1846 to 83,000 tons in 1854, the difference all being traffic via Preston Brook.

On 29th April 1870, the NSR agreed to charge 3d and 2d per ton on white salt and rock salt respectively, provided either that a minimum quantity of 135,000 tons of white salt and 55,000 tons of rock salt were sent annually by the Preston Brook route for shipment on the Mersey, or that the gross toll amounted to £2,145 per annum.

Apart from other shipment traffic, salt provided a return cargo to Cornwall, Devon and Dorset for coasters bringing in china clay and stone.

In 1888, the Salt Union, a cartel of salt producers in Cheshire, Staffordshire and Worcestershire, was set up and most of the works on the T&M and Weaver were included. The Salt Union operated about eighty canal boats and a fleet of Weaver barges.

The 1891 enlargement of the canal between Anderton and Middlewich meant that barges carrying 60 tons could travel from Middlewich to Liverpool without transshipment. There is no evidence, however, that any such craft were introduced by the salt carriers and the Croxton aqueduct was later rebuilt to a width of 8 feet 2 inches.[7]

The growth of refrigeration and canning resulted in a decline in the home trade, and the railways and coastal shipping took much of the inland traffic away from the canal. By the end of the 19th century, the canal carried little salt south from Cheshire. There remained, however, a large trade in salt to the Mersey ports for export and for onwards movement by coastal shipping. By the 1890s, the London market was under pressure from Middlesbrough producers, who enjoyed a coastal shipping freight of about 5s per ton. In 1894, there was a *'considerable traffic'* in Cheshire salt to London by rail and by coastal shipping, some being transshipped into barges at London and conveyed to City Road Basin on the Regent's Canal,

A salt works alongside the River Weaver at Winsford.
BASIL JEUDA COLLECTION

Newbridge Salt Works around 1908. The swing bridge in the foreground spans the River Weaver at the site of Newbridge Lock but this had been removed in 1880. NEIL PARKHOUSE COLLECTION

where only one salt buyer remained. The Salt Union was struggling to retain a trade in Droitwich salt to London by canal but had to move their distribution point from City Road to Paddington to avoid the high tolls on the Regent's Canal.[8]

Around 1892, the Marbury pipeline was laid by the Marbury Salt & Brine Company, from Marston to Marbury pumping station and thence to Weston Point, some 11 miles. At the time this was thought to be a minor construction by a small company. The NSR, as owner of the T&M Canal, objected to the pipe crossing their canal, under the clauses in the T&M 1766 and 1831 Acts that prohibited conveyance of brine in pipes in, on or under any part of the Company's land but later reached an agreement for the Marbury Company to pay them £5 per year and remove the pipe on being given three months notice.

Over the years, the pipeline and pumping equipment was greatly improved. In 1888, the Marbury Company became part of the Salt Union which, in 1909, started to build a large new works at Weston, where they also supplied brine to the Castner Kellner Company's works. This was a major threat to the NSR's canal toll income and they sought Counsel's opinion on the legality of the pipe crossing their canal. The opinion expressed was:

1. Authorities or traders could only proceed with

Salt being transshiped from canal boats to a steam packet in the basin below the Anderton Lift circa 1950. The motor boat, having been emptied, has been pushed out of the way alongside the flat across the basin and work has just started on the butty's cargo using the packet's steam derrick. BASIL JEUDA COLLECTION

The Anderton Lift showing one of the adjacent salt chutes. The photograph is believed to have been taken in early 1906, shortly before work began on rebuilding the lift for electrical operation. The salt chute was in the way of the expanded new structure and was removed as a result. THE WATERWAYS TRUST

the removal of the pipe in the name and instance of the Attorney General.

2. The NSR were not entitled to authorize the use of the existing or any future pipeline crossing their canal.
3. The NSR had the remedy of removing the pipe with the Salt Union having no right of action. If this were likely to result in serious damage it would be better to seek a declaration and mandatory injunction compelling the Salt Union to remove the pipe.
4. The Salt Union could not construct a bridge over the canal.
5. The owners of any mine under the canal could authorize the Salt Union to carry the pipe under the canal through their mine.

In 1910 the NSR gave notice to the Salt Union to remove the pipe by the 1st March but no action followed.[9]

The last Cheshire salt traffic, from Middlewich to Anderton, ceased in 1960.

Chemicals

The T&M carried a large and varied trade in chemicals. Sulphuric acid was used in pottery manufacture and caustic soda was used in paper making. The ready

The Brunner, Mond chemical works at Middlewich around 1930, by which time the company was part of Imperial Chemical Industries. The works manufactured sodium carnonate and was purchased by Brunner Mond in 1894. The building in the left background is the King's Lock public house and just this side of it is the entrance to the canal arm into the works. BASIL JEUDA COLLECTION

Salt, Chemicals and Liquid Fuels

Imperial Chemical Industries steam packets on the River Weaver at Winnington between 1923 and 1927. BASIL JEUDA COLLECTION

availability of salt and limestone led to the growth of a large alkali industry at Sandbach, Middlewich and on the Weaver, near the Anderton Lift.

The alkali industry was started by James Muspratt at the beginning of the 19th century, using the Leblanc process and was concentrated around Widnes, on the St. Helens coalfield in Lancashire, where the first chemical works opened in 1847. This was superseded by the Solvay process, introduced by Ludwig Mond, which was more economically carried out on the saltfield. John Brunner opened a works at Winnington, on the Weaver opposite the Anderton Lift in 1873, to be followed by an adjacent works at Wallerscote. The partnership became Brunner, Mond & Co. in 1881 and absorbed similar firms at Lostock Gralam, Middlewich and Sandbach in the 1880s and 1890s. The Solvay process used brine, limestone, ammonia and coke. The two works on the Weaver and that at Lostock had rail connections from the beginning but some raw materials were

Brunner, Mond's works at Northwich circa 1908. Narrow boats carried soda from here to north and south Staffordshire and Manchester. BASIL JEUDA COLLECTION

A Brunner, Mond boat loading limestone at Froghall circa 1905. The smoke behind is coming from the limestone kilns. The Churnet Valley is outstandingly scenic but throughout the 19th century and for the first half of the 20th century it was dominated by heavy industry. Very little of it remains today. BASIL JEUDA COLLECTION

brought by canal. The Sandbach works were only served by canal and Brunner, Mond had their own fleet of boats, bringing in limestone from Froghall, a traffic that finished when the works closed in 1920. An interchange basin between the L&NWR and the canal was built at Sandbach.

Most of the company's enormous waterborne traffic was carried on the Weaver but significant quantities used the T&M. The earliest supplies of ammonia for Winnington came from Manchester in a double-ended boat owned by Samuel Buckley, pulled by two mules named 'Sankey' and 'Moody'. Subsequent ammonia supplies came from Liverpool via the Weaver. 'Light' soda ash was sent from Lostock to Gossages soap works at Widnes. Wide beam craft were used, loading 30 tons at Lostock, going down the lift and completing to 70 tons at Winnington. The *Eva* and the *Paddy*, built for this

The ICI works at Wallerscote, seen from Barnton Bridge on the T&M Canal in the late 1920s. JOHN RYAN COLLECTION

A circa 1905 view of the General Electrolitic Alkali Company's works at Middlewich. JOHN RYAN COLLECTION

traffic in 1914, were steel craft 74 feet 3 inches length by 14 feet 3 inches beam.

Brunner, Mond asked for a toll credit account with the Coventry Canal on 21st May 1914 and with the Oxford Canal on the same day. Soda was passing onto both these canals in 1913, en route to Northampton, carried by John Griffiths of Bedworth.

In 1926, Brunner, Mond became part of Imperial Chemical Industries. The Gossages traffic ceased in 1932 but soda ash continued to be taken from Lostock to Winnington by the motor barge *Benzidene* and dumb barges *Atlantic*, *Pacific* and *Ann Elizabeth*. There was also a narrow boat named *Ethel*. The Mersey, Weaver Company carried light soda ash from Lostock to Runcorn into the 1950s.[10]

Brunner, Mond, Midlands & Coast Canal Carriers Ltd and later FMC carried soda ash to Monument Lane Soap Works, Birmingham, and soda crystals and other products to warehouses at Birmingham (Worcester Wharf and Dudley Road Wharf) and Wolverhampton. They also carried salt cake from Oldbury to the northwest. Mersey, Weaver carried soda to the Potteries, Manchester and Coventry and 'light' soda ash from Lostock to Runcorn.

The Stanton Iron Company carried 'heavy' soda ash from Winnington to Stanton Iron Works on the Erewash Canal. Through chemical related traffic on the T&M included bones for a fertilizer works on the Hatherton Branch of the Staffs & Worcs Canal carried by FMC and acid to Stourbridge,

A different aspect of the Wallerscote ICI Works again in the 1920s. JOHN RYAN COLLECTION

A forest of chimneys alludes to Middlewich's industrial heyday in this 1930s view, taken from a footbridge over the canal on the south side of Town Bridge. An Anderton Company boat is unloading on the right, as a crate boat bound for Runcorn passes. BASIL JEUDA COLLECTION

In the late 1930s, cows graze in a canal-side field by Middlewich Chemical Works, which has expanded since the view shown on page 142. JOHN RYAN COLLECTION

Birmingham (Shadwell Street) and Titford Locks by the Union Acid Company.

Other chemical works on the T&M were the Runcorn-based Union Acid Company's works at Wincham (they had their own fleet of boats) and the Davis Chlorine Company, Lostock, established in 1893, for whom a new basin was dug in 1898. There were also bone works in the Lostock area, at Weston and elsewhere on the canal, that produced ammonia and ammonia based fertilisers. In 1899, the General Electrolytic Alkali Company started production of chlorine and caustic soda at a canalside works at Cledford Bridge, Middlewich, using electrolysis of brine.

On 26th November 1884, the boat *Charity* was registered with the T&M. She belonged to the Riverside Chemical Company, Phoenix Alkali Works, Widnes, and was intended to carry chemicals in 'bottles' (carboys) between Ambergate, on the Cromford Canal, and Widnes.[11] *Charity* poses an interesting question; did narrowboats actually cross the Mersey? The crossing between Runcorn and

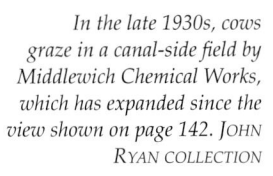

SALT, CHEMICALS AND LIQUID FUELS

Stanton Iron Works at Ilkeston around 1906, with narrow boats alongside on the Erewash Canal. Soda ash was brought here from Northwich by canal, whilst cast iron pipes and tubes were sent to various canal-side sites and exported via Preston Brook. Stanton also had a big trade in tubes and slag to London. NEIL PARKHOUSE COLLECTION

Widnes is quite short and there seems no reason why boats should not be towed across at slack water.

The term 'bottle boat' is one that lasted right to the end of canal carrying days. The carboys were not necessarily taken out of the boat but the liquid cargo could be run in and sucked out. Chemicals were also carried in sacks or drums and later some boats were equipped with large cylindrical tanks.

Following research into coal tar derivatives in 1838-1860, a valuable canal trade in the liquid by-products from producing gas (gas water and tar) sprang up between gas works, steel works, shale oil works and chemical works. The firm of Thos Clayton (Oldbury) Ltd used to take creosote from Oldbury, in 50-gallon barrels, to Kerr, Stuart & Co. Ltd in Stoke-on-Trent. They took tar from Etruria, Stone and Rugeley gas works to Oldbury and there was a trade in Naptha from Oldbury to Manchester

*William Preston's **Rushmere** at Hardingswood Junction, near Kidsgrove, sometime in the 1930s. The junction is where the T&M's Hall Green Branch, in the foreground, meets the main line beyond the towpath bridge. The branch leads 1.5 miles to the Macclesfield Canal and was built, like the Wardle Canal at Middlewich, under Trent & Mersey Acts that prohibited other canals connecting with its main line. BASIL JEUDA COLLECTION*

A Chance & Hunt boat, laden with chemical carboys from south Staffordshire, enters the Trent at Derwentmouth bound for Leicester. As was usual when narrow boats worked on rivers, the towline passes through a block on the mast and is led back to a stud in front of the steerer, who can adjust its length as necessary. The strap rope for stopping the boat in downhill wide locks is attached to the anser pin and coiled on the cabin roof. For working narrow locks it would have been attached to the stern stud. CHRISTOPHER M. JONES

in which they participated.[12] The tar and gas water traffic from the Potteries declined after the closure of the smaller plants and concentration of gas production at the enlarged, rail served, Etruria Gas Works, which had its own distillation plant. Tar for road surfacing was also carried; for example the Brownhills Chemical Company sent a load to Rugeley in June 1914.

The Tunstall Chemical Company, later Staffordshire Chemicals Ltd, had a plant at Tunstall, supplied with gas water from Shelton Iron & Steel Works by their own boats, which were among the last to trade on the canal.

Josiah Hardman Ltd had a chemical works at Milton, supplied with gas water from a number of gas works including that at Stone. Its last waterborne traffic was gas water from Leek, which finished in 1939. Hardmans had another tar distillery at Nechells, Birmingham, bought in 1904 and occasional Hardman boats were bringing tar from here to Milton in 1918.

There was a shale oil works at Chatterley, producing ammonia and paraffin.

One of the major chemical carriers on the T&M was the Manchester firm of W. H. Cowburn & Cowpar Ltd, descendant of a chemical merchant and his partnership in a chemical manufacturing company. W.H. Cowburn was at Radcliffe on the Manchester, Bolton & Bury Canal during the 1880s and was receiving cargoes of waste salt from Runcorn. Their first narrowboats were introduced in the early 1900s, in response to the introduction of man-made fibre manufacture by Samuel Courtauld. Courtauld built canalside works at Coventry and Wolverhampton, and the business rapidly expanded. Cowpars' original chemical plant at Castlefield moved to Trafford Park, was considerably extended during the First World War and was sold to Courtaulds. By 1928, Cowburn & Cowpar had about eighteen boats, all horse-drawn. Between 1932 and 1936, eight motor boats were built for them. Cowpars also carried acid from Chance & Hunt's Leabrook Works to Coventry.

In its early years, Cowburn & Cowpar's cargoes had been mixed, carboys of acid, drums of acetone and oils, bagged lime and salt. The principal commodity handled was highly inflammable carbon disulphide, carried in drums. From 1934, Cowburn & Cowpar installed cylindrical tanks into their boats, the cargo being blown in by air pressure at Trafford Park and discharged at Courtaulds viscose fibres plants by introducing water into the tanks.

Figures for May 1928 show that Cowburn &

*Cowburn & Cowpar's **Swift** and **Judie** at W.J. Yarwood's shipyard at Northwich, where the motor boat had been built, having called for minor repairs in the 1930s. They are loaded with empty barrels being returned from Courtauld's man-made fibres factory at Coventry to Trafford Park on the Bridgewater Canal.* BASIL JEUDA COLLECTION

*Jim Preston with W.H. Cowburn & Cowpar's motor boat **Swan** waits at the Dutton portal of Preston Brook Tunnel, on his journey back to his employers' Trafford Park Works in Manchester with empty carboys from Courtaulds' man-made fibres plant in Coventry. Boats were allowed to pass in either direction at scheduled times.*
EUAN CORRIE COLLECTION

Cowpar carried 175 tons of lime, 17 tons of chloride, 130 tons of carbon disulphide, 20 tons of caustic soda, 36 tons of sulphuric acid and 4 tons of empties to Courtaulds' Coventry Works, returning with 50 tons of 'acid' and 20 tons of soda. They also carried 24 tons of bagged lime onto the Grand Union Canal at Salford Junction, destination unknown. FMC also carried chemicals to Courtaulds.[13] In 1925, the Runcorn carrier Joseph Rayner was carrying wood pulp and starch to Courtaulds at Coventry and, two years later, J. Horsfield, also of Runcorn, was delivering chlorine sulphide and caustic soda. Mersey, Weaver brought soda ash from ICI.[14]

On the eastern end of the canal, the chemical manufacturers Chance & Hunt operated their own boats between Leabrook Works (Wednesbury) and Nottingham, and between Oldbury and Leicester. Their cargoes included sulphuric acid, hydrochloric acid, ammonia and nitre cake. Their boats also went to Rugeley Gas Works for cargoes of gas water for Oldbury. Rugeley gas water also went to the Brownhills Chemical Works.[15]

Barytes (barium sulphate) was being sent from Runcorn to Messrs Pegg, Harpur & Company, paint manufacturers of Derby, in the 1850s. It originated from the small port of Clonakilty, in the extreme south of Ireland.

One of the more unusual toll enquiries was that made by the Union Acid Company, in September 1913, for tolls on hydrogen in cylinders from Weston Point to Daventry. The gas was for a Government balloon factory and was being carried by rail. It is not recorded whether this traffic was actually gained for the canal.

Liquid Fuels

From 1924, Thos Clayton carried liquid fuels by boat from Trafford Park, Manchester to the Shell Mex depot at Langley Green and to a number of works on the BCN. When Shell opened a new plant at Stanlow, near Ellesmere Port, this traffic was transferred away from the T&M. However, during the 1939-45 war, Claytons carried oil from Ellesmere Port to Nottingham. Although these oil traffics were carried in Thos Clayton boats, the tolls were paid by Fellows, Morton & Clayton. In May 1928, 2,201 tons were carried from Manchester to seven works on the BCN and to Shell Mex.[16]

NOTES TO CHAPTER SEVEN
1. Lead P., *Agents of Revolution*, Keele 1989
2. Ibid
3. *Pigot's Directory of Cheshire*, 1822
4. BW GLOS, WM 72.568, Light Boats through Fradley
5. Faulkner A., 'Seddons of Middlewich', *NarrowBoat* magazine, Autumn 2009
6. Foxon T., 'Staffordshire Salt Works on the Trent & Mersey Canal', *Journal of the Railway & Canal Historical Society*, July 2002, pp88-91
7. Royal Commission on Canals 1906, Minutes of Evidence 1 (PtII), pp83-84

Subsidence caused by brine extraction coupled with a period of heavy rain caused this serious breach in the T&M Canal at Marston, near Northwich, on 21st July 1907. Two maintenance boats were sucked down to the bottom as the water rushed out. In the background, an NSR maintenance boat sits on the bottom of the canal and beyond the onlookers is the gang's house boat. Work was clearly taking place on this unstable length of embankment when the breach occurred. JOHN RYAN COLLECTION

Cowburn & Cowpar horse boat **Ethel***, laden with chemicals from Trafford Park, Manchester, for Courtauld's works at Coventry, about to turn right at Fradley Junction.* WATERWAY IMAGES COLLECTION

8. WRO, CR 1590/198, Salt Union to Oxford Canal Co, 30th October 1894
9. Information contributed by Mr Pat McCarthy
10. Leathwood Bill, 'The Brunners', *Waterways World* magazine, September and October 1978
11. BW GLOS, BW 234.96, Stoke Boat Register
12. Faulkner A., *Clayton's of Oldbury*, Robert Wilson, 1978
13. Corrie E., 'Cowburn & Cowpar', *NarrowBoat* magazine, Autumn 2008
14. BW GLOS, Coventry Canal Letter Book, not catalogued
15. BW GLOS, BW1628.96, Coventry Canal Traffic Sheets
16. Birmingham Central Library, Box 18 Ms86

CHAPTER EIGHT
A Working Waterway

Every waterway had its own traffic arrangements and methods of working, and the Trent & Mersey Canal was no exception. The originating and destination points for its through traffic were outside its own waters, and consideration has to be given to the effect this had on the T&M's traders.

Of all the terminals for T&M traffic, Liverpool was the most important. The direct route across the Mersey estuary was unsuitable for narrow boats, so this part of a through journey had to be made by Mersey flat.

A flat is the local name for a barge which might be rigged for sailing or unrigged for inland waterway work. Besides providing the link between canal narrowboats and Liverpool and Birkenhead docks, flats could work as far as Manchester, Winsford on the River Weaver, and Chester. There were also coastal flats that traded between the Mersey and Cumberland and North Wales.

Large consignments were transshipped overside between ship and flat, and smaller consignments were loaded at depots devoted to this traffic. Nearly all the traffic between Liverpool and Preston Brook was handled by the flats of the Duke of Bridgewater and his successors. The Bridgewater concern had a depot at Duke's Dock and many of the canal carriers maintained agents there. It had other depots at Manchester Dock, Stanley Dock and Carrier's Dock.

Of the carriers on the competing Weaver route, the Salt Union and its associated general carrying companies used a depot at the north west end of West Waterloo Dock. Goods for the Shropshire Union route were handled at Manchester Dock and Chester Basin.

Tate & Lyle sugar was loaded into flats at their refinery on the Leeds & Liverpool Canal in Liverpool, for shipment to the transshipment points on the other side of the Mersey.

Traffic via Preston Brook had an unusual obstacle to surmount. Horse haulage through Runcorn Locks was prohibited, so flats and narrow boats had to be manhandled. When the canal had been planned, it had been agreed that Liverpool traffic would be transshipped at Preston Brook, thus securing the tolls and freight between Preston Brook and Liverpool to the Bridgewater. Runcorn was then only a village. Docks were later built at Runcorn, to encourage coasters to use the port instead of Liverpool and, under the pressure of competition, it became clear that some revision of the original arrangements was desirable.

*A busy scene at Winsford on the River Weaver circa 1906. In the right foreground, the Weaver flats **Cayman** and **Victory** are tied up alongside the boat yard whilst beyond, another craft is loading with salt. The warehouses of Winsford Wharf are on the left.* NEIL PARKHOUSE COLLECTION

To aid in the passage of traffic through the three canal tunnels at Barnton, Saltersford and Preston Brook, the T&M provided a steam towage service and a steam tug was used for working boats from Barton to Saltersford, with a second towing through Preston Brook. In the heyday, boats were worked in trains, nine trips a day each way. The third tug was available to cover for maintenance. As horse drawn traffic declined and the tugs got older and in need of replacement, they were withdrawn from service, in 1943, 1944 and 1946 respectively. This view shows a tug, with an Anderton boat as leader of the tow, leaving Saltersford Tunnel and crossing the wide to Barnton Tunnel. THE WATERWAYS ARCHIVE

Everything was heavy on the canal except the wage packet! Right up to the end of the carrying age, some warehouse hoists were still manually operated by vertical capstans, like this one. SHARDLOW HERITAGE CENTRE

Runcorn Docks became a terminal for many narrowboats carrying onto the Trent & Mersey, raw materials for the Potteries, ores and grain arriving by coastal vessel, being stored there and sent forward by canal boat as required. Warehouses for the storage of earthenware were provided. In 1848, the NSR claimed to be the only carrier of any note to take earthenware as far as Runcorn, having a special arrangement whereby the Bridgewater paid them the cost of haulage, the rates of freight being calculated between the Potteries and Preston Brook by the NSR, and between Preston Brook and Liverpool by the Bridgewater. The general rule was that the Bridgewater had control over all goods delivered to them with a Liverpool consignment or a consignment in favour of a Liverpool firm, and the NSR over all goods consigned or transferred to them for carriage, as well as over all potter's manufactured goods brought to Runcorn by them to await the manufacturers' orders.[1] Six years later:

> 'The pottery manufacturers generally despatch the crates as soon as packed, in small lots to the depots at Anderton, Runcorn or Ellesmere Port where they remain until the entire order is complete, when the merchant or shipbroker at his convenience either writes or sends a messenger directing the whole to be forwarded alongside some outward bound vessel then loading at Liverpool docks. This is accomplished by flats or lighters towed down the river.'[2]

This indicates that sending crates through to Runcorn rather than storing them at Preston Brook had by then become standard practice for all carriers.

After the completion of the Manchester Ship Canal, some crates were sent from the Runcorn warehouses to vessels in Manchester docks. The situation there was different because narrow boats could enter the docks and transfer their cargoes alongside the ship.

Crates sent from the Potteries at the last moment to catch a ship were despatched by flyboat. As indicated above, shipment ware traffic was also dealt with at Anderton and Ellesmere Port although Runcorn remained the main depot until 1948.

In the early days of the T&M, earthenware had been transshipped at Preston Brook until railway competition forced improved arrangements on the canal companies. Preston Brook, however, remained the main depot for general merchandise, grain and export iron. A substantial inland port grew up where goods were transshipped either directly between the Bridgewater flats and the canal boats of many carriers or stored awaiting orders.[3]

On leaving Preston Brook, southbound boats were confronted with the 1,239 yards long Preston Brook Tunnel. For some unexplained reason, this had been built to a width of 13 feet 7 inches, too narrow for a Bridgewater flat or for two narrow boats to pass. The actual boundary between the T&M and the Bridgewater was the north end of the tunnel, and boats were gauged and a toll ticket issued at Dutton Stop Lock and toll office at the south end of the tunnel. Four miles south was Saltersford Tunnel (424 yards), closely followed by Barnton Tunnel (572 yards), both of similar width to Preston Brook Tunnel. Before the introduction of steam tugs in 1864, boats were legged through all three tunnels, entering the south end of Preston Brook every even hour and the north end every odd hour and the shorter tunnels when they were clear. The tunnel tugs at Preston Brook made nine return trips per day in 1904 and a tug ran through between the north end of Saltersford and the south end of Barnton, also making nine trips daily. There were no tugs between 8.30pm and 6.00am, and boats wishing to pass between these hours had to be manhandled. The tugs were withdrawn in 1943, the few remaining horse boats usually being able to get a tow behind powered craft. The country between Preston Brook and Anderton was rural, the only wharf of note being at Acton Bridge on the Chester to Warrington road.

At Anderton, 6 miles 6 furlongs from Preston Brook, traffic from the River Weaver joined the canal via the lift. Narrow boats ran through to Weston Point Docks for some cargoes, others being transshipped to and from flats below the lift. The Weaver was subject to sudden floods and could be difficult for horse boats, which had to use an extra long towline. If a boat got out of control and caught the bottom, the force of water could turn it over. On one occasion, two boats tied abreast went over Saltersford weir and broke their backs. Horse boats were still going down to Weston Point in 1949.[4]

One traffic transshipped below the lift was the

ABOVE: The north end of Preston Brook Tunnel in August 1958. By this date, traffic lights, triggered by rollers on the wooden fendering, had been installed to control the passage of boats.

BELOW: Since the actual boundary between the Bridgewater and T&M canals was the north portal of the tunnel, this site at Dutton was selected for the stop lock and toll office between the two waterways. There was also a dry dock for the tugs, beyond, on the left. The two boats in the foreground are NSR Engineers Department maintenance craft. BOTH WATERWAY IMAGES COLLECTION

Steam powered tunnel tug No. 2 emerging from the north end of Barnton Tunnel in the 1920s. The spring loaded wheels prominant near the boat's fore end were an aid to steering through the twisty Saltersford Tunnel, without causing damage to the brickwork. The brickwork of the portal seen here had been protected from the towing lines of horses continuing up the path over the hill by the substantial metal-bound post in the days before through steam towage. BASIL JEUDA COLLECTION

'Staffordshire Goods'. This was a flyboat service, operated by the Mersey, Weaver & Ship Canal Carrying Company between Liverpool and the Potteries. In the 1930s, a steam 'packet' would leave the north end of Waterloo Dock every Wednesday and Friday night. The cargo included bags of flour and sugar, boxes of apples, crates of oranges, new empty bags, sides of bacon and Chinese eggs. This would be transshipped to narrow boats that worked nonstop to the Potteries.[5] The Anderton Company operated a similar service from Liverpool via Preston Brook.

The wide, deep, 9 1/2 mile section from Anderton to the Big Lock at Middlewich was known as the Big Lock Pound. There were many salt and chemical works, and an important wharf at Wincham on the outskirts of Northwich. The canalside at Middlewich was also industrialised. At Wardle Junction, the short Wardle Lock Branch connected with the Shropshire Union Canal's Middlewich Branch. Traffic from Chester and Ellesmere Port joined the T&M here. The Shropshire Union, until it discontinued carrying in 1921, ran regular flyboats to the Potteries. One horse brought the boat from

A 1960s view of Willow Wren boats waiting to load at Weston Point Docks. WATERWAY IMAGES COLLECTION

Margaret in Etruria Top Lock on 25th June 1962. The overall roofs here and at Dutton protected the Gauging Clerk and his paperwork as he measured the freeboard of the boats to ascertain their liability for tolls. WATERWAY IMAGES COLLECTION

Ellesmere Port to Minshull, where it was changed for another horse which worked through to Tunstall. A third horse hauled the boat for the final leg, delivering to Burslem, Etruria and Stoke.

Many boatmen lived at Middlewich and the town was a popular overnight stopping place, boats mooring above and below the Big Lock, and above Wardle and King's Locks. There were many boatmen's houses above King's Lock, so some boatmen could tie up outside their front door. King's Lock marked the start of the 'Cheshire Locks', as the thirty-one locks from here up to Harecastle were known. The T&M was one of the first canals to be built and its locks were far from handy, being very deep. Most, but not all, canals fitted the top gates of their locks with an upwardly projecting post, protected by iron bands or an iron casing, known as a strapping post. On entering the lock, the boatman would stop the boat using a rope known as a 'strap'. On a horseboat he would drop the bight of the strap over the post and take a turn on a stud on the boat's stern. On a motorboat he would step ashore and take two or three turns on the strapping post. This action, known as 'strapping' would simultaneously bring the boat to a stand and close the gate. There were no proper strapping posts on

British Waterways Crewe unloading at Henry Seddon's Salt Works on 18th March 1965. She was bought from British Railways in 1954. WATERWAY IMAGES COLLECTION

ABOVE: Wheelock Wharf, warehouse and stables, on 14th June 2002. WATERWAY IMAGES COLLECTION

BELOW: A modern view of Red Bull wharf and warehouse. Located where the Newcastle-under-Lyme to Congleton road crosses the T&M Canal, Red Bull once handled a variety of traffic, including millstones. During the period of government food control during and just after WW2, it was one of several wharves along the canal where strategic stores of flour were kept. It later became a British Waterways maintenance depot. The remains of the hand-crane can be seen. WATERWAY IMAGES COLLECTION

*BELOW RIGHT: Potter & Son's motor **Silver Jubilee** and crew. BASIL JEUDA COLLECTION*

the T&M top gates, merely a horizontally projecting iron plate that caused a lot of wear on the straps. The North Staffordshire Railway 1867 Bye-laws forbade strapping the gates, downhill boats being required to use a line from the bow. This was done by flicking the horse towline over the fore end stud and taking a turn around a suitably placed stump. Uphill boats were supposed to use a strap on the same stump, probably attached to the boat's anser pin for this purpose. The anser pin is not a pin at all but a shackle attached to the side of the boat, some way forward from the stern. The date when these rules were abandoned is not known but in later years downhill boats strapped the gates and uphill boats were stopped by drawing a top paddle. When one craft met another, the uphill boat kept to the towpath side when passing.

At Ettiley Heath, where the L&NWR crossed the canal, there was a rail/canal transshipment basin. Boats transferred goods between local factories and the railway. Above Wheelock, with its salt, chemical and iron works, the nearest point on the canal to Sandbach and once a calling point for flyboats, boatmen encountered the first of the duplicated locks. A paddle connected each side-by-side pair of locks, enabling either lock to be used as a side pound to the other. Drawing this paddle would admit water behind the bottom gates of the other lock, thus closing them without effort. These locks were later to be of great benefit when pairs of boats, a motorboat towing an unpowered butty, were introduced on the T&M in the late 1920s, as both locks could be filled or emptied and the butty, when cast off, would have enough way to float into one of them while the motor went in the other. Wheelock was another place with a large population of boatmen, as were the villages of Malkins Bank, Hassall Green, Rode Heath and Harding's Wood. Just before reaching Harding's Wood was Red Bull Wharf, on the Congleton to Newcastle-under-Lyme road at Kidsgrove. Flyboats called here and there were two cranes, one of them of 3-tons capacity. Among the outward cargoes handled here were millstones. The Manchester, Sheffield & Lincolnshire (later the Great Central) Railway had a wharf here on the Hall Green Branch of the T&M. This railway operated a boat service, in competition with Fellows Morton & Clayton, between South Staffordshire and Macclesfield until 1908.

This was the top of the Cheshire Locks and the next obstacle was Harecastle Tunnel. When the two tunnels were in use, southbound traffic took the new tunnel, which had a towpath, and northbound traffic, which was usually more heavily laden, less bulky and consequently lower in the water, legged through the old tunnel. Boatmen recalled that when going through the old tunnel with a high, bulky cargo, they had to leave a space for the legger to retreat into at places where subsidence had lowered the roof. In 1904, the headroom was 5 feet 10 inches. Horses going through the new tunnel would be nervous so, in order to calm them, the towline would be shortened and attached to a backward

*British Waterways' maintenance boat **Badger** at Limekiln (or Stone Top) Lock, on 25th June 1962. WATERWAY IMAGES COLLECTION*

curving peg in the cabin roof just forward of the slide when open. The horse would be by the mast beam, on which the horse driver would sit and talk to it while going through the tunnel. In the case of boats that were clothed up, the horse would be by the deck and the driver would sit there talking to it. Many of the boats using the tunnel regularly were fitted with these cabintop pegs, which enabled the line to slip off if it became fouled. Boats not so fitted had to use their removeable cabin top tee stud.

An electric tug was put on in the new tunnel in 1914 and the old tunnel soon became impassable. The tug took power from an overhead wire by means of a tramcar-style trolley pole and dragged itself along on a chain laid on the bed of the canal. It could tow up to seventeen boats. Haulage through the tunnel took about 45 minutes and departures from each end were usually at one hour, fifty minute intervals. The new tunnel was also affected by subsidence and motor boats had to protect the corner of their engine rooms by lashing a plank from the stern beam to project slightly outside the engine room.

The south end of Harecastle Tunnels on 25th June 1962, with Brindley's 'legging' Tunnel to the left and showing the fan house over the entrance to Telford's Tunnel; this was built after the electric tug was withdrawn in 1954 so that internal combustion engines could be used through the tunnel. WATERWAY IMAGES COLLECTION

Engines had to be stopped while being towed through the tunnel and fires were supposed to be extinguished. If there was only a small tow the fires were often left in. Horses were walked over the hill. The ends of the tunnel were scenes of great activity, with engines being started, horses attached, and, at the north end, a queue of boats waiting their turn for the top locks.

Those boats which were bound beyond the Potteries continued their journey on a much less busy waterway. For those unloading in the Five Towns, work had not finished. Cargoes of flint and stone lay heavy on the shovel and china clay was solid and had to be sliced into. Some firms provided unloaders to do this work. After the boats had been emptied, their holds had to be thoroughly cleaned so as not to contaminate the next cargo.

East of the Potteries, flyboats usually called only at Stone, Haywood (to transship), Rugeley, King's Bromley (for Lichfield), Fradley (to transship), Burton on Trent, Cuttle Bridge (No. 13) at Swarkestone and Shardlow. The three miles between Rugeley and Armitage were industrialised, there being iron works, plaster works and a tannery at Rugeley, a coal loading basin at Brereton and a pottery at Armitage. At Burton on Trent, there was a rail/canal transshipment interchange with the Midland Railway at Bond End (1847). Brewers could access this via their internal railways. Bond

*An aerial view from the late 1920s of Stone boat yard with its four drydocks. The dock, owned by the canal company, dates back at least as far as 1789. When the **Cornwall** was built here in February 1888, she cost £127 9s 9d. Bottom left is the Grand Trunk Wharf, whilst far right is Yard Lock No. 28, sometimes known as 'Workhouse Lock' after the buildings at the extreme bottom of the picture that later became part of Stone Hospital. ROY LEWIS COLLECTION*

End was last used in 1962 to send canal engineer's materials to Fradley maintenance depot. At Burton, flyboats used wharves at Horninglow, Shobnall, at the Trent end of the Bond End Canal and on the Upper Trent Navigation in Burton. Pickfords and the Grand Junction Canal Company had a wharf on the river.

Boats served Wychnor Forge by an arm from the main canal entered by a single lock gate in the upstream end of the weir opposite Wychnor Lock cottage, passing under the then single-carriageway A38. Below Wychnor the canal entered the Trent which it used for 200 yards, leaving the river immediately above Alrewas lock and weir. Below the lock a millstream gave access to Alrewas mill.

The original system of paying boatmen was by mileage but, in later years, a system of payment based on tons carried was introduced. This was

OPPOSITE PAGE TOP: Inside Telford's Harecastle Tunnel on 25th June 1962. The collapsed towing-path can be seen. WATERWAY IMAGES COLLECTION

OPPOSITE PAGE BOTTOM: Anderton Company boatman Edward Gorton and horse passing Meakin's Eastwood Pottery in the late 1940s. The pottery later passed into Johnson Bros' ownership, as seen on page 45. BASIL JEUDA COLLECTION

***Aston** at Fradley Junction on 26th August 1963. From left to right are the warehouses, the Swan Inn and the stables. Fradley was an important transshipment centre and also handled some traffic for Lichfield. An early British Waterways 'Water Baby' hire boat is tied at the head of Junction Lock in the foreground. WATERWAY IMAGES COLLECTION*

Fradley maintenance yard on 26th August 1963. The small boat to the right of the crane is a weed-cutter. In the 1950s, export traffic from Derby was brought here by road and loaded to boats. WATERWAY IMAGES COLLECTION

Armitage (known to boatmen as 'Plum Pudding') Tunnel on 4th May 1970. It has since been opened out. WATERWAY IMAGES COLLECTION

meant to encourage boatmen to load their boats fully. The Anderton Company stuck to mileage payments to the end. It was the rule, after motorboats and butties had been introduced, for boats to load 20 tons each and this gave the tonnage-paid Mersey, Weaver boatmen an exact equivalent to the mileage based Anderton men. In horseboat days, loads were generally of 23 tons but carriers of coal from the T&M onto the Staffs & Worcs Canal around 1900 were recorded with as much as 31 tons.[6] For light, bulky cargos, a minimum payment for 20 tons was made. Boatmen's wages are a specialist subject[7] but suffice it to say that boatmen were not paid when their boats were stopped for lack of cargo or other reason, until a fallback of £2 10s per boat per week was introduced during the 1939-45 war. Under this system, some boatmen led a precarious life but others prospered, bought houses and sometimes set up their own businesses. They were adept at living off the land, fishing, poaching and raiding farmers' potato crops, and were also expert at pilfering from their cargoes. The old style of pottery crate was easily broached and the crew would wriggle their hands through the straw until they found what they wanted. Teapots were a useful article of exchange. In the days when canals were crowded with coal boats, to buy coal was unthinkable and a small amount of coal taken from each cargo and sold was never noticed.

On 9th January 1846, the *North Staffordshire Mercury* reported that at

> 'Staffordshire Epiphany Sessions, Joseph Nickson and George Jones, Boatmen, [were] accused of robbing crates of earthenware at Burslem wharf. Joseph Batkin, wharfinger, testified to fact that crates had been broken open. James Martin, a packer in the employ of Bowers & Lloyd said he had packed crates similar to those broken open. Jabez Smith, clerk to the T&M Canal said he had found items in boat where Jones was. Nickson was master of same boat. Jones claimed he was ignorant of the theft and was acquitted. Nickson was sentenced to two months in prison.'

The freezing of canals in winter was a regular occurrence and the T&M was organised to deal with this efficiently. Icebreakers were kept at strategic points and the canal company hired horses and boatmen from the carriers to man them. There was a particular problem in locks, where lumps of ice would jam boats and prevent the gates from being

A WORKING WATERWAY

Brindley's Bank aqueduct near Rugeley. The canal made a sharp right angle turn here in order to cross the River Trent. The former flint wharf is out of sight on the left. WATERWAY IMAGES COLLECTION

ABOVE LEFT: *The Crown Inn at Handsacre. This was a favourite overnight stop for boatmen.* TOM FOXON COLLECTION

ABOVE: *The back of the Crown Inn. The 'boat doors' enabled goods to be unloaded from boats and stored here to await collection. This was one of the functions of many canal-side inns which sometimes also acted as a place where business was done between local carriers and prospective customers.* TOM FOXON COLLECTION

LEFT: *The wharfinger's house at Gaskell's Wharf, Alrewas.* WATERWAY IMAGES COLLECTION

*The author's boat, **New Hope**, near Fradley in 1955.*
TOM FOXON COLLECTION

Ice-bound boats at Wall Grange, on the Caldon Canal between Endon and Cheddleton, in the 1920s.
BASIL JEUDA COLLECTION

opened. The company's workmen would place a board in the stop plank grooves above the lock before removing all the ice from the chamber and opening the top gate, taking up the board only to admit a boat. Ice could be flushed out of empty locks ready for an uphill boat to enter. The men were equipped with special icebreaking cudgels called podgers. In a severe freeze up, the canal would be stopped entirely and the carriers would forward urgent goods by road.

Delays caused by ice were expected and, in former times, traders carried large stocks to meet this eventuality. The year 1795 was one in which there was prolonged and heavy frost. The Trent was frozen over and no ships were able to arrive at or sail from Gainsborough until 7th March.[8] Stafford County Infirmary ran out of coal and, on 7th February, the temperature was reported 11 degrees below freezing point at Macclesfield. The thaw, when it came, caused a great deal of damage, particularly at Burton where breweries, timber yards, wharves and warehouses were affected. Mr Clifford had a boatload of cokes worth £30 washed away. Remarkably, the boat was later found full of timber.[9]

Delays were compounded by the effect of a coastal shipping embargo, the result of the threat of war with France. According to the *Staffordshire Advertiser* of 21st March 1795:

'An order of Council is issued permitting all ships and vessels laden with clay for the Potteries in Staffordshire to sail. The Manufactures have been much in want of clay the whole winter due to the extreme boisterous and unsettled weather that has been of late and the embargo still increasing their distress.'

The normal pattern of trade could be affected by poor harvests. Normally there was a substantial trade in cereals through the canal from east to west, supplemented by supplies brought by coaster to Liverpool. In 1795, however, it was necessary to import 60,000 quarters of Canadian wheat in eighty vessels.[10]

The canal could be a dangerous place, as the *Staffordshire Advertiser* of 16th January 1795 described: '*Boy drowned in the navigation near Hanley. He was whipping a top on the ice and, approaching too near the side in that part where the water from the steam engine empties itself, the ice gave way.*'

There were many accidents to boatmen. They were killed and injured by being kicked or crushed by horses, drowned in the canal, and in handling cargo. Fingers could be caught in ropes. On 25th April 1849, the canal company agreed to compensate, up to a sum of £5, Jno Riley, a boatman employed by Mr Gerard of Hanley, who had been injured by the breakage of a crane chain.[11] Nearly all transport workers were exposed to greater dangers than the rest of the population but boatmen were the most accident prone of all transport men, the dangers even exceeding those experienced by seamen.[12]

There were, at one time, many boatbuilding yards on the canal. There are known to have been at least thirteen between Stone and Anderton. It was the sort of business that could be set up almost anywhere, work was usually done in the open and the boats winched out of and slid into the canal on ironshod, greased timbers. A feature of the T&M is the relatively large number of drydocks. Early canal boats were small, carrying only 20 tons but competition and design innovation later led to them being built to the full size the locks could accommodate. However, the fuller shaped designs found in the south found little favour on the northern narrow canals, probably because it was considered essential for them to enter and leave the numerous narrow locks quickly. There was little standardisation in design and some boats were particularly small. The Anderton Company's motor boat **Bedford** was said to be 'sunk' with 20 tons on, meaning she was very low in the water. The boatyard at Barlaston is said to have been responsible for the 'Barlaston bow', a shape of fore end peculiar to the north Trent & Mersey, whereby the striking point of the fore end on the lock cills was brought below the top bends. This gave a canoe shaped stempost. Although empty motor boats with the normal height of cabin could negotiate Harecastle Tunnel, those built locally had lower cabins than usual. The slight difference was enough to make the steerer feel uncomfortably exposed.

Some intrepid skaters take advantage of the frozen canal at Wheelock Wharf. GRAHAM HOVEY

Ice breaking at Fradley in the 1930s, with the crane and warehouses in the background. The boat is being violently rolled from side to side by her large crew, in order to break a wider passage through the ice for the larger carrying craft that will follow. WATERWAY IMAGES COLLECTION

Brindley's aqueduct carrying the T&M Canal over the River Dove near Egginton in Derbyshire. The shallows here were popular with young swimmers. WATERWAY IMAGES COLLECTION

Mersey Weaver motor boat **Joan**, *which had joined the fleet from Henry Johnson of Birmingham in October 1941, passing under the ex-NSR line at Kidsgrove in the late 1950s. The steerer is Bill Wain and his niece, Alice Lapworth, is on the cabin top.* GORDON BRIGGS

Boatbuilders often owned boats, Samuel Turner of Barlaston, Geo Archer of Tunstall and John Jackson of Baddeley Green being among them. Some of these boats were change boats, hired to a carrier while his own craft was being docked, some were hired to owner boatmen and carriers for longer periods, and a few boatbuilders acted as carriers themselves. Boats required rope and there were canalside rope walks including those at Shardlow, Tunstall and two at Middlewich.

The northern part of the T&M was heavily affected by subsidence from coalmining and brine pumping. This meant many low bridges, making it necessary to dismantle the cratch on empty boats. For this reason, boats in the potteries trade were built with low cratches and stands, so that when loaded with light cargoes they would have sufficient headroom. A horseboat loaded with light earthenware would only carry eight tons weight and would be high out of the water. As the cratches had to be taken down altogether on empty boats, few of the Potteries boatmen bothered with the finer points of appearance. The sidecloths would be tied across the front of the cratch (which made an unsightly bulge under the deckcloth) and the deckcloth only used if the cargo required it, otherwise left rolled up on the foredeck. If not required to be fully clothed up, sidecloths would be pulled up to the minimum extent necessary to prevent water coming aboard when the paddles were drawn in uphill locks. Many photographs show them pulled up to the middle beam only and the planks behind this laid on the beams instead of on the stands. Downhill boats with heavy cargoes of coal or gravel would not put the cratch up at all. With coal boats, where the coal was piled up high in the middle of the hold, it was common to put the planks up between the mast and the 'stern middle' stand (over the heap of coal), and lay the mast plank and sternplank on the beams. There was a wide variety of different arrangements and, if you examine old photographss carefully, you can work out why the planks and cloths are arranged as depicted. By contrast, the long distance boats working through from Preston Brook to the East or West Midlands would have their cratches carefully erected, pains being taken to avoid wrinkles in the deckcloth, and would decorate them with lengths of scrubbed white canvas hosepipe and cotton strings and have all their top planks up. Some boats were not fitted with sidecloths and had to exercise great care when drawing the upper paddles in a lock.

Apart from this, the boats in the potteries trade were painted in the much same way as other cabin boats and the crews decorated their cabins with brass, crotchet work and hanging up plates as elsewhere. However, brass bands on the cabin chimneys, a decoration widely used elsewhere, were rarely seen because of the corrosive effect of the chemical laden air.

Disposing of worn out boats could be a problem as the oak timbers were difficult to cut up and only the iron knees could be reused. On the T&M, the number of 'wides' or 'flashes' caused by mining subsidence provided graveyards for old boats at no expense.

To depict the operation of wharves, Wincham and Middlewich can be taken as examples. Wincham was the nearest T&M wharf to Northwich and Middlewich was an important market for cheese and a transshipment point to the Shropshire Union system. Flyboats called at both places. Before the invention of the telephone and the availability of next day postal deliveries, there were obvious difficulties in organising the nationwide transport service that the merchandise carriers of the canal age provided. Carriers had their own agents at large depots such as Preston Brook but at smaller wharves, responsibility fell on the wharfinger, a canal company employee. He would receive goods, sometimes consigned to a specific carrier but often unconsigned, in which case he had to decide which service to use. A great deal of transport required transshipment en route, often more than once. He had to arrange this, besides storing goods, raising wharf charges, collecting

Potter & Son's motor Sunshine *departing Lock 57 at Hassall Green, in 1957, a few moments after the picture on page 83 was taken. Note the hand operated klaxon horn on the cabin slide next to steerer George Radford.* GORDON BRIGGS

charges on behalf of carriers, and often supervising smaller wharves and toll clerks.

The key document in the operation of sundries traffic was the roadnote, later to be known as the waybill. Made out at the starting point of each voyage, it contained a list of all the goods on board with their destinations and transshipment instructions. Each consignment had to be signed for by the wharfinger at its destination. The roadnote was a versatile document and might be used to note space booked at wharves further along the line, in the hope that wharfingers would not occupy that space to clear their own cargoes. This happened sometimes and would provoke a sharp note from the carrier not to load goods on their boats without prior arrangement but, generally speaking, in the absence of contrary instructions, wharfingers would use space on any boat that called. At times, there was considerable difficulty in clearing traffic and there were complaints about boats failing to call when they had space. Wharfingers would sometimes annotate the roadnote with a message to the carrier's nearest agent, asking for space on a boat in the other direction. Invoices usually accompanied the cargo, advice notes often going to customers by post. Carriers' letters and messages were often carried by boat.

We, in the 21st century, may marvel that this system worked at all. Yet work it did and the nation's transport was conducted with a regularity that might be envied in these 'advanced' days.

Mr William Mosely was the wharfinger at Middlewich in 1846-47. He dealt with five main carriers: Suttons, Soresbys, Henshalls, the Anderton Carrying Company and Pickfords. The Ellesmere & Chester Canal Company provided connecting services to Barbridge Junction and beyond. Middlewich had a large and varied trade but the commodity which caused most problems was cheese, for which he often had difficulty in finding space on boats. Goods were sometimes unloaded at the wrong wharf. Mr Mosely had close contacts with his colleagues, Arthur Shenstone at Wincham and S. Clowes at Barbridge. He also supervised a toll clerk at Wardle Junction.[13]

British Waterways somewhat untidy maintenance boat Gailey *in Thurlwood steel lock on 11th August 1966.* Gailey *had been converted from a butty at W.J. Yarwoods River Weaver shipyard in August 1937.* WATERWAY IMAGES COLLECTION

Mountbatten, one of British Waterways' 'Admiral' Class motor boats, had been built as recently as July 1960 by W.J. Yarwood at Northwich but seems to be lacking any indication of ownership on the cabin side, so the photograph probably dates from after 1964 when she was hired to Willow Wren. These all-welded craft would carry a greater tonnage on the same draft than the older, more finely shaped but riveted boats, which was useful as canal dredging came to be neglected after nationalisation. Mountbatten is seen here at Middlewich, near the gas works. WATERWAY IMAGES COLLECTION

A close up of John Walley's **Dunstan** *(built as* **Dunstable** *for the Grand Union Canal Carrying Co. in 1937, ex-John Knill, 1952) and* **Margaret** *(ex-FMC) at the north end of Harecastle Tunnel.* GORDON BRIGGS

Twenty years later, well into the railway age, we find Geo Caldwell, wharfinger at Wincham, still busy with part load traffic. In fact, the only itemised full load traffic in his ledger[14] is 50 tons of manure and some roadstone. By now, the number of large carriers had fallen to three: the Anderton Carrying Company, the Bridgewater Trustees and the Shropshire Union. Other regular carriers were Mellor, Colsell & Co. and James Cockshott. Among Caldwell's customers was James Hesketh, who had a nearby mill. Small consignments were still the order of the day. Hesketh had a varied trade including wheat, oats, meal, tiles, pottery crates, maize, flour, bran, castings, ironwork, millstones (from Red Bull), machinery, roadstone and cotton cake.

The Ocklestone Bros (later John Ocklestone) were another customer. Their trade included hides, tanning agents, oilcloth, rope, mats, castings and leather. James Ocklestone dealt with bones, corn and sacks. The Ocklestones had other canal connections. In 1818, Thos Ocklestone was the Manchester agent for Coffield & Company, carriers to Chester, Shrewsbury and North Wales. The family also had a wharf at Runcorn. There were some smaller customers, including the carriers Whitehouse and Hargreaves, and Mr Forshaw, a timber merchant. Caldwell himself is debited with charges for some goods. He was responsible for accounting for traffic from the nearby Cheshire Amalgamated Salt Works and for the tolls on traffic transshipped to the canal at Anderton.

Cheddleton was an important wharf on the Caldon Canal. In 1830, when Jno Shaw was wharfinger, one of its customers was Jos Wardle, who had a dyeworks at Leekbrook, one and a quarter miles from the wharf. The business was dependent on canal transport and two boatloads a month of slack, carted from the wharf, were used. Silk came from London, valonia (acorn cups), shumac and soap from Liverpool, and casks and carboys of chemicals from Geo Pratt's Lifford Chemical Works near Birmingham. Other cargoes were soda from Shardlow, copperas from Shelton and Derby, bark from Uttoxeter, gravel, straw, archill, fuller's earth, bricks, timber, logwood, oil and safflower. Finished goods were sent outwards.

Wardle used a number of carriers including Alexander Reid, the Anderton Carrying Company, Pickfords, Suttons, Thos Henshall and the Trent & Mersey Navigation Co. Mathew Heath brought bags of Bristol dye from Stourport. Wardle's account with Pickford's shows carriage to and from London, Macclesfield, Manchester, Liverpool, Derby, Stone and Bristol. Occasionally, goods were sent to Leek Wharf instead of Cheddleton. In the month ended 29th January 1837, Wardle paid 10s 9d in wharfage and cranage.[15]

NOTES TO CHAPTER EIGHT
1. PRO RAIL 532/4, NSR Report, 1848
2. Braithwaite Poole, *The Commerce of Liverpool*, 1854
3. Lewery, Tony, 'Preston Brook', *Waterways World* magazine, July 1976, p34
4. Barnett R., 'Narrowboats on the Weaver', *Waterways World* magazine, September 1979, p48-51
5. Lightfoot, T.S., *The Weaver Watermen*, Chester Museums & Libraries, undated
6. SRO D3900/2, Haywood Permits
7. Hanson H., *The Canal Boatmen*, Manchester 1975
8. *Staffordshire Advertiser*, 16th January and 7th March 1795
9. *Staffordshire Advertiser*, 21st February 1795
10. *Staffordshire Advertiser*, 16th May 1795
11. PRO RAIL 532/140, NSR Minutes
12. Hanson H, op cit, p134
13. Moss G., *The Middlewich Letters*, Oldham, 1989
14. BW GLOS, WM77.51 Wincham Wharf Ledger
15. SRO D1313/2, Carriage Vouchers

CHAPTER NINE
THE DECLINING YEARS 1913-1970

Traffic on the Trent & Mersey had reached an all time high in 1863, of 1,652,530 tons, albeit against a background of declining toll receipts. Twelve years later, in 1874, traffic had declined to 1,187,047 tons and it was to remain close to this figure for four decades, with a figure for 1913 of 1,051,930 tons. Inland waterway transport had, by then, long been superseded as the national transport system by the railways and canal carriers only operated in niche markets. Because of the inflexibility of their track and the fact that extensions to the canal system to tap new traffic sources were no longer viable, they were vulnerable to both the decline of existing canal served industries and mineral deposits, and to any alterations in the patterns of trade. To a large extent, canal traffic depended on industrial inertia and the number of firms who considered it advantageous to site new premises to use canal transport was already negligible.

It is not surprising that the upheaval of the First World War destroyed the status quo of forty years and left the T&M with a 42% fall in its traffic by 1919, when the figure was 605,307 tons. Wartime government control, first of all under the Railway Executive Committee, then from March 1917 under the Canal Control Committee of the Board of Trade, did nothing to preserve the traffic of canals and the opportunity of higher earnings in wartime industries led to a loss of boatmen, many of whom also joined the armed services, where their skills were in considerable demand both on the Continent and in Mesopotamia.

Nor was there any recovery after the war. The decline of heavy industry continued, canal connected mineral workings became worked out and the canals were unable to offer an attractive service to the new light industries that sprang up between the wars. Inflation created a huge increase in costs but the canals were often unable to apply the increased tolls and charges for which they had obtained powers. For instance, on 23rd July 1920, the Bridgewater Department of the Manchester Ship Canal agreed with the NSR to retain charges at the level authorised by the T&M Enabling Act, despite having obtained powers for a 50% increase. By 1938, a further fall of 36% in T&M traffic had occurred.

Among the principal carriers on the T&M, the Anderton Company, the Mersey, Weaver Co., Potter & Sons and Fellows, Morton & Clayton survived throughout this period of decline, although with reduced fleets. The Shropshire Union discontinued its carrying department in 1921. Its boats and equipment had been handed back by the Canal Control Committee in a very worn state and with virtually no compensation. It had sustained an average loss of £153,318 for 1920-21, on average receipts of £227,845 and had rarely shown a profit in the previous twenty years, being subsidised by the L&NWR. Its bulk cargo trade and some of its boats were taken over by the other T&M carriers and owner boatmen, helping to keep them in business, but its flyboat services ceased.

An early postwar problem was a temporary transfer of South Staffordshire traffic from Preston Brook to Ellesmere Port. Traffic transshipped at Preston Brook to and from Liverpool in 1919 had been 43,788 tons. In 1920, it fell to 34,412 tons. In 1922, South Staffordshire traffic to and from Liverpool via Ellesmere Port was 16,352 tons, against 46,769 tons via the Bridgewater route. The year 1923 was disastrous for Preston Brook, with only 1,019 tons from and 4 tons to Liverpool

A Potter & Son boat unloading china clay at Twyford's Cliffe Vale Pottery, Stoke in the 1930s. Potters were based at Runcorn and owned a fleet of around thirty boats, the names of which all began with the letter 'S'.
BASIL JEUDA COLLECTION

North Staffordshire Railway spoon dredger **Lawton** *tied in the approach to Brindley's Harecastle Tunnel on the T&M Canal at Kidsgrove around 1910. JOHN RYAN COLLECTION*

(Ellesmere Port 18,878 and 21,640 tons). These figures refer only to FMC traffic. By then, they were the only important carriers between the Mersey and South Staffordshire. Thereafter, the Bridgewater route trade recovered, whilst import traffic for South Staffordshire (excluding grain) via Ellesmere Port fell to nothing by 1930. Preston Brook was helped through this difficult time by a regular traffic in borate of lime, carried by Joseph Rayner.

Pottery materials traffic from Runcorn Docks, which had been 89,555 tons in 1913, was 5,773 tons in 1920, rising to 10,440 tons in 1921 but only to fall to 8,229 tons in the following year.[1] On the Weaver route, the five-yearly average for 1911-15 had been 90,223 tons, falling to an average of 34,541 tons for 1916-20 and recovering slightly to 59,224 tons for 1921-25.

Another major change affecting the Trent & Mersey was as a result of the Railway Grouping that came into effect in 1923. Under this scheme, the North Staffordshire Railway, owner of the T&M, and the London & North Western Railway (lessee of the Shropshire Union) became part of the newly formed London, Midland & Scottish Railway (LM&SR). As both canals were now under the same ownership, there was no reason why the South Staffordshire trade could not be routed over the T&M between Preston Brook and Wardle Junction, and thence via the Shropshire Union. At a stroke, a substantial amount of traffic disappeared from the T&M between Wardle Junction and Haywood Junction.

There had been a motor lorry service for export pottery ware since 1906 but the aftermath of war created a whole new class of small road hauliers using war surplus lorries. Initially, however, they concentrated on creaming off high value traffics (it will be remembered that at this time carriage charges were based on the value of the goods) and at first made little impact on the canals' preponderant low value traffic, although by the end of the inter war period, lorries were taking pottery raw materials from the docks to the Potteries. Where works were not sited on a canal, lorries had the advantage of providing door to door transport. It was another story where goods had to be received in large quantities, stored and subsequently delivered. Here, the canals, with their large wharves and warehouses, still held their own.

A horse-drawn wagon crosses the Caldon Canal at Ivy House Bridge, Hanley. BASIL JEUDA COLLECTION

*Captain Primrose Thorley, one of the partners in Bowers & Thorley, lime burners of Froghall, on one of their boats, **Farmers Friend**, circa 1904. The boat is in the first pound of the former Uttoxeter Canal at Froghall and the building behind is a former warehouse. The Bowers had begun lime burning in 1858 and Bowers & Thorley traded until 1920, when the incline down to Froghall Wharf was closed. BASIL JEUDA COLLECTION*

Soot Hill Wharf on the T&M Canal near Anderton circa 1910. The bridge carries Soot Hill across the canal, whilst one of the properties, which still survive today, housed a shop. The Anderton Lift can be seen in the right background.
JOHN RYAN COLLECTION

Among the factors affecting the decline in T&M trade was the closure of many of the smaller salt and alkali works on the Cheshire section of the canal. Of the twenty-three works between Lawton and Anderton that existed in 1894, only six survived in 1950. Of these, only Henry Seddon's works at Middlewich made any great use of the canal. All the others were rail connected, although some soda ash continued to be boated between the Imperial Chemical Industries' Lostock Works and Runcorn by the Mersey, Weaver & Ship Canal Carrying Company, whilst Ingram Thompsons at Marston despatched a little salt to Anderton for export. It must be remembered that the process of salt making consumed enormous quantities of coal that, except for the supply to Seddons, was lost to the canal. Seddons' salt traffic ceased in October 1962.

The large number of colliery loading places that once existed on the canal has already been described. By 1924, Foxley, Stoke New Wharf, Sideway and Brereton were among the few that survived, the latter closing in that year. Just before the closure of Brereton Basin, in addition to local traffic, coal was being sent from there to Plume Street, Aston; Birmingham Old Wharf; Wednesbury and the Cape Arm (Smethwick).

Coal and roadstone brought onto the canal from the Bridgewater and Coventry canals had ended by 1950. That from the Coventry Canal was short distance traffic and vulnerable to road competition, as merchants sent their delivery lorries to the collieries' landsale sites. In the early 1920s, King's Bromley received coal from West Cannock Colliery on the Cannock Extension Canal and from Wednesbury, slag from Toll End and also roadstone. Coal also went to the nearby Lichfield Creamery from Tibberly. There was also a coal trade to Barton Turn and Burton on Trent from the Coventry Canal.[2]

The development of gas firing for pottery kilns was another factor affecting coal traffic. The last coal trade on the T&M was between Sideway and Seddon's salt works at Middlewich, amounting to 5,160 tons in 1966. The last shipment was delivered on 11th November 1967.[3]

As far as the iron trade was concerned, in 1927, FMC reported an almost total loss of iron from South Staffordshire to both north and south. In the same year, the Anderton Company was still delivering substantial quantities of Shelton steel to the Black Country. In July of that year, there were forty boatloads to Baylis, Jones & Baylis at Wolverhampton, two boatloads to the District Iron & Steel Company at Smethwick, and three boatloads to Stewarts & Lloyds at Coombswood. The boats returned to the Potteries with clay from Dudley Port or firebricks from Brierley Hill.[4] Mersey, Weaver's

The north end of Saltersford Tunnel around 1908, showing the horse-path over the top. NEIL PARKHOUSE COLLECTION

boats also visited the West Midlands, carrying bentonite clay to Wolverhampton and zinc ashes to Coombswood.

The Anderton Company acquired its first motorboat in 1923 and went on to build a total of sixteen, all converted from horseboats. Some of these had 9hp Bolinder engines and were designed to run singly, replacing the horsedrawn flyboats. Others had 20hp Bolinders and towed butties. The Mersey, Weaver Company did not start building motors until 1939. Although Fellows, Morton & Clayton had built its first motorboat in 1912, it mechanised its services between London, Birmingham, Leicester and Nottingham first, and it was not until 1933 that motorboats were built specifically for the Preston Brook trade. L.T.C. Rolt, passing through the canal in 1939, commented on the large number of horse boats and there were still some operating between Middlewich and Anderton in 1954, and on local traffic in the Potteries into the 1960s.

The slump of the late 1920s caused the pottery carriers to seek traffic outside their normal area of operation and the boats of Joseph Rayner, J. Horsfield, Simpson Davies, Potter & Son, Mersey, Weaver and the Anderton Company appeared on the Coventry and London route, carrying such cargoes as washing powder, woodpulp, starch, chemicals, flour, aluminium and furniture.[5] In the late 1920s, a new carrier appeared on the canal. This was the Midlands & Coast Canal Carrying

A view across the T&M Canal at Barnton circa 1908, a short distance west of Soot Hill Wharf and looking towards the River Weaver down below. Barnton Bridge and coal wharf are just off to the right with the tunnel beyond. NEIL PARKHOUSE COLLECTION

*British Waterways **Aberystwyth**, built at Rickmansworth in 1951, leaving Runcorn ('New') Top Lock and Waterloo Bridge with a cargo of feldspar for the Potteries. The drydock seen on page 15 is through the centre arch. When the Runcorn-Widnes Bridge spanning the River Mersey was constructed in 1960-61, an approach road to it was built right across the canal immediately beyond Waterloo Bridge, blocking the waterway off completely. However, construction of a new crossing of the river – the Mersey Gateway project – began in 2014 and this includes plans to remove some of the roads leading to the Runcorn-Widnes Bridge (renamed Silver Jubilee Bridge on widening in 1977), which will once again open up the line of the canal.* BASIL JEUDA COLLECTION

Cottages at Thurlwood Upper Lock. These small canal-side settlements were typical of the northern section of the T&M, where boatmen often followed the tradition of keeping Sunday as a day of rest. Many of them owned cottages, although they may only have tied up there once or twice a week and rarely slept on the land. BASIL JEUDA COLLECTION

Company. Although set up to compete with FMC by using the Ellesmere Port route, it also traded on the Trent & Mersey. In 1929, this company carried nearly 1,000 tons of firebricks from Brierley Hill, on the Stourbridge Canal, to Johnsons for lining kilns. It also carried grain from Liverpool to Hovis' mill at Macclesfield and flour from Price's mill at Bloxwich to Burslem.

The year 1935 saw the last traffic between the Derby Canal and the T&M when, on 20th February, an FMC boat went through Swarkestone Junction with 5cwt of empty drums. In the four preceding years, the route had only seen occasional loads of cast iron pipes, wood pulp, sugar and mousetraps.[6]

In 1938, the LM&SR prepared an engineers' plan of the T&M showing intended dredging and engineering work. It was accompanied by details of the number of boats moving on the canal in May of that year. Boats are listed as horse, motor or butty but I have found it more convenient to convert this into horse, single motor and pairs of boats. The canal is divided into sections and the number of boats through each section is given in the table below, loaded craft being separated from empties by a forward slash.[7]

Of the Potteries traders, only the Anderton Company had any motorboats at this time (sixteen in 1940). Most motorboats on the canal belonged to Fellows, Morton & Clayton, who were engaged in through traffic to and from Preston Brook or Anderton and Wardle Junction, the Coventry Canal and the River Trent.

Section	Horse	Single Motors	Pairs
Preston Brook-Anderton	259/74	93/21	48/1
Anderton-Middlewich	453/224	97/21	51/1
Middlewich-Wheelock	503/174	99/20	51/1

The above figures should include traffic between the Bridgewater Canal and the Weaver to and from the Wardle Branch. As they show no net traffic in single motors or pairs leaving or entering the T&M at Wardle, i.e. the same number of pairs and almost the same number of single motors passed between Anderton and Wheelock, it would appear that the South Staffordshire via Wardle traffic was not included in this survey.

Wheelock-Etruria	568/238	106/26	51/1

This was the busiest section of the canal and included traffic to and from the Hall Green and Etruria branches.

Hall Green Branch	23/22	6/6	5/6
Etruria-Milton	176/100	15/20	2/7
Etruria-Sideway	484/280	67/32	36/16
Sideway-Stone	13/12	40/19	14/3
Stone-Great Haywood	9/11	40/19	14/3

It appears that only four boats unloaded at Stone this month.

Great Haywood-Fradley	7/11	40/19	14/3

Only two boats joined or left the Staffs & Worcs Canal at Great Haywood, probably vessels carrying firebricks from the Stourbridge Canal to the Potteries.

Fradley-Derwentmouth	4/5	32/16	3/3
Milton Branch	66/66	–	–
Milton-Hazlehurst	53/53	–	–
Hazlehurst-Froghall	49/49	–	–
Leek Branch	4/4	–	–

An aerial view of Kidsgrove circa 1960, which shows much of interest. In the centre is Kidsgrove Central station, where the main lines from Crewe (bottom left) and Manchester (bottom right) joined to head through Harecastle Tunnel and in to Stoke. The T&M Canal can be seen at Plant's Lock coming in past the gas works (bottom right), going under the Crewe line and then curving round to pass under the railway again. The entrance to Harecastle canal tunnel is just to the right of this second railway bridge. The Macclesfield Canal runs behind the larger gas holder and then swings round to join the T&M at Hardingswood Junction. Kidsgrove Liverpool Road station can be seen bottom left, at the start of the Potteries Loop Line. BASIL JEUDA COLLECTION

*The later, or Norton, part of the Preston Brook complex, with the Anderton Canal Carrying Company (not to be confused with the original Anderton Company) fleet. The boats are lying beside Stitt's Shed with the Black Shed in the background. Identifiable are **Argo**, on the left, and **Mountbatten**, on the right.* WATERWAY IMAGES COLLECTION

On the outbreak of war in 1939, all railway owned canals again came under the authority of the Railway Executive Committee. In June 1940, the government gave carriers a toll subsidy equal to 50% of tolls. In 1942, eighteen canal companies and forty-two carriers were brought under the control of the Ministry of War Transport and crewing canal boats became a reserved occupation, although not in time to prevent many boatmen leaving the canals in the first two years of the war. The wartime period saw several changes in the pattern of trade, to adjust to the reduction in use of the East Coast ports. Thus, for a time, Thomas Clayton took fuel oil from Ellesmere Port to Nottingham and FMC carried

Wardle Junction, Middlewich in the late 1950s. JOHN RYAN COLLECTION

flour from the CWS Sun Mills at Manchester to the Nottingham and Long Eaton Cooperative Societies. Imported Canadian cheese became a feature of the trade being carried to the East and West Midlands, reserve stocks being held in the long disused warehouses at Shardlow. Grain and flour were also carried from Ellesmere Port, to maintain buffer stocks in warehouses at Wheelock, Rode Heath, Red Bull, Tunstall, Middleport, Burslem, Etruria, Stoke, Stone Shardlow and Coventry. Pig lead and brass for making munitions were sent from the Mersey to Nottingham in 1941-43.[8]

Despite attempts to use the canals as much as possible, traffic fell from 385,870 tons in 1938 to 198,136 tons in 1945. The LM&SR took advantage of the distraction caused by the war to obtain an Act in 1944, allowing it to abandon many miles of canal including the Leek Branch, which appears to have seen its last regular trade in 1939 – tar from Leek Gas Works to Hardman's chemical works at Milton. Trade on the Caldon Canal east of Milton had ended by 1951, when Brittain's Cheddleton Paper Mills ceased to have coal by canal.

A feature of wartime control was that traffic to and from South Staffordshire and Liverpool was worked through Ellesmere Port, Weston Point, Preston Brook and Runcorn indiscriminately.[9]

Government control ceased on 31st December 1947, in which year an Act was passed to nationalise all the major inland waterways and their carrying departments.

The very first day of 1948 saw the take-over of most British canals, including the Trent & Mersey, by the British Transport Commission, who operated them under its Docks & Inland Waterways Executive. In the same year, the Manchester Ship Canal (Bridgewater Department), which had, since the end of the war, been making losses on its lighterage and transshipment operations between Liverpool and Preston Brook, withdrew from its agreements with FMC and the Anderton Company. FMC almost immediately went into liquidation and the BTC bought its stock and took over most of its depots.

The Anderton Company started to sell off boats from 1948, in which year it sold seven of its sixteen motorboats, but struggled on until 1953, by which year traffic on the canal had fallen to 89,183 tons. That year saw the last boatload of ware leave the Potteries and, on 31st December, Elizabeth Boddington sold the thirteen remaining Anderton Company boats to Mersey, Weaver. At its height, around the turn of the century, the Anderton Company had operated some 200 boats. In the same year, Cowburn & Cowpar took off their chemical boats between Manchester and the Courtauld factories at Coventry and Dunstall Park at Wolverhampton.

With the closure of Preston Brook depot in 1948, the FMC (later British Waterways Northern Fleet) boats and the Anderton Company used Weston Point, and occasionally Anderton, for transshipping their Liverpool traffic. Transshipment traffic at Ellesmere Port was discontinued.

Nationalisation had brought the railways, inland waterways and some of the larger road hauliers under one umbrella, the British Transport Commission. The smaller hauliers were controlled

Hyperion waiting to unload coal at Seddon's, Middlewich on 18th March 1965. The boatman's beret and the lady's pinafore were typical items of boat people's dress in the period after WW2. WATERWAY IMAGES COLLECTION

*FMC motor boat **Dragon** at Hem Heath Bridge in the early 1960s. TOM FOXON COLLECTION*

*Potter & Son's **Sunshine** about to leave Booth Lane Top or Crows Nest Lock on 30th July 1958. John E. Lynam, courtesy Philippa Corrie*

*Mr and Mrs Moore on their Potter motor boat **Silver Jubilee** at Runcorn in 1958. Basil Jeuda collection*

by a system of licences issued by the Road Transport Executive. At the same time, the coal mining and electricity industries were also nationalised. It was expected that each mode of transport would be used for the traffic for which it was most suitable and the canal interest hoped that they would acquire additional bulk, low value traffic. This was not to be. New power stations, such as that at Meaford on the Trent & Mersey, were built on waterside sites so as to access cooling water but were supplied entirely by rail, while the National Coal Board quickly imposed surcharges for loading coal to boats.

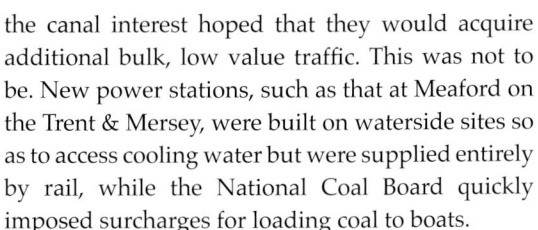

On 31st October 1948, representatives of the Docks & Inland Waterways Executive (D&IWE), the Railway Executive (RE), the Road Transport Executive (RTE) and the National Association of Inland Waterways Carriers (NAIWC) met to consider proposals for cooperation and coordination. The NAIWC was represented by John Iremonger of Fellows, Morton & Clayton and Stewart Boddington of the Anderton Company. Iremonger had been Chairman of the Association between 1933 and 1942, and Boddington had served on its Executive Committee since its early days. The Association's secretary was Norman Bird, Manager of the Manchester Ship Canal, Bridgewater Department.

A rail/road/canal conference was set up for each of the four D&IWE divisions. This was a revival of the pre-government control rail/canal conference enlarged by the inclusion of the RTE. Among its other functions, the conference published rates schedules for road, rail and canal carriage of specific traffics. There was an immediate problem so far as the Potteries trade was concerned. The conference rates were from Manchester, Runcorn or Weston Point to the Potteries, not rates inclusive of the coastal shipping section of the total movement. The railways and the RTE could adhere to the conference schedules and at the same time undercut the canal on the through carriage of raw materials

*Sunshine, originally the Anderton Company's **Portugal**, at Hawkesbury Junction on 11th July 1959. The author bought this boat when Potters ceased to carry in 1957 and used her on short-distance work around Birmingham. Here she is seen about to set off with a passenger day trip. She had a 20hp single cylinder Bolinder engine. Hawkesbury Junction, also known as Sutton Stop Lock, is where the Oxford Canal meets the Coventry Canal.* BASIL JEUDA COLLECTION

from South West England. The RTE tried to get a share of the existing canal traffic by reducing rates on this route and was only hampered by the then small size of lorries and their being subject to low speed restrictions.[10]

In November 1951, Shirley wrote to Boddington and to C.M. Marsh, the British Waterways Divisional Manager at Liverpool, to advise him that the RTE had offered special rates on china clay to the Pottery Manufacturers Association. It turned out that these rates only applied to ball clay which, he later wrote, 'No longer interests the canal'.

The RTE had another means of taking traffic from the waterways. As the Licensing Authority for road transport, it could rescind the 'A' and 'B' licences of hauliers who were employed by canal carriers to provide ancillary services. This threat became a reality in October 1950, when notices of licence revocation (under the provisions of the Transport Act 1947, Sections 52 and 53) were sent to large numbers of hauliers. On consulting British Waterways about this threat, the NAIWC stated that through waterway rates had no margin for the employment of contractors' or RTE vehicles and cited the necessity to continue to provide a service in cases of flood, drought or frost. As it happened, BW had a lever against the RTE as, if the effect on carriers businesses was such as to result in a loss of

Thurlwood Steel Lock was at Upper Thurlwood Lock No. 53, between Wheelock and Hardingswood Junction. It was built by British Waterways in 1957, to replace one of the pair of locks here which had been affected by subsidence. Built as an experiment, it was both slow and complicated to use, so became something of a failure, the remaining traditional lock alongside tending to get used instead. The steel lock was taken out of use in 1981 and subsequently scrapped in 1988. WATERWAY IMAGES COLLECTION

traffic to the canal, then BW would suffer a reduction in toll income. Looked at from this point of view, the RHTE was competing, outside the conference system, with another part of the British Transport Commission, one of whose remits was to promote cooperation and coordination between modes.

In October, the Trent & Mersey was particularly affected by licence problems concerning the Anderton Company. Harrison & Sons, stated at the time to be the Anderton Company's best account, had three works in North Staffordshire: Trent Works and Joiners Square Works manufactured pottery, whilst Victoria Mill, at Stanley on the Caldon Canal, ground flints, feldspar, quartz and china stone. Victoria was originally a watermill, later converted to steam power and had a siding put in by the 1890s to supplement its canal wharf.

At Victoria, it was the practice to unload canal borne china stone, feldspar and quartz into railway wagons at a canalside siding belonging to the firm, for movement to the point of production in the mill. Flints and coal had long been carried throughout by rail. Unloading from boat to railway wagon eventually became uneconomic and Harrison's then experimented with having their materials brought from Runcorn or Weston Point docks by rail. The

The once busy wharf and warehouses at Leek in 1958. A lorry is parked on the bed of the in filled canal. BASIL JEUDA COLLECTION

*Potter & Son's **Sunlight** on the new cut at Marston in 1957. This section of canal was cut in the 1950s to avoid an area of subsidence caused by brine pumping. The chimneys of Ingram, Thompson's Salt Works are in the background.* GORDON BRIGGS

*A view at Hardingswood Junction near Kidsgrove on 4th November 1960. The T&M's Hall Green Branch, leading to the Macclesfield Canal is entered under the side-bridge on which the photographer is standing, shortly to make a right angle turn and be carried over the main line on an aqueduct. The only identifiable boat is **Sunbeam**, front left.* WATERWAY IMAGES COLLECTION

service given by the railway from these ports proved to be unsatisfactory so, as this part of the canal had become badly silted, the Anderton Company, who arranged all Harrison's transport, resorted to delivering by road from their Stoke Wharf. This also became uneconomic so the Anderton Company arranged for the 50 tons per week of materials from the docks to be carried by road by a small haulier, Turner Bros. Their relationship with Turners, who also performed their local cartage, was such that they could rely on them not to interfere in canal business. This arrangement safeguarded the Anderton Company's relationship with Harrisons and enabled them to retain on the canal the 150 tons per week of china clay boated to the Hanley works.

Turners required a licence for the Victoria Mill traffic, the distance from Weston Point being about 31 miles from their base. Boddington was extremely concerned when it was advised that Turners' licence had been withdrawn from the end of October 1951 and that the RTE had applied for the traffic for their own lorries. Harrisons said that, under no circumstances would they use British Road Services, its rates being higher than those of private hauliers, and that they would, if the situation was not resolved, be forced either to take china stone direct from Cornwall by rail or acquire their own vehicles. Firms that operated vehicles only for their own traffic had 'C' licences, with no distance restrictions.

The danger, which Boddington clearly perceived, was that a lorry acquired by Harrison's would not be fully utilised carrying to Victoria Mill and, in order to occupy the rest of its time, might be used on the traffic carried by boat to Harrisons' other works at Hanley.

This process had already started to abstract traffic from the canal. Johnsons, a large firm of potters,

Etruria Junction in April 1963, showing the entrance to the canal company's gauging dock on the left and the overall roof over the Top Lock. The lock was provided with a canopy to protect the toll collector from the weather as he calculated the tonnage loaded aboard cargo craft passing through. The gauging dock was where craft were measured to facilitate the future calculation of tolls. Etruria Basin is on the left.
BASIL JEUDA COLLECTION

used local hauliers for its earthenware traffic to Liverpool. When the RTE withdrew their licences, Johnsons bought its own vehicles and had, about three weeks previously, begun to use the spare capacity of these vehicles to carry clay from Weston Point, taking at least 100 tons per week from the canal. Similarly, Colin McNeal, a pottery material and ware merchant, had obtained a 'C' licence, originally because the RTE distance restriction on his hauliers was affecting his Birmingham traffic, and was now using it to carry from Runcorn and Weston Point, again to the detriment of the canal.

Regaining Turners' licence was a protracted process, because the vehicles were not owned by the canal carrier but by a separate haulier. The D&IWE was involved at its highest level. Meanwhile, Victoria Mill used its stockpile, supplemented by occasional cargoes boated to Stoke Wharf and thence delivered by road. Turners' licence to go to the docks was restored from the beginning of 1952.[11]

In retrospect, it can be seen that failure to control 'C' licences was a fateful omission from the 1947 Transport Act, resulting in far more serious damage to both the canals and railways than competition from professional hauliers. This was a political decision, proposed restrictions on 'C' licences being violently opposed by certain influential supporters of the Labour Party.

Etruria Top Lock viewed from below the lock. The footbridge has a slot to allow the passage of towlines. WATERWAY IMAGES COLLECTION

The Decling Years 1913-1970

The lower chamber of Bedford Street staircase locks on the Caldon Canal at Etruria. Geo Mellor's mineral mill is in the background. There were formerly carrier's wharves on part of this site and on the arm to the right. Today, the arm has been filled in and a housing development now occupies the site of the mineral mill. BASIL JEUDA COLLECTION

Another problem for carriers was the widespread adoption of the five day week in the years after the war. Although boatmen continued to work a seven day week, most collieries, docks, wharf staff and factories did not work on Saturdays, causing delays to craft and reduced productivity. To this was added the cost of the fall back wage introduced during the war.

On 1st February 1958, the Mersey, Weaver & Ship Canal Carrying Company was sold to British Waterways (BW). Sixteen motors and eleven butties were transferred, of which six motors and six butties were immediately disposed of. The Shirley family retained the warehousing in the Potteries and some of the contracts, which were subcontracted to BW. Their boatyard, the former Anderton Company dock at Middleport, was closed, some of the equipment being sold to the Samuel Barlow Coal Company dock at Braunston.

British Waterways was called upon to defend its takeover of Mersey, Weaver and said that the latter had suffered from adverse trading conditions created by low road rates and 'C' licences. They had asked Leslie Shirley to delay the sale until the publication of the Bowes Committee report but he would not do so. The NAIWC made the usual reference to unrealistic tolls and stated that the RRC conference was under strain from the freedom accorded to British Railways under the Charges Scheme. They claimed that it was the reduced railway rates on clay from Cornwall to the Potteries that had affected Mersey, Weaver. As we have seen, the RRC conference schedules only provided for rates between Runcorn or Weston Point and the Potteries. The railways and road hauliers could therefore reduce their rates from Cornwall without contravening the conference arrangements.[12] Leslie Shirley, in speaking to the author, blamed through road haulage from Cornwall.

Pleas for a general reduction in tolls reached a climax in 1958, the carriers blaming high tolls for the alarming decline of canal traffic as the 1950s wore on. BW continued to take the view that no general reduction in tolls could be made but they were always ready to consider special tolls for individual traffics, such as the 10s per ton Special Through Toll for salt between Middlewich and Oxford granted in 1950. The carriers accepted that no genuine request for a Special Toll had been refused. BW North Western Division tolls were 1d per ton-mile on all

E. John's Armitage Sanitary Pottery. China clay was brought here by Sproston's, a small carrier based at Haywood, and ware was carried away. TOM FOXON COLLECTION.

*Shovels and barrows in use unloading coal from **Crewe** at Seddon's Salt Works on 18th March 1965.* WATERWAY IMAGES COLLECTION

classes of traffic or 3s 4d per ton from Weston Point to Etruria. In 1952, the RRC conference canal rate for clay from Weston Point or Runcorn to customers' wharves in the Potteries was 20s 9d.[13]

By the end of the 1950s, through road haulage from Cornwall had become well established and block trains, known as 'Clayliners', with road delivery from a depot at Longport throughout the Potteries, were to eventually gain the railways a large share of the china clay trade. Harrisons' clay was soon being brought by rail to Cockshute Sidings (Shelton) and delivered from there to Hanley by boat until the traffic ceased in 1961.

So much for the Cornwall trade but what of the

British Waterways boats, including three of the comparatively new 'Admiral' Class butties, of which **Howard** *and* **Frobisher** *are prominent, moored in Anderton Bottom Basin, below the lift, in the late 1950s.*
BASIL JEUDA COLLECTION

British Waterways ex LM&SR boat **Crewe** *approaching Stoke Bottom Lock circa 1958.*
J. PARKINSON/BASIL JEUDA COLLECTION

British Waterways Lindsay, Aberystwyth and Cypress waiting for orders above the Anderton Lift on 1st July 1962. They were captained by Ken Nixon, who was one of the fourteen children of 'Jumpabout Ernie' Nixon and his wife Jane. Ken's wife Emma was born into the Shaw family. The name of Nixon or Nickson appears early in T&M Canal records, while the Shaws were a Lancashire family. WATERWAY IMAGES COLLECTION

other traffics on the canal? The bentonite clay, borax and flour traffics had all finished by 1966, leaving only one company receiving raw materials in the Potteries. This was Dolbeys, potters millers of Stoke, whose feldspar traffic from Runcorn ended in 1969 when the works closed. In 1966, this traffic had amounted to 9,000 tons.

British Waterways disbanded their North Western fleet on 6th October 1964, leasing 20 boats to Willow Wren Canal Transport Services who took over the remaining traffic. By this time tolls had been replaced by an annual licence of £21 per boat. They gave up from the end of November 1967 following the loss of the Seddon's coal traffic and the business was handed over to their local manager who formed the (second) Anderton Canal Carrying

Sunlight was another Potter & Sons boat which ended up doing short-distance work in Staffordshire. Here she is at Ken Keay's boat dock at Bloxwich in either 1966 or 1967. GORDON BRIGGS

Company.[14] After the loss of Dolbey's feldspar, they had a small trade in grinding powder to Norbury and some traffic between Weston Point and his warehouse at Preston Brook, via Anderton as Runcorn locks had been closed.

By 1970, all regular trade had left the Trent & Mersey Canal, except for a small interworks traffic operated by Johnson Bros from 1987 between several of their Hanley works and a packing plant at Milton. There were at one time three boats in use, specially designed to carry ware in cages and making six daily trips. The traffic finished in July 1995, by which time the ware was being carried to a packing plant at the former J. & G. Meakin's Eagle Pottery. One boat was in use doing two trips per day. The traffic ceased when the Hanley works closed.[15] This minor traffic was really only a postscript to the main story of carrying on the T&M which ended in 1970.

NOTES TO CHAPTER NINE
1. Manchester City Archives, M300, Bridgewater Tolls and Freight 1894-1922
2. BW GLOS, BW1628.96, Coventry Canal Traffic Sheets
3. Faulkner A., *Willow Wren*, Waterway Productions Ltd, Burton on Trent, 1986
4. Birmingham Central Library Archives MS86 Box 18
5. BW GLOS, Coventry Canal Correspondence Books, not catalogued
6. Derby Record Office, Box 12, Derby Canal Permit Book
7. BW GLOS, BW 191.8
8. BW GLOS, WM 72.197
9. BW GLOS, WM 548.72
10. BW GLOS, BW 113.95
11. Ibid
12. Ibid
13. BW GLOS, BW 47.62, R/R/C Conference Rate Schedules.
14. Faulkner A., op cit
15. Boughey J., 'Final days on the Caldon', *Waterways World* magazine, November 1995

Above: Three Fellows Carrying Company **Banbury** *crossing the Trent at Alrewas. The Long Bridge on the left carries the towpath.* WATERWAY IMAGES COLLECTION
Below: Modern industry. **Cypress** *passes Steventon's Sanitary Pottery, Middlewich in the early 1960s.* BASIL JEUDA COLLECTION

27th February 1970. The last cargo to be carried by the Anderton Carrying Company and the last regular commercial traffic on this part of the T&M Canal. **Mountbatten** *leaves the southern portal of Preston Brook Tunnel.* WATERWAY IMAGES COLLECTION

After the rest of the trade had left the canal, in the 1970s Johnson Bros operated several craft to transfer ware between their works in Hanley. This is **Milton Maid**, *which had a shallow draught and turned over three times when fully loaded with pottery, although each time the ware was rescued from the canal and losses were minimal.* BASIL JEUDA COLLECTION

APPENDIX I

THE TRENT VALLEY LINE

When the Trent Valley Line of the London & North Western Railway (L&NWR) was in course of construction in 1845, rails and fastenings were delivered by boat to points along the adjacent Trent & Mersey Canal, as listed in this summary. There were wharves at all these places but it is possible that some of this material was unloaded at places where there were no wharves, the place names being for toll purposes. This was often done in the case of round timber using a make-shift derrick, with a convenient tree used as an upright, to which the jib was secured.

The rails were supplied from the Chillington Iron Works at Wolverhampton and from the Birkenhead Iron Works, the latter being transshipped to canal boats at Runcorn.

On completion of the line in 1847, the L&NWR proposed a joint wharf at Colwich with the North Staffordshire Railway. The NSR were uninterested so it was never constructed but it would have been sited in the triangle between the two railways at Colwich Junction. The L&NWR Goods Agent expected a considerable traffic, which would have come from canal-side works and been transshipped to the railway.

SHIPMENTS OF RAIL MATERIALS TO SITES

This is a transcript of a tabular record of rail materials shipped to parts of the Trent Valley Railway construction site. The document is on the headed notepaper of the Trent Valley Railway Co. Contractors' Department – Mckenzie, Stephenson & Brassey (see note below). It is marked as having been received from Mr [Thomas] Berkley on December 12th 1845. Mr Berkley was the site engineer for the northern section of the railway. The materials marked from Runcorn were supplied by the Birkenhead Iron Co. [now Cammel Laird]. The materials marked from Chillington (Wolverhampton) were supplied by the Chillington Iron Co.

Trent Valley Railway
Contractor's Department – McKenzie, Stephenson & Brassey
Tamworth 10th December 1845

From	Place of Delivery	Date of Receipt	No. Rails	No. Chairs	Spikes
Runcorn	Baswich	Nov. 4th	205	1,025	–
Runcorn	Milford	Dec. 5th	650	3,290	–
Runcorn	Gt Haywood	Oct. 30th	210	1,090	–
Runcorn	Little Haywood	Oct. 29th	525	2,625	–
Runcorn	Bellamour	Oct. 31st	321	1,605	–
Runcorn	Colwich	Oct. 29th	120	600	–
Runcorn	Rugeley	Nov 17th	1,115	5,575	–
Runcorn	Armitage	Nov 26th	324	1,620	–
Runcorn	Hansacre	Dec 10th	564	2,820	–
Runcorn	Kings Bromley	Dec 8th	324	1,620	–
Runcorn	Streethay	Dec 4th	1,282	8,845	–
Chillington	Whittington	Dec 8th	546	–	23 bags
Chillington	Hopwas	Dec 2nd	108	2,955	–
Chillington	Fazeley	Nov 4th	1,194	–	–
			7,504	33,670	

The document is signed by James Reekie who was probably a clerk

Notes

The original document is held in and is the copyright of the National Archives, Kew, under the reference RAIL 410/1570, which contains miscellaneous items of correspondence and other small documents referring to the Trent Valley Railway. The document was transcribed by Robin Mathams

The contractors for the civil engineering and building of the permanent way were the London Railway Contractors partnership of William McKenzie, John Stephenson and Thomas Brassey.

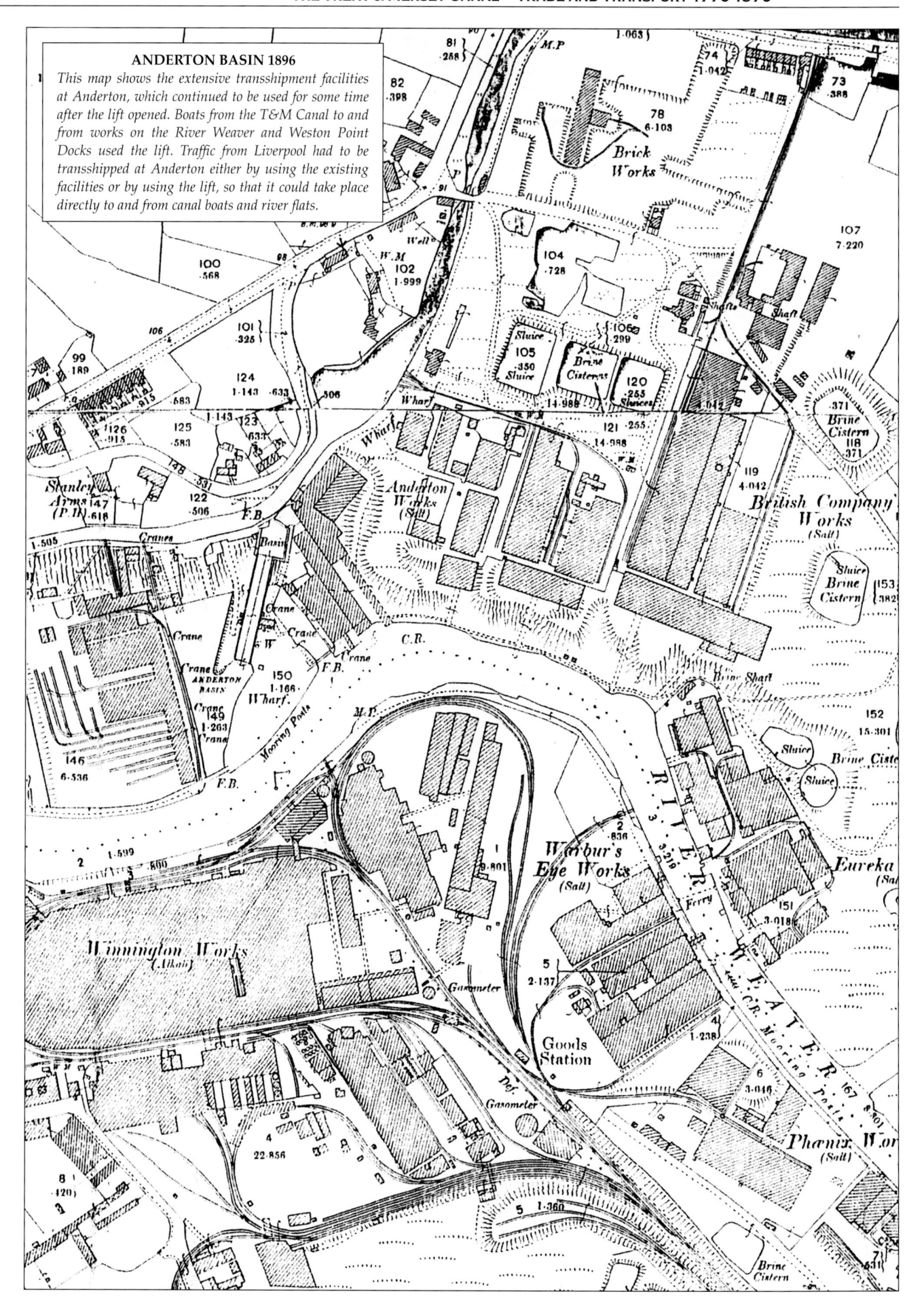

The Trent & Mersey Canal – Trade and Transport 1770-1970

ANDERTON BASIN 1896

This map shows the extensive transshipment facilities at Anderton, which continued to be used for some time after the lift opened. Boats from the T&M Canal to and from works on the River Weaver and Weston Point Docks used the lift. Traffic from Liverpool had to be transshipped at Anderton either by using the existing facilities or by using the lift, so that it could take place directly to and from canal boats and river flats.

INDEX

Agreements and Legislation

Agreements, 9, 39, 49, 69, 71, 84-86, 89, 102-3, 119, 129, 151
Board of Trade, 88-9, 167
Bowes Committee, 181
Canal Control Committee, 167
Embargoes, 162
Leases, 35, 39, 43, 47, 52, 69, 71, 84, 102-3, 167
National Association of Inland Waterway Carriers, 177, 181
North Staffordshire Conference, 87
Northern Alliance Conference, 103,
NSR & Bridgewater Trustees Traffic Committee, 87
Railway & Canal Commission, 88-9
Railway & Canal Traffic Act 1888, 88-9
Railway & Canal Traffic Act 1894, 89
Rail/Road/Canal Conference, 176, 181, 183
Railway (Rates & Charges) Act, 1891 & 1892, 88
Road Traffic Act 1930, 90
Royal Commission on Canals and Inland Navigation, 1906, 89, 105
Tariff barriers, 74, 132
Transport Act 1947, 177, 180

Boats and Vessels

Coasters, 59, 63-4, 69, 92, 103, 113, 118, 129, 140, 152, 162, 176
Flats, 14, 27, 59-60, 62-4, 69, 71, 85-6, 102-3, 115, 126, 138-9, 143, 151-3
Flyboats, 23, 27, 42, 44, 52, 57, 59, 71-2, 103, 114, 117-8, 152, 154, 156, 158-9, 164, 167, 171
Lighterage, 49, 64, 85, 152
Schooners, 55, 77
Steamers, 59, 72
Trent Boats, 49, 52-3, 74, 110, 116-8, 135
Tugs, 69, 88-9, 152-4

Boat Names

Aberystwyth, 107, 109, 111, 172, 184
Action, 22
Agnes, 56
Alice, 87
Alsager, 102
America, 65
Ann Elizabeth, 145
Anson, 103
Argo, 174
Aston, 159
Atlantic, 145
Badger, 157
Banbury, 185
Bedford, 73, 163
Benzidene, 145
Bethune, 84, 85
Cayman, 151
Charity, 146
Cheshire, 106
Clarrie, 118
Columba, 25
Cornwall, 159
Crewe, 155, 182, 183
Cypress, 107, 109, 111, 184, 185
Dane, 118
Dragon, 175
Dunstable, 50, 166
Dunstan, 50, 166
Effingham, 23, 25
Empire, 31
Enterprise, 77
Epsom, 50
Ethel, 145, 150
Eva, 144
Farmers Friend, 169
Fitton, 31
Frobisher, 183
Gailey, 165
Goldenlily, 121
Gowanburn, 20
Hendra, 16
Henshall & Co's boat No. 2, 101
Howard, 107, 183
Hyperion, 175
Ireland, 70
Joan, 164
Judy, 148
Jupiter, 112
Kate, 8
Kenelm, 25, 50
Keppel, 23, 25, 103
Kildare, 103
Lamprey, 88
Lawton, 168
Lindsay, 184
Margaret, 39, 155, 166
Marston, 115
Mendip, 138
Mersey, 85
Millicent, 65
Milton Maid, 186
Monarch, 120
Mountbatten, 166, 174, 186
Nelly, 79
New Hope, 162, 196
Nora, 19
North Staffordshire Railway (NSR), 55, 66, 150, 153, 168
Pacific, 145
Paddy, 144
Perch, 22, 138
Perseverance, 130
Portugal, 177
Protection, 8
Raven, 29
Roach, 107, 114
Romford, 120
Rushmere, 147
Saxon, 74
Silver Jubilee, 156, 176
Snipe, 103
Spain, 8
Speedwell, 79
Stretford, 15
Sunbeam, 179
Sunlight, 179, 184
Sunshine, 83, 165, 176
Swan, 75, 149
Sweden, 138
Swift, 148
Swiftsure, 74
Tench, 29
Thames, 15
Three Sisters, 76
Trout, 111
Tunnel tug No. 2, 154
Victory, 151
Weaver Belle, 20
Westminster, 31
Whale, 78

Canal Carriers

Adams & Sothern, 49
Alexander Reid, 26, 42, 63, 113, 166
Ames, J. & G., 55
Anderton Carrying Company, 27, 63, 65, 72, 84, 165-6
Anderton Carrying Co. (*second of this name*), 184
Anderton Company, 8, 14-5, 18, 22, 24, 26, 28-30, 34-5, 38-9, 40, 42-3, 52, 64, 72-3, 76, 84-7, 93, 118-20, 124, 138, 152, 154, 159-60, 163, 167, 170-1, 173, 175-9, 181
Appleby, G., 27-8, 30 ,69
Bache, W., 31, 43, 69, 73, 113-4
Barlow, S., Tamworth, 76
Barrow & Simpson, 118
Beckett, W., 119
Bowater, 109, 112
Bridgewater Trustees, 9, 15, 28, 40-2, 52, 60, 63-4, 69, 72-4, 76, 101-4, 115, 117-9, 151-2, 166
Bridgewater Navigation Co., 84-7, 104, 151-2
British Waterways 22-3, 25, 28, 30, 35, 155, 171, 175, 177-8, 181, 183-4
Brown, D., 74, 119
Buckingham Company, 107
Burton Boat Co., 42, 49-52, 65
Cavendish Bridge Boat Co., 53
Charles, W., 109
Chesworth, G., 137
Clifford, J., 117, 162
Cockshott, J., 118, 166
Cockshott & Gandy, 118
Colclough, J., 112
Colsall, Walley & Co., 40, 74
Cowburn & Cowper, 148-50, 175
Cowlishaw, G., 52, 74, 110-1, 118
Crockett & Salkeld, 28, 42, 114
Crosby, W., 27, 53-4
Crowley, Hicklin & Co., 40, 69, 115, 119
Davenport, J., 112

Dickenson & Henshall, 106, 111
Ebbern, W., 40
Element, T. & S., 109
Ellesmere & Chester Canal, Carriers, 69, 101-2, 118, 165
Emery, York & Co., 55
Fellows, J., 74, 102, 104, 118-9
Fellows, Morton & Co., 118-9
Fellows, Morton & Clayton, 59, 105, 119-20, 123-4, 129, 136, 145, 149, 156, 167, 169-76
Fletcher, W., 93
Flixborough Shipping Co., 50
Gainsborough Boat Co., 48, 53
Gandy, J., 118-20, 124
Gilbert, J., 107, 133, 137
Gothard & Co., 113
Grand Junction Canal Carrying Dept., 30, 52, 59, 73-5, 118-9, 159
Great Central Railway, 156
Green, J., 109
Griffiths, J., 119, 124, 145
Heath, M. & Co., 55, 166
Heath, R. & Son, 49, 96
Heath, Tyler, Danks & Co., 63, 65, 114
Hendra Company, 16, 18, 30, 49
Henshall, H. & Co., 30, 43, 49, 52-3, 55-7, 61-6, 71, 96, 101, 102, 113-4, 165
Henshall T., 166
Henshall, W., 28, 30, 60
Horsfield, J., 149, 171
Jackson, T., 64
Johnson, F. & R.H., 108, 185-6
Joules, F., 109
Kenworthy & Co., 40, 63-4, 69, 71, 73, 111, 115-6, 129
Kenwright & Co., 27-8, 42, 129
Knill, John, 25, 50
Lester, W.U., 41, 126
Lloyd, S., 48
Lowe, J., 137
Manchester, Sheffield & Lincolnshire Railway, 118, 156
Manchester Ship Canal, Bridgewater Department, 85-6, 105, 152, 175-6
Mellor, Colsell & Co., 30, 42, 75-6, 119, 166
Mellor, G. & J., 36, 42, 75
Mersey, Weaver & Ship Canal Carrying Co., 7, 8, 27, 30-1, 34-5, 42, 75, 84-7, 109, 118-9, 123-4, 139, 145, 149, 154, 160, 164, 167, 170-1, 175, 181
Midland & Coast Canal Carrying Co., 145, 171
Moore, C., 138
Moore, H., 48
Morris & Carter, 137
Morris, Herbert & Co., 129
North Staffordshire Railway & Canal Carrying Co., 28, 43, 71-4, 84, 89, 102, 118, 152-3
Perry, J., 109
Pickford & Co., 30, 40-1, 43, 49, 52, 57, 59, 63-4, 65, 69, 73, 113-5, 116-8, 129, 159, 165-6
Podmore, R., 27, 49
Potter & Son., 40, 49, 75-6, 86, 156, 165, 171, 176-7, 179, 184
Price & Son, 91-2, 102
Rayner, J., 87, 137, 149, 169, 171
Redesdale, Walker & Co., 118
Robins, Mills & Co., 40, 69, 73
Salt Union, 69, 85-6, 139-41, 151
Seddon, H. & Son, 137-8, 155, 170, 175
Shardlow Boat Co., 117
Sharp, S., 93
Shipton & Co., 101-2, 129
Shropshire Union Railway & Canal Co., 26-7, 30, 34-5, 38-44, 69, 84-7, 96, 102-3, 106, 118-20, 151, 154, 166-7
Simpson & Potter, 49, 76
Simpson, Davies & Co., 76, 171
Smith, J. & Sons, 40, 52-3, 73
Soresby & Co., 52, 55, 74, 111, 117-8, 165
Soresby & Flack, 117
Sparrow, J., 107
Spilsbury & Smith, 49, 53
Sproston, J.H. & W., 109, 124, 181
Sutton & Co., 31, 52, 64, 71, 74, 109, 116-7, 138, 165-6
Swanwick & Co., 63
Thos Clayton (Oldbury) Ltd, 147-8, 174
Traders (North Staffordshire) Canal Carrying Co., 26
Trent & Mersey Navigation Co., 166
Trent Navigation Co., 74
Walker, T., 108
Walley, J., 30, 50, 74, 76
Weston Salt Co., 26, 49, 55-6, 85, 139
Wheatcroft, G. & N., 73, 117-8
Whitehouse, J. & Sons, 40, 102, 119, 166
Williams, E., 126
Williamson, Robert, 96
Willow Wren Transport Services, 154, 184
Worthington & Gilbert, 49, 62, 65, 113
Worthington, J. & Co., 62

CANALS AND RIVERS

Ashby de la Zouch Canal, 97
Ashton Canal, 65, 72, 118
Birmingham Canal Navigations, 9, 20, 93, 96, 103-4, 109, 111, 129, 130, 134, 149
Birmingham & Liverpool Junction Canal, 66, 69, 101, 116
Birmingham & Liverpool Ship Canal, 88
Bond End Canal, 50-2, 158-9
Bridgewater Canal, 6, 9, 13, 60, 64-5, 69, 71-2, 85-7, 100-5, 108, 113-5, 152-3, 167, 169-70, 173, 175
British Waterways, 175-8
Burslem Arm, 27, 31, 34-5, 42, 46, 92, 95, 106

Subsidence caused pools of water, some of considerable area, known as 'flashes'. This one is at Shelton in the Potteries, in 1952. Disposing of old boats could be a nuisance to carriers. Sometimes some ironwork was salvaged and reused or sold for scrap. The oak timbers of wooden boats were too hard to be economically cut up for firewood, although whole planks and the cabins might be used as makeshift sheds or hovels. These pools provided a useful boat graveyard. BASIL JEUDA COLLECTION

Caldon Canal, 10, 20, 39, 44, 46-7, 66, 76, 87, 91, 100-1, 106, 109, 124, 130-4, 162, 169, 175, 178, 181
Commercial Canal, 97
Coventry Canal, 51, 57, 75-7, 93, 107-9, 113-5, 124, 129-30, 145, 170, 173, 177
Cromford Canal, 59, 65, 93, 116, 118, 134, 146
Derby Canal, 59-60, 108, 117, 171
Ellesmere & Chester Canal, 65, 69, 98, 101, 165
Erewash Canal, 93, 145, 147
Foxley Branch, 47, 99-100, 133
Grand Junction Canal, 49, 53, 75-7, 114
Grand Union Canal, 149
Grantham Canal, 18, 135
Hall Green Branch, 106, 156, 173, 179
Kennet River, 131
Leeds & Liverpool Canal, 151
Leicester & Northampton Union Canal, 76-7
Macclesfield Canal, 63-5, 72, 100-1, 107, 109, 112, 116, 118, 136, 147, 173, 179
Manchester, Bolton & Bury Canal, 148
Manchester Ship Canal, 6, 39, 85-7, 100, 152, 167, 176
Mersey & Irwell Navigation, 64, 102, 114
Newcastle Junction Canal, 97-8
Newcastle-under-Lyme Canal, 40-1, 43-4, 92, 97, 99, 133
Nutbrook Canal, 111
Oxford Canal, 57, 75-6, 113, 145, 177
Peak Forest Canal, 64-5, 118, 135
Regent's Canal, 49, 59, 72, 75-6
Rochdale Canal, 109
Runcorn & Weston Canal, 85
Shropshire Union Canal, 6, 66, 69, 73, 77, 92, 102-5, 120, 134, 154, 164, 169
Sir Nigel Gresley's Canal, 97-8
Soar, River, 18, 130, 135-6
Severn, River, 54-7, 72, 75, 114, 139

Staffordshire & Worcestershire Canal, 6, 54, 57, 71, 103, 105, 108, 111, 123, 129, 134, 145, 160, 173
Stourbridge Canal, 57, 172-3
Stourbridge Extension Canal, 92, 133
Thames, River, 49, 57, 76, 113-4, 126
Trent, River, 6, 13, 48-9, 53, 55, 59-60, 65, 68, 74, 88-9, 102, 116-9, 126, 135, 148, 159, 162, 173, 185
Trent & Mersey Canal, 6-7, 9, 11, 13-4, 22, 42-3, 46-8, 50-2, 54, 59-66, 69, 71, 75-7, 85-7, 89-90, 93, 95-7, 101-9, 111, 113-4, 117, 119-120, 129, 133, 135, 138, 140-4, 146-51, 153-6, 160-2, 164, 167, 169, 170-3, 176, 178, 185-6
Upper Trent Navigation, 49-50, 52, 159
Uttoxeter Canal, 47, 66, 131, 169
Wardle Branch, 6, 65-6, 69, 87, 102, 105, 114, 129, 140, 154, 164, 169, 173-4,
Weaver Navigation, 11, 13, 27, 60-1, 63-5, 73, 76, 85, 87, 98, 100, 102, 105, 114, 123, 126, 137-41, 144, 151, 153, 169, 171, 173
Weston Canal, 63
Worcester & Birmingham Canal, 72
Wyrley & Essington Canal, 42, 93

Costs, Charges and Revenue

Charges, 53, 60, 62, 69, 75-6, 85, 87-8, 167, 169
Canal/Sea Rates, 52, 103, 176
Classification of Merchandise, 85, 88
Costs, 66, 89
Cranage, 166
Credit, 71
Dividends, 66, 71, 90
Drawbacks, 134
Five day week, 181
Freights, 56, 61-4, 69, 71-2, 74, 76-7, 151-2
Haulage, 103, 152

Import duties, 74
Licences, 114, 176-181, 184
Mileage payments, 159-60
Pooling, 86-7, 104
Rate Cutting, 53, 62, 64, 89, 177
Rates, 52, 71-2, 75-7, 85, 87-9, 103, 107, 111, 113, 116, 177, 181, 183
Reductions, 60, 62-4, 67-9, 76, 87, 93, 117, 140, 181
Revenue, 53, 104
Subsidies, 87, 167, 174
Tolls, 25, 53, 57, 59-60, 62-5, 68-9, 72-3, 75-7, 87, 89, 92-3, 96, 102-5, 113-4, 116-7, 129, 134, 136, 140-1, 151, 153, 166-7, 174, 180-1, 184
Tonnage, 60-1, 73, 89, 159-60, 167
Undue Preference, 62, 88
Wages, 89-90, 160, 181
Wharfage, 39, 56, 62, 113, 166

Companies and Public Bodies

Banbury Co-operative Society, 109
Bass, 40
Bayliss, Jones & Bayliss, 105, 170
Birmingham Wagon Co., 109
Boulton, W. & Co., 107
British Patent & Rock Salt Co., 138
British Transport Commission, 175
Brownhills Chemical C., 148-9
Brunner, Mond & Co., 131, 134, 142-5
Burgess & Leigh, 31
Burslem Co-operative Society, 34
Butterley Company, 59
Cauldon Lime Co., 133
Chance & Hunt, 148-9
Cheadle Brass Co., 131
Cheddleton Lime Co., 133
Cheshire Amalgamated Salt Co., 138, 166

A boat graveyard in a 'flash' at Billings Green near Northwich, photographed on 13th April 1971. WATERWAY IMAGES COLLECTION

Cockshead Colliery, 106-7
Coles, Shadbolt & Co., 76
Courtauld, S., 148-50
Cotton, Elijah, 42, 46
Dairy & Domestic Salt Co., 137
Daniel & Co., 93
Davis Chlorine Co., 146
Dimmock J. & T., 129
District Iron & Steel Co., 105, 170
Docks & Inland Waterways Executive, 176, 179
Fitton & Pidduck, 28, 31, 124
Fourdrinier, Hunt & Co., 130
General Electrolytic Alkali Company, 145-6
Hardman, J., Ltd, 133, 148, 175
Harrison & Sons, 45, 47, 178-9, 183
Hendra Company, 16, 18, 30, 49
Imperial Chemical Industries, 134, 143-5, 170
Ingram, Thompson & Sons, 138, 170, 179
Johnson Bros, 25, 45-6, 172, 180, 185-6
Keeling & Adams, 45
Kerr, Stuart & Co., 147
Lever Bros, 119
Meakin, J. & G., 45-6, 49, 87, 159, 184
Marbury Salt & Brine Co., 141
Mersey Wheel & Axle Co., 109
Midland Tar Distillers, 133
National Association of Inland Waterway Carriers, 176-7
National Coal Board, 176
Newton, W.H. & Co., 135
North Staffordshire Chamber of Commerce, 89
Podmore, W. & Sons, 25, 73
Pottery Manufacturers Association, 177
Railway Executive, 176
Riverside Chemical Co., 146
Road Transport Executive, 176-7
Salt Union, 69, 85-6, 139, 142
Seddon, H. & Son, 137, 154, 175, 182, 184
Silvertown Co-operative Society, 38
Shelton Iron, Steel & Coal Co., 36-7, 92, 96, 105, 148
Smith, Stone & Knight, 136
Staffordshire Chemicals, 26, 148
Stanton Iron Co., 145, 147
Staton & Co., 109, 135
Stewarts & Lloyds, 170
Stoke, Fenton & Longton Gasworks Co., 111
Stubbs & Co., 124
Summers, J. & Co., 92, 96
Tunstall Chemical Co., 148
Turner Bros, 179, 180
Twyford & Co., 40, 167
Union Acid Co., 146, 149
Weaver Trustees, 60-1, 64
Wedgwood & Byerley, 61
Weston Salt Co., 109, 135-6, 138-9
Wheelock Iron & Salt Co., 49, 100

Company Premises and Works

Albion Ironworks, 109
Alrewas Mill, 159
Apedale Ironworks, 97-8
Armitage Pottery, 48, 109, 158, 181
Atlas Iron Works, 26-7, 86,
Birchills Ironworks, 93
Bolton's Ironworks, 101
Bolton's Brass Works, 101
Bradwell Pottery, 27-8,
Brereton Colliery, 92, 108-9, 158
Brindley's Bank Waterworks, 109
Brownhills Chemical Works, 27, 148-9
Burnell's Iron Works, 92
Butterly Ironworks, 93
Cauldon Place Pottery, 40, 44-5
Chatterley Ironworks, 96
Colton Mill, 48, 56, 89, 135
Consall Forge, 47, 91, 132
Consall Flint Mill, 25, 47, 73
Copeland's Pottery, 43
Cheddleton Flint Mills, 47
Church Lane Ironworks, 93
Corbyns Hall Furnaces, 91-2
Crowgutter Mill, 25
Croxton Mill, 48
Cupola Mill, 47
Dale Hall Works, 28, 30,
Dolbey's Mill, 23, 25, 36, 42, 184
Eagle Pottery, 45-6, 87, 185
Eastwood Pottery, 45-6, 159
Eastwood Electricity Power Station, 109
Epstein Electric Accumulator Works, 47
Etruria Bone & Flint Mill, 39, 86, 181
Etruria Gas Works, 40, 42, 109, 112, 147-8
Falcon Glass Works, 44
Fenton Gasworks, 109
Fitton & Pidduck's Flour Mill, 28, 31, 124
Florence Colliery, 107, 109
Furnival's Flint Mill, 38
Furlong Flint Mill, 34, 75
Goldendale Iron Works, 96
Goldenhill Iron Works, 96
Gossages Soap Works, 145
Grazebrook Iron Works, 92
Hanley Pottery, 46
Hardman's Chemical Works, 47, 133, 148, 175
Hayes Colliery, 108-9
Imperial Pottery, Hanley, 46
Ivy House Paper Mills, 46
Ivy House Iron Works, 46
Johnson's Flint Mill, 28, 30,
Joules' Brewery, 109
King's Mill, 48, 116, 135
Joiner's Square Pottery, 45
Leabrook Iron Works, 93
Lawton Salt Works, 137
Leekbrook Dye Works, 166
Leighton's Pottery, 28, 31,
Lichfield Creamery, 109, 170
Lifford Chemical Works, 166
Linley Cement Works, 42, 111, 129
Macclesfield Mill, 172
Malkin's Flint Mills, 31,
Malkin's Flour Mill, 34,
Marston Salt Works, 137, 141
Middleport Mill, 31
Middleport Pottery, 28, 31
Milton Aluminium Works, 47, 132-3
Minton's Pottery, 43-4, 129
Monument Lane Soap Works, 145
Mousecroft Brick Works, 45
Nelson Pottery, 46
Newport Pottery, 22, 32
Norton Colliery, 100
Norton Iron Works, 100
Oak Farm Furnaces, 91
Phoenix Alkali Works, 146
Phoenix Pottery, 48
Ravensdale Iron Works 96
Red Bull Lime Works, 134
Ridgeway's Flour Mill, 36, 40, 124
Royal Staffordshire Pottery, 31, 32
Rugeley Gas Works, 112, 147, 149
Seddon's Salt Works, 137-8, 155, 175, 182
Sideway Colliery, 7, 106-7, 109, 111, 170, 173
Shardlow Mills, 123
Shelton Bar Ironworks, 36-7, 93, 148
Shut End Furnaces, 92, 133
Silverdale Ironworks, 97
Stanton Ironworks, 93, 147
Stoke Gasworks, 42, 111
Stoke Pottery, 40
Stone Gas Works, 109, 147-8
Sun Mills, 175
Top Bridge Works, 28, 30
Trent New Works Pottery, 34, 35
Trent Sanitary Works, Hanley, 45-6, 178
Twyford's Pottery, 36, 167
Unicorn Works, 28, 30
Victoria Flint Mill, Stanley, 47, 178-80
Walsall District Ironworks, 93
Waterloo Flint Mill, 46
Waterloo Pottery, 46
Wedgwood's Etruria Pottery, 36-8, 51, 95, 107
West Cannock Colliery, 109
Weston Salt Works, 109, 135-6, 138-9
Winkle's Colonial Pottery, 43
Winkle's Wheildon Sanitary Pottery, 43
Wolverhampton Corrugated Iron Co., 77, 92
Wood's Pottery, 24, 34
Wychnor Iron Works, 100, 159
Zouch Mills, 136

People

Adams, C.H., 45-6
Adams, W., 19, 57, 107
Allport, J., 138
Alsopp, S., 129
Bastard, R., 42
Bentley, T., 19
Bentley, W., 56-7
Bill, R., 133
Bill, W., 47
Bird, N., 176
Boddington, E., 175
Boddington, H., 84
Boddington, S., 176-7, 179
Boddington, W., 83-4
Boulton, D., 134
Brassington, J., 41-2
Bridgewater, Duke of, 60-2, 151

Brindley, J., 106-7
Broughton, H., 138
Broughton, Sir T., 137
Caldwell, G., 166
Cartledge, S. & T., 19, 46
Clowes, S., 165
Davenport, J., 28, 49, 112, 134
Davenport, W., 64
Edge R., 84
Firmstone, Thos, 99
Firmstone, W., 98
Fitton, S., 28, 31, 124
Faringdon, Lord, 96
Foster, 104
Furnival, W., 43, 138
Gilbert, J., 61-2, 96, 107, 133, 137, 139
Gilbert, T., 62, 106, 133, 137
Gower, Earl, 62
Granville, Earl, 36-7, 49, 92-3, 96
Gresley, Sir Nigel, 97
Griffin, T., 47
Harrison & Co., 46-7
Heath, R., 49, 96
Henshall, H., 106, 113
Hesketh, J., 166
Hindle, T., 42,
Iremonger, J., 176
Johns, E., 48, 181
Johnson Bros, 25, 45-6, 185-6
Kinnersley, T. 49, 92
Leigh, F., 47
Loch, James, 72
Loch, Henry, 72
McIntyre, J., 72
Malkin, James, 72, 84
Marsh, C., 177
Meakin, A., 25
Mellor, Geo., 36, 75, 181
Moore, C., 59, 138-9
Moore, H., 48, 135
Morton, F., 104
Mosely, W., 165
Ockleston Bros, 166
Paget, Lord, 49, 51
Pamphilon, E., 83
Peake, T., 92, 106
Podmore, R., 49
Ridgeway, G., 36, 43-4, 49, 124
Seddon, H., 137
Shaw, J., 166
Shenstone, A., 165
Shirley, C., 86
Shirley, Councillor H.B., 39
Shirley, Alderman J., 39
Shirley, L., 177, 181
Smith, J., 52-3
Sneyd, W., 98-9
Sparrow, J., 107
Spode, J., 107
Stevens, F., 123
Stubbs, T., 42, 56, 124
Sutherland, Duke of, 109
Thompson, A., 138
Vernon, G., 131

Vernon, W., 42,
Waite, W., 42-3,
Wardle, J., 166
Wedgwood, J., 16, 20, 36-8, 51, 55-6, 62, 107
Wheildon, S., 133
Wheildon T., 44
Williamson, H., 26, 30, 92
Williamson, R., 96, 106
Wood, Enoch & Sons, 34-5

PLACES

Acton Bridge, 65, 133
Alrewas, 51-2, 109, 112, 159, 161
Ambergate, 146
Anderton, 7, 11, 16, 20, 61, 63, 65, 72, 84, 86-7, 89, 100, 104, 113, 119, 124, 126, 129, 137-8, 140-3, 152-4, 163, 166, 170-1, 173, 175, 183-6
Apedale, 97, 99, 107
Armitage, 12, 20, 48, 116, 124, 158, 160, 181
Ashton under Lyne, 111
Aston, 56, 135
Australia, 73, 132
Baltic, 129
Barlaston, 68, 163
Barnton, 8, 21, 61-2, 90, 98, 115, 126, 152-4, 171
Barrow on Soar, 134, 136
Bewdley, 13, 57
Birkenhead, 74, 103, 151
Birmingham, 14, 27, 30, 50, 53-4, 57, 68, 72-3, 91, 99, 102, 111-3, 115-9, 124, 129-32, 145-6, 148, 166, 170, 180
Bloxwich, 129, 184
Boothen Bridge, 47, 99
Braunston, 7, 57-9, 113-4, 181
Brereton, 134, 139, 170
Brierly Hill, 71, 91, 102, 172
Bristol, 13-4, 50, 56, 72, 75, 113, 115, 131, 166
Broken Cross, 61, 84
Buckland Hollow, 118
Bugsworth, 134-6
Burslem, 13-4, 20-1, 27, 34-5, 39, 46, 72, 75, 92, 118, 155, 160, 172, 175
Burton-on-Trent, 49-53, 63, 71, 88, 109, 118-20, 129, 136, 158-9, 162, 170
Brindley's Bank, 48, 89, 130, 161
Bromley, see Kings Bromley
Caldon Low, 11, 67, 132
Cavendish Bridge, 27, 49-50, 53-4, 116-7
Cheddleton, 47, 66-7, 130, 133, 162, 166, 175
Chester, 27, 30, 60, 73, 101, 103, 113, 118, 151, 154, 166
Cheshire, 98, 137-8, 140
Chirk, 134
Churchbridge, 111
Clay Mills, 135-6
Colwich, 71
Congleton, 64, 72, 95, 112, 156
Consall, 47, 91, 106
Coombswood, 171
Cornwall, 13, 16, 55-6, 140, 179, 181, 183
Coventry, 50-3, 57, 73, 119, 145, 148-50, 171, 175
Cromford, 117-8, 131
Cumberland, 92-3, 103-4, 151

Derby, 48, 60, 71, 74, 113, 116-20, 126, 135, 138, 149, 166
Derwentmouth, 6, 13, 49, 52, 54, 88, 117, 137, 148, 173, 185
Devon, 55, 140
Dorset, 13, 55, 140
Dudley, 72, 134, 170
Eastwood, 44-5, 109
Ellesmere Port, 6, 11, 15-6, 69, 77, 85, 87, 92, 101-5, 116, 118, 123, 137, 149, 152, 154-5, 167, 174-5
Endon, 47, 134, 162, 169, 172
Ettiley Heath, 156
Etruria, 9, 20-1, 35-40, 44, 46-7, 62-3, 71-2, 75, 84, 86, 96, 102, 106-7, 109, 124, 129, 133, 147-8, 155, 173, 175, 180-1, 183
Fenton, 13, 43,
Foxley, 100, 106, 133, 170
Fradley, 7, 51, 57, 68, 73, 93, 102, 108-9, 112, 115, 124, 129, 136, 150, 157, 159-60, 162-3
France, 18, 73, 162
Frodsham, 60
Froghall, 9, 10-1, 14, 47, 67, 91-2, 100, 106, 131-4, 144, 169, 173
Gainsborough, 13, 18, 49, 52-3, 57, 74, 113, 118, 139, 162
Germany, 73-4
Goldenhill, 92
Grantham, 118
Great Haywood, 52, 54-5, 71, 73, 93, 96, 101-2, 104-5, 108-9, 124, 126, 136, 158, 169, 173, 181
Gravesend, 26, 42, 49, 57, 60
Hall Green, 14, 65, 72, 101, 106, 136, 173, 179
Hanley, 13, 20, 37, 39, 44-6, 92, 106-7, 129-30, 163, 169, 179, 183, 185-6
Handsacre, 109, 129, 161
Harecastle, 7, 69, 71, 86, 88-9, 92-3, 96, 106-7, 111, 134, 137, 155-7, 159, 163, 166-7, 173
Harefield, 76, 130
Harding's Wood, 147, 156, 173, 179
Harefield, 42
Hassal Green, 103, 156, 165, 176
Haywood Junction, see Great Haywood
Hem Heath, 106, 109, 134
High Peak Junction, 116
Hull, 13, 71, 74, 102, 113, 117-8, 120, 132
Ireland, 12, 86, 92-3, 149
Kettlebrook, 76
Kingswinford, 91
Kings Bromley, 109, 115-6, 124, 129, 134, 158, 170
Kidderminster, 72, 123
Kidsgrove, 10, 69, 92, 100, 106-7, 118, 133, 137, 147, 156, 164, 167, 173, 179
Lancashire, 28, 49, 54, 58, 98, 102, 105, 119-20
Lane End, 19, 20, 46, 107
Lawton, 10, 88, 100, 130, 137, 170
Leek, 14, 44, 134, 148, 166, 173, 175, 178
Leicester, 113, 119, 131, 138, 148-9, 171
Leigh, 100
Lichfield, 109, 115, 158-9
Liverpool, 9, 13, 16, 19, 27-8, 30, 50, 56-7, 60, 62-5, 68-9, 71-2, 75, 77, 84, 90, 93, 100-4, 113-20, 123, 126, 129, 132, 140, 144, 151-2, 154, 163, 166-7, 172, 175, 177

London, 13-4, 30, 49-50, 52-3, 57-9, 63, 68, 71-4, 76, 107, 113-4, 116-7, 119, 126, 129, 137, 139-41, 147, 166, 171
Longport, 16, 20, 27, 30, 35, 48, 62, 69, 72, 96, 106, 113, 124, 129, 133, 183
Longton, 12-3, 43, 47
Lostock, 133, 143-6, 170
Macclesfield, 42, 63-4, 71-2, 116, 130, 156, 162, 166
Marple, 109
Malkin's Bank, 156
Manchester, 13, 16, 28, 30, 34, 50, 53-4, 60-3, 65, 72, 92, 99-103, 109, 113-4, 116-20, 129, 132, 137-8, 143-5, 147-9, 151, 166, 173, 175-6
Marston, 107, 138, 150, 170, 179
Meaford, 10, 55, 101, 176
Middleport, 7, 19, 27, 30-1, 75, 181
Middlesbrough, 140
Middlewich, 22, 48, 60-2, 66, 89, 98, 101, 103, 111-2, 124, 126, 129, 137-8, 140, 142-3, 145-6, 154-5, 164-6, 170-1, 173-5, 181, 185
Milton, 9, 47, 124, 132-3, 148, 173, 175, 185
Mountsorrel, 130
Nantwich, 97-8
Newark, 74, 118
Newcastle-under-Lyme, 14, 28, 43-4, 96-7, 99, 156
Newhaven 26,42,49,57,60
Newport, nr Burslem, 20, 31, 72, 75
Northampton, 145
Northwich, 72, 86, 137, 143, 147, 150, 154, 164
Norton, 96, 103, 106-7
Nottingham, 74, 113, 118-9, 138, 149, 171, 174, 175
Oakamoor, 131
Oldbury, 145-7, 149
Oxford, 50, 59, 107, 114, 119, 181
Preston Brook, 6-7, 9, 11, 13-4, 16, 21, 48, 54, 60, 62, 64-5, 71-3, 85, 87, 93, 96, 98, 101-5, 113-20, 123, 126, 129, 134, 137, 140, 147, 149, 151-4, 164, 167, 169, 171, 173-5, 185
Poole, 75
Pool Dam, Newcastle-under-Lyme, 99
Reading, 59
Red Bull, 48, 134, 156, 166, 175
Rode Heath, 156, 175
Rugeley, 7, 48, 56, 89, 100, 108-9, 112-3, 116, 129, 135-6, 147-9, 158, 161
Runcorn, 8, 11, 22, 15, 34, 59, 63-5, 72-3, 76, 84-7, 92-3, 103-4, 119-20, 129, 137-40, 145-6, 148-9, 151-2, 166-7, 169-70, 172, 175-6, 178, 180-1, 183-4
Russia, 73-4
Saltersford, 62, 99, 126, 152-3
Sandbach, 60, 134, 138, 143-4, 156
Sandiacre, 118
Sandon, 75, 109, 134
Scandinavia, 93
Scotland, 93, 101
Shardlow, 4, 11, 27, 49, 52-4, 60-1, 74, 93, 110-1, 113, 116-8, 124, 126, 129, 131, 134, 137, 158, 164, 166, 175
Shelton, 20, 25, 36, 40, 46, 53, 75, 84, 93, 96, 113, 129, 130, 166, 170, 183
Shirleywich, 138
Shobnall, 51, 129, 135-6
Shrewsbury, 30, 129, 166

Sideway, 48, 106-7, 109, 111, 170, 173
Silverdale, 97-9, 107
Spain, 73, 92
Stafford, 98, 133, 162
Stanley, 46-7, 178
Stanton, 145
Stockport, 109
Stockton Quay, 113, 119-20
Stoke-on-Trent, 7, 13, 18, 20, 25, 36, 39-43, 46, 50, 62, 70, 72, 75, 84, 86, 93, 97, 99, 106-7, 124, 126, 129, 147, 154, 167, 170, 173, 175, 179-80, 183-4
Stone, 7, 9-10, 48, 50, 52, 55-6, 71, 109, 124, 129, 131-3, 147-8, 158-9, 163, 166, 173, 175
Stourbridge, 145
Stourport, 55, 63, 72-3, 75, 113, 117, 129, 166
Streethay (for Lichfield), 115
Swarkestone, 93, 108, 116, 120, 129, 135-6, 158, 172
Tipton, 102, 119
Trentham, 47-8, 70, 109
Tunstall, 7, 13, 19, 21, 25, 48, 75, 86, 92, 96, 106, 133, 148, 155, 164, 175
Uttoxeter, 44, 47, 71, 97, 134, 166
USA, 73
Vale Royal, 100
Wales, 93, 96, 101-2, 104, 118, 129, 151, 166
Wallerscote, 143, 145
Walton, 102, 114
Wardle Junction, 6-7, 14, 66, 69, 87,104-5, 114, 118, 154-5, 165, 173
Warrington, 111, 153
West Bromwich, 102
Weston Cliff, 48-9, 52, 106, 116, 135
Weston Point, 11, 15-6, 86-7, 92, 141, 149, 153, 175-6, 178-81, 183, 185-6
Widnes, 143-4, 146-7, 172
Wheelock, 9, 22, 27, 60, 69, 100, 129, 133, 156, 163, 173, 175
Whittington Brook, 51, 109, 129
Wilden Ferry, 13, 50
Willington, 13, 49, 53, 71, 134
Wincham, 46, 108, 129, 138, 140, 146, 154, 164-6
Winnington, 143-5
Winsford, 13, 60-1, 86, 102, 105, 139-40, 151
Wolverhampton, 27, 57, 72, 101-2, 104-5,113-4, 117, 124, 129, 131, 145, 148, 171, 175
Worcester, 75
Worsley, 111
Wychnor, 52, 63, 159
Wyre Forest, 56-7
Yorkshire, 71, 116-8, 129

Railways

Birkenhead Railway, 103
Birmingham & Derby Railway, 71
Birmingham & Derby Junction Railway, 71
Birmingham & Gloucester Railway, 74
Brereton Colliery Railway, 109
British Railways, 181
Canal Extension Railway, 99
Cockshute Sidings, 36, 183
Cromford & High Peak Railway, 65, 116-8
Grand Junction Railway, 28, 66, 69, 71, 98, 102

Great Central Railway, 96, 156
Great Western Railway, 103
Liverpool & Manchester Railway, 6, 66, 69
London & Birmingham Railway, 111
London, Midland & Scottish Railway, 6, 14, 29, 30, 40, 87, 105, 169, 172, 175
London & North Western Railway, 6, 41, 76-7, 87, 102-3, 144, 167, 169
Manchester & Birmingham Railway 71
Manchester & Leeds Railway, 117
Manchester, Sheffield & Lincolnshire Railway, 118, 156
Midland Railway 28, 30, 36, 39, 41, 43, 52, 87, 103, 134
North Staffordshire Railway 6, 14, 21, 28, 41, 43, 71, 76, 87, 99, 102, 129, 131, 134, 140-2, 156, 167-9
Shrewsbury & Birmingham Railway, 102-3
Silverdale & Newcastle Railway, 99
South Staffordshire Railway, 103
Stour Valley Railway, 104
Trent Valley Railway, 71

Road Transport

British Road Services, 179
Cartage, 46, 61, 69, 72, 100, 107, 110, 123, 179
Delivery lorries, 84, 170, 177, 179
Licences, 176-7, 179-81
Motor lorries, 90, 169
Road Transport Executive, 176-80
Road Carriers, 61, 63, 113, 169, 181
Wagons, 46-7, 57, 60, 113, 117-8

Traffic

Acid, 15, 142, 148-9
Alkali, 133, 137, 142-3, 145, 170
Aluminium, 47, 132-3, 171
Ammonia, 133, 143-4, 146, 149
Ale, 63, 128-9
Apples, 154
Bacon, 154
Ball Clay, 15, 18, 35, 55, 75, 177
Barytes, 149
Beans, 117
Bentonite, 15, 86, 171, 184
Bones, 16, 25, 31, 39, 166
Bone Ash, 15, 86
Borax, 15, 86, 184
Bottles, 116
Bricks, 69, 129-30, 166
Brass, 101, 131, 175
Building Materials, 113, 136
Butterpots, 47
Calamine, 131
Carbon disulphide, 148-9
Caustic soda, 146, 149
Cement, 40, 42, 75-6, 111, 129, 135
Cheese, 53, 62, 114-6, 129, 137-8, 164-5, 175
Chemicals, 47, 49, 142-3, 145, 148-50, 154, 156, 166, 171, 175
Chert, 60
China stone, 15, 18, 21, 25, 31, 39, 48, 55, 85-6, 89, 139, 140, 178

China clay, 15-6, 18, 24, 35, 39-40, 42, 45-6, 55, 76, 85-6, 140, 158, 162, 177, 179
Cinders, 96
Clay, 13, 20-1, 23, 31, 52-3, 60-4, 68, 85-6, 97, 108, 129, 180-1, 183
Coal, 13, 20, 24, 34, 36, 43-4, 49, 60, 63, 65, 76, 91, 96-8, 106-112, 123-4, 126, 140, 158, 160, 162, 164, 166, 170, 175-6, 178, 182
Coins, 57
Condensed Milk, 125-6
Coke, 42, 97, 99, 111-2, 143, 162
Copper, 53, 131-2
Copperas, 40, 166
Cotton, 116
Crates, 18, 23-5, 35, 55-7, 60-1, 63-4, 72, 85, 87, 114, 120, 152, 166
Creosote, 147
Dyeing agents, 115, 166
Earthenware, 108, 116, 120, 152
Eggs, 154
Feldspar, 15 ,23, 25, 172, 178, 184
Fertiliser, 145, 146, 166
Firebricks, 57, 172
Flints, 15-8, 21, 23, 25-6, 31, 34-5, 39-40, 42-3, 45-9, 52-3, 57, 59-63, 68, 72,74-6, 86, 89, 126, 139, 158, 161, 178
Flour, 27, 28, 31, 34, 38, 40, 72, 104, 117, 123-4, 154, 166, 171-2, 175, 184
Furniture, 171
Gas Water, 147-8
General Merchandise, 27, 42, 57, 63, 65, 69, 86, 113, 136, 153
Grain, 104, 115, 120, 123-4, 126, 152-3, 169, 172, 175
Granite, 15
Gravel, 164, 166
Groceries, 27, 64, 114-6
Gypsum, 15, 18, 48, 135
Hardware, 115-6
Hosiery, 116
Iron, 36, 46, 53, 59, 64, 91-105, 116, 133, 134, 153, 156, 158, 166, 170-2
Iron Ore, 43, 91-105, 118
Ironstone, 34, 91-105, 108, 126
Lead, 15, 53, 116, 131, 175
Leather, 116, 166
Lime and Limestone, 63, 96, 100, 130, 132-5, 143-4, 148-9, 169
Liquid Fuels, 149
Machinery, 18,
Malt, 53, 117
Manchester packs, 114
Manchester goods, 64
Marl, 12,
Meal, 123-4, 166
Millstones, 156
Nails, 114
Naptha, 147
Nickel and Nickel Ore, 132
Oats, 166
Oil, 116, 148-9, 166
Oranges, 154
Paper, 46, 130-1, 136
Passengers, 28, 116

Plaster, 15, 48, 75, 116, 126, 135-6, 158
Porter, 28, 54
Quartz, 15, 178
Sacks, 166
Saggars, 15
Salt, 15, 25, 31, 49, 53, 59-63, 65, 70, 74, 85-6, 98, 116, 137-8, 140-1, 148, 151, 154, 156, 166, 170, 181
Salt Cake, 145
Shoes, 132
Silicon metal, 132
Silk, 116, 166
Slag, 93, 147
Slates, 53, 114, 129
Slop, 18, 22, 25, 47
Soap, 114, 144, 166
Soda, 15, 142-5, 149, 166, 170
Soda ash, 145, 147
Starch, 171
Steel, 36, 105, 170
Stone, 126, 130, 158, 166
Sugar, 126, 154
Syenite, 15
Tanning agents, 166
Tar, 133, 147-8, 175
Timber, 28, 40, 53-4, 56-7, 63, 69-70, 117, 120, 123, 126, 129, 162, 166
Tiles, 26-7, 40, 46, 69, 72, 129
Tubes, 93, 105, 147
Vinegar, 117
Ware, 18, 21, 23-4, 27, 31, 34, 42-3, 49, 53, 56-7, 60, 63-5, 68-9, 74-7, 84-5, 87, 169, 175, 185-6
Washing Powder, 171
Wheat, 166
Whiting, 15, 40, 135
Wines & Spirits, 64, 114
Wood pulp, 171-2
Wool, 116, 129
Zinc, 131
Zinc ash, 171

TRAMROADS AND INCLINED PLANES

Tramroads, 34, 37-8, 43-4, 46-7, 65, 67, 87, 92, 96, 98, 108-9, 135, 137-8
Inclined Planes, 97

WHARVES, BASINS AND WAREHOUSES

Acton Bridge, 65, 153
Anderton, 27, 61 ,72, 84-5, 87, 124, 138, 141
Appleby's, 28
Aston, Birmingham, 50
Barton Turn, 170
Barlaston, 21
Bellamoor, 134-5
Belmont Road, Etruria, 37, 86
Bond End, 158-9
Bordesley Street, Birmingham, 129
Braunston, 58, 113
Brindley's Bank, 56, 161
Broken Cross, 61
Bromley, 109, 116, 170

Brook Lane, Newcastle-under-Lyme, 43-4, 97-9
Buckland Hollow, 118
Burslem, 21, 24, 34-5, 46, 74, 87, 160, 175
Castlefield, 61, 63
Cauldon Place, 43
Cavendish Bridge, 116-7
Cheddleton, 66-7, 130-1, 166
Cherry Eye, 91
City Road Basin, 49, 59, 75, 140
Cockshute Sidings, 36, 183
Copeland Street, Stoke, 75
Cotton's, Stoke, 42
Cuttle Bridge, 116, 134-35
Ducie Streeet, 65
Dudley Road, Birmingham, 145
Duke of Sutherland's, 134
Earl Granville's, 92-3, 96, 106
Etruria, 21, 35-6, 38, 43, 46, 57, 84, 87, 175, 180
Fradley, 124, 163
Froghall, 67, 91, 101, 131, 169
Grand Junction Canal Carrying Dept, 30, 159
Hall Green, MS&LR, 156
Hal o'Lee, 107
Horninglow, 49-53, 129, 135, 159
Imperial Wharf, Stoke, 36, 42
Ivy House, 20, 46-7, 92, 106, 131
Joiner's Square, 43, 45
Leek, 134, 166
Liverpool Road Basin, Apedale, 97
Little Eaton, 108
Longport, 28-9, 30, 64,
Lytton Street, Stoke, 41, 75
Macclesfield, 72
Middleport, 28, 30, 31, 75, 87, 175
Middlewich, 22, 59, 124, 164-5
Navigation Road, Burslem, 35, 42, 84, 86-7
Paddington Basin, 75, 137, 141
Peake's, 26
Pickford's, 30
Port Vale, 25, 28, 30, 31, 86
Preston Brook, 60, 62-4, 71, 102, 113, 115, 152-3
Raddle Wharf, 104
Rail/canal interchanges, 36, 52-3, 104, 144, 156, 158-9
Red Bull, 156, 166, 175
Rigby's, 106
Severn Wharf, Stoke, 43
Shardlow, 93, 117-8, 124, 152, 175
Shelton, 36-7, 53, 75, 113, 129
Sandbach Interchange Basin, 144, 156
Shobnall Interchange Basin (Bond End), 52-3, 158-9
Shobnall, 50-1, 59, 159
Stoke-on-Trent, 21, 24, 41, 43-4, 84, 86-7, 175, 179-80
Stoke Station Interchange Wharf, 36,
Stone, 109, 124, 175
Tunstall, 26-8, 87, 92, 96, 175
Weston Cliffe, 50, 116, 135
Wheelock, 156, 163, 175
Williamson's, 92
Wincham, 164-6
Winsford, 151
Wolseley, 134

THE AUTHOR

Tom Foxon was born in 1933. In 1950, he left his first job in an insurance office to work as a mate on a canal boat. After three years service in the RAF, he successfully traded as an owner boatman until 1959, when he sold out and became a Captain in the British Waterways Midland Fleet. With the fleet's main contract about to end, Tom spent the next few years working on dry cargo barges and tankers on the River Severn. Three years after his marriage in 1962 (his late wife, Jeanne, worked on a horse-drawn hostel boat), Tom 'swallowed the anchor', and after a period as a lock-keeper, spent the rest of his working life on the railway as a Goods Guard, Signalman and finally as a Platform Supervisor at Worcester.

Imbued with a life-long fascination for transport and industrial landscapes, Tom is a member of the Railway & Canal Historical Society and contributes papers to its Journal and to waterway magazines. After retirement he spent ten years as a volunteer tram driver and conductor at the National Tramway Museum. He is a member of the Prayer Book Society and of his local station promotion group. A keen sailor, Tom can often be found at his local sailing club on the River Avon. He is also a Vice-President of the Commercial Boat Operators Association

ALSO BY TOM FOXON
Anderton for Orders
No. 1
Following the Trade
The Industrial Canal. Vol. 2: The Railway Interchange Trade

The author on **New Hope** *in 1955.* TOM FOXON COLLECTION

FURTHER CANAL AND INLAND WATERWAY TITLES FROM BLACK DWARF LIGHTMOOR PUBLICATIONS

| Vol. 1: 272 pages. ISBN 97809533028 9 5. Price £30.00 + £5 p&p | Vol. 2: 352 pages. ISBN 9781903599 12 9. Price £30.00 + £5 p&p | 176 pages. ISBN 97809533028 6 4 Price £22.50 + £5.00 p&p | 180 pages. ISBN 9781903599 20 4. Price £22.50 + £5.00 p&p | 180 pages incl. 4 in colour. ISBN 97809533028 2 6 Price £26.95 |

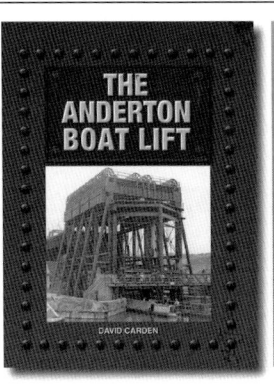

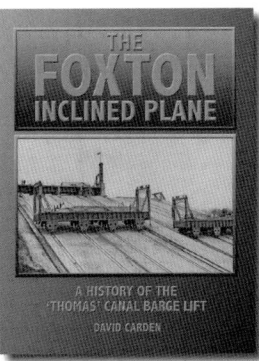

FULL DETAILS OF ALL BLACK DWARF LIGHTMOOR TITLES CAN BE FOUND AT WWW.LIGHTMOOR.CO.UK

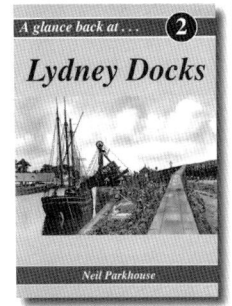

| 80 pages. ISBN 9781903599 00 6. Price £7.50 + £2 p&p | 48 pages. ISBN 9781903599 15 0. Price £5.00 + £2 p&p | 48 pages. ISBN 9781903599 05 1. Price £5.00 + £2 p&p |

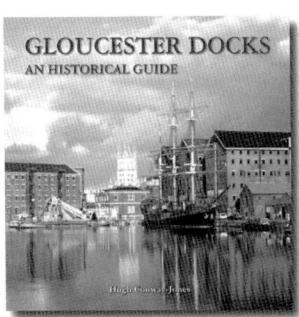

ORDER FROM
BLACK DWARF LIGHTMOOR PUBLICATIONS LTD

BY POST: 120 Farmers Close, Witney, Oxon OX28 1NR
FROM WEBSITE: www.lightmoor.co.uk
BY PHONE: 01993 773927 / 01594 844789
EMAIL: info@lightmoor.co.uk

PLEASE NOTE: If ordering more than one book, postage discounts apply. Please contact us first for a quote. If ordering via the website, our secure payment facility will automatically apply the correct postage rate.